IMAGES
of Modern America

JACKSONVILLE

On the Front Cover: Independent Life and Accident Insurance Company, a trademark name in the Northbank skyline until 1995, had a significant role in Jacksonville's corporate culture, and its claim to fame was the "Hartford of the South" (courtesy of the City of Jacksonville Historic Preservation Office); the historic Elks Club Building at 201–213 North Laura Street was in need of a makeover when this photograph was taken in the late 1980s (courtesy of the City of Jacksonville Historic Preservation Office); a sailor aboard the guided-missile frigate USS *Stephen W. Groves* (FFG-29) throws a heaving line to moor the ship at the Northbank of the Riverwalk in downtown Jacksonville on October 10, 2008 (courtesy of the US Navy and Mass Communication Sp2c. Daniel Gay); an automobile-filled Jacksonville Beach scene is captured from above (courtesy of the Jacksonville Public Library Special Collections Department); the Jacksonville Zoo and Gardens features 2,400 rare and exotic animals and over 1,500 unique plant species on 117 acres (courtesy of Daniel Herbin).

On the Back Cover: From left to right, the 2012 Florida East Coast Railway (FEC) "Toys for Tots Christmas Train" completes its trip from Jacksonville to Miami, distributing over 11,000 toys annually to representatives of the US Marine Corps for local Toys for Tots programs (courtesy of Robert Mann); Mayor Hans Tanzler poses with actress Lee Meredith, a photograph that over time has become an icon for Jacksonville's consolidation, transforming the city into the largest in the continental United States by land area (see page 30, courtesy of the Jacksonville Historic Society); the Jacksonville Jaguars prepare to take the field against the Dallas Cowboys at Wembley Stadium (courtesy of the US Government).

IMAGES
of Modern America

JACKSONVILLE

Ennis Armon Davis

ARCADIA
PUBLISHING

ISBN 978-1-4671-1468-4

Published by Arcadia Publishing
Charleston, South Carolina

Printed in the United States of America

Library of Congress Control Number: 2015935747

For all general information, please contact Arcadia Publishing:
Telephone 843-853-2070
Fax 843-853-0044
E-mail sales@arcadiapublishing.com
For customer service and orders:
Toll-Free 1-888-313-2665

Visit us on the Internet at www.arcadiapublishing.com

I dedicate this book to all my loved ones and those who have supported me along the way. I would not be where I am in my life without you. I am forever grateful.

Contents

Acknowledgments

Special acknowledgment is extended to the following individuals, organizations, and businesses that have served as major resources for the preparation of this book: Boston Public Library, Burger King, City of Jacksonville Historic Preservation Office, CozyCornerRadio.com, Daniel Herbin, Edward Graham, Eduardo Fernandez, Edwin and Erma Davis Jr., Ernie Oest via Bob Kay and Beercanhistory.com, First Coast Section of the Florida chapter of the American Planning Association, Jacksonville Farmers Market, Jacksonville Fire Department, Jacksonville Public Library Special Collections Department, JAXPORT, Jax Truckies, Leware Construction Company, Library of Congress, Mattie Davis, MetroJacksonville.com, Robert Mann, Sarah Gojekian, Simon Property Group, Inc., State Archives of Florida, Shorpy.com, UF Health Jacksonville, US government, US Navy, Whiteway Corner, Wikipedia, and Visit Jacksonville.

INTRODUCTION

The first 50 years of the 20th century saw Jacksonville explode to life after the devastating Great Fire of 1901, rising from a small town of 28,429 to one of the South's largest cities with a population of 204,275 by 1950. Enjoying an economic boost provided by World War II, the city's population had increased 33.6 percent over the previous 10 years. Over 25 percent of its workforce was employed in the manufacturing, logistics, and wholesale industries; furthermore, NAS Jacksonville, Mayport, and Cecil Field had been commissioned, creating a housing boom throughout the county. The 1952 opening of the Mathews Bridge led to the rapid development of Arlington.

At the center of Florida's gateway city was its vibrant downtown. Here, millions would get their first glimpse of urban life in Florida by arriving at the Jacksonville Terminal, the largest passenger rail station south of Washington, DC. Stepping outside the terminal's doors, visitors were exposed to an atmosphere filled with 24-hour life and activity, featuring four flag-ranked hotels. The heart of the city bustled with blocks filled with restaurants, theaters, bars, and flagship department stores. While downtown bustled, its congested streets and decaying wharfs resulted in a push for change. Mayor Haydon Burns's "Jacksonville Story" resulted in a new look for the downtown waterfront by replacing decaying wharfs and piers with new skyscrapers, a new government complex, and riverfront parking. In addition, established in 1955, the Jacksonville Expressway Authority's first wave of transportation projects would lay the foundation for establishment of the sprawling metropolis most recognize in the 21st century.

By 1960, the city had already become known for its substantial freeway and expressway program, which preceded the enactment of the accelerated interstate highway program of 1956. Hoping to meet anticipated demand for downtown growth, plans were even proposed for a downtown loop consisting of a "double central business district belt." This unique loop would include an elevated freeway with a surface expressway at the lower level. While this loop was never built, two additional loops eventually became reality: the Twentieth Street Expressway (MLK Parkway) and Interstate 295. Jacksonville's road-building program was utilized as an urban-renewal program to remove vibrant African American neighborhoods such as the ritzy Sugar Hill and the working-class community of Campbell's Addition, both of which had mysteriously been determined as blights.

While Duval County's population exploded to 455,411 by 1960, Jacksonville had become a troubled city. Defined by race riots, urban blight, corrupt politics, disaccredited public high schools, a declining manufacturing and tax base, and white flight, the city saw its population decline to 201,030. Determined to change the city's fortunes, a meeting in the Robert Meyer Hotel's Windsor Room on January 18, 1965, set the wheels in motion for a new beginning. Here, chamber of commerce president Claude Yates secured 22 signatures petitioning the legislature for the consolidation of city and county governments. Approved by voters in 1967, Jacksonville's consolidation became official on October 1, 1968. Once a stagnant and troubled 30-square-mile urban city, consolidation had transformed Jacksonville into the nation's largest city by land area. While the original city would continue to decline in population, those figures were forever hidden through consolidation. Instead of having an estimated population of 164,739, in the 1970 census, combined with its booming suburbs, Jacksonville's official population had boomed to 528,865. It had become the Southeast's second-largest city and the nation's 23rd largest. The Isaiah Hart Bridge and new Jacksonville International Airport both opened the same year as consolidation. In 1969, the largest professionally planned road-construction program in the city's history and a $126 million water/sewer improvement program were launched. A recent recipient of the All America City Award, Jacksonville had truly become the "Bold City of the South."

In the midst of celebrating its sesquicentennial, new towers with names of Gulf Life, Atlantic Bank, and Blue Cross Blue Shield would rise, signifying the city's transition into a major financial and insurance center and helping the city live up to its Bold City of the South moniker. This scene culminated with the completion of the iconic Independent Life Building in 1975. As Florida's tallest, stretching 535 feet into the sky, it instantly became a postcard image for Jacksonville's progress and was anticipated to spur major growth. Growth would come, but not in the form of what many civic boosters had anticipated. Anchored by a new University of North Florida campus and booming shopping centers such as Regency Square, Gateway, Philips, Normandy, Roosevelt, and Orange Park Malls, Jacksonville's suburban areas exploded with growth as Arlington had done with the opening of the Mathews Bridge two decades earlier. Suffering at their expense was downtown Jacksonville, which saw its historic passenger rail station and most of its major hotels close by the end of the decade. With its downtown department stores threatening to follow suit, city leaders went as far as proposing a makeshift downtown mall above city streets to provide its struggling retail scene with the conveniences its suburban counterparts enjoyed.

The 1980s would become known as the "Billion-Dollar Decade" due to the amount of new development completed in downtown. This decade would be capped with the construction of the JTA Skyway people-mover system, the completion of the Prime Osborn Convention Center, and the Rouse Company's opening of the Jacksonville Landing. However, while the Northbank skyline literally changed overnight with the completion of the AT&T Tower, Omni Hotel, and Enterprise Center, downtown's department stores all closed, finally unable to compete with suburban shopping centers and a riverfront festival marketplace that turned its back to the downtown core.

With downtown still in need of help, Mayor Ed Austin's River City Renaissance program led to the purchase and restoration of the historic St. James Building into a new city hall, Gator Bowl renovations, and the transformation of the civic auditorium into the Times-Union Center for the Performing Arts; however, the controversial program also resulted in the significant loss of the city's most-storied African American district, LaVilla. Intended to revitalize what was once known as the "Harlem of the South," the urban-renewal program ultimately ended up displacing longtime residents and demolishing most of its storied buildings, leaving empty lots behind.

The 1990s will forever be known as the decade Jacksonville overcame the odds to win a National Football League (NFL) franchise. Playing their first game in 1995, the Jacksonville Jaguars delighted fans by making the playoffs in four of their first five years. Ushering in the 21st century was Mayor John Delaney's Better Jacksonville Plan. Approved by voters in 2000 and promoted as a blueprint for Jacksonville's future, the $2.25-billion package of capital projects became a case study for peer cities across the country seeking to improve their own quality of life and capital improvement–funding challenges. This decade, fueled by a real estate boom, also placed the city in the eyes of an estimated 86 million viewers when it hosted Super Bowl XXXIX on February 6, 2005. Another historic event occurred on July 1, 2011, when Mayor Alvin Brown assumed office, becoming the first African American elected to the position since the city's incorporation in 1832.

With a bright future ahead, Jacksonville has come a long way since the mid-20th century. This installation in Arcadia Publishing's Images of Modern America series is intended to take you on a visual journey of Jacksonville's transformation from a compact 30-square-mile, mid-20th-century city into a 21st-century metropolis while exposing what makes this city a culturally unique and special place.

One

1950s

The Jacksonville Story

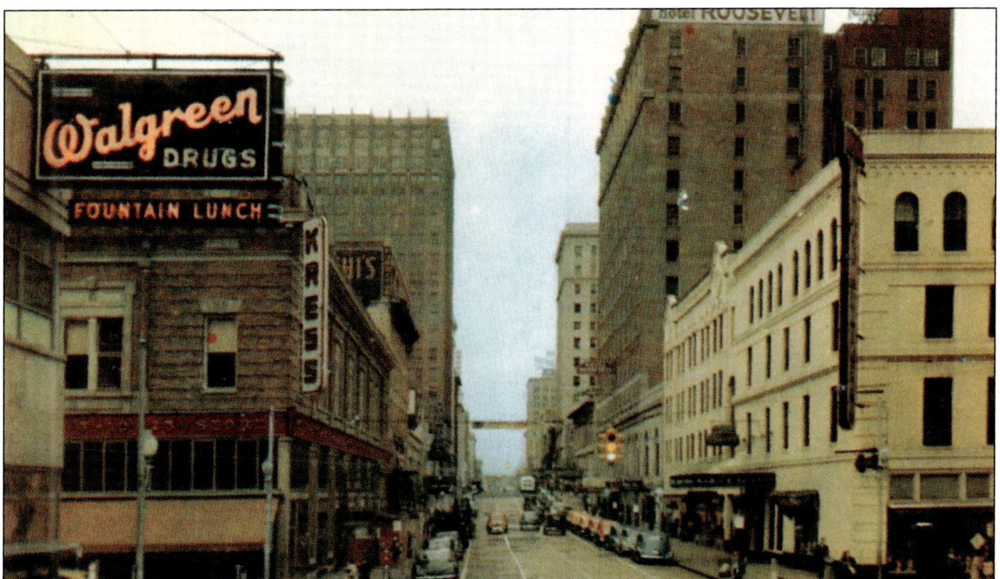

Pictured is Adams Street, looking west from Main Street, in 1941. Prior to World War II, downtown was the undisputed retail center of the city and walkable urban environment in the state of Florida. Things would rapidly change over the next 20 years. In 1940, some 173,065 of Duval County's 210,143 residents lived in Jacksonville. By the 1960 census, Duval's population increased to 455,411, while Jacksonville's declined to 201,030 after maxing out in 1950 at 204,275. (Courtesy of the Jacksonville Public Library Special Collections Department.)

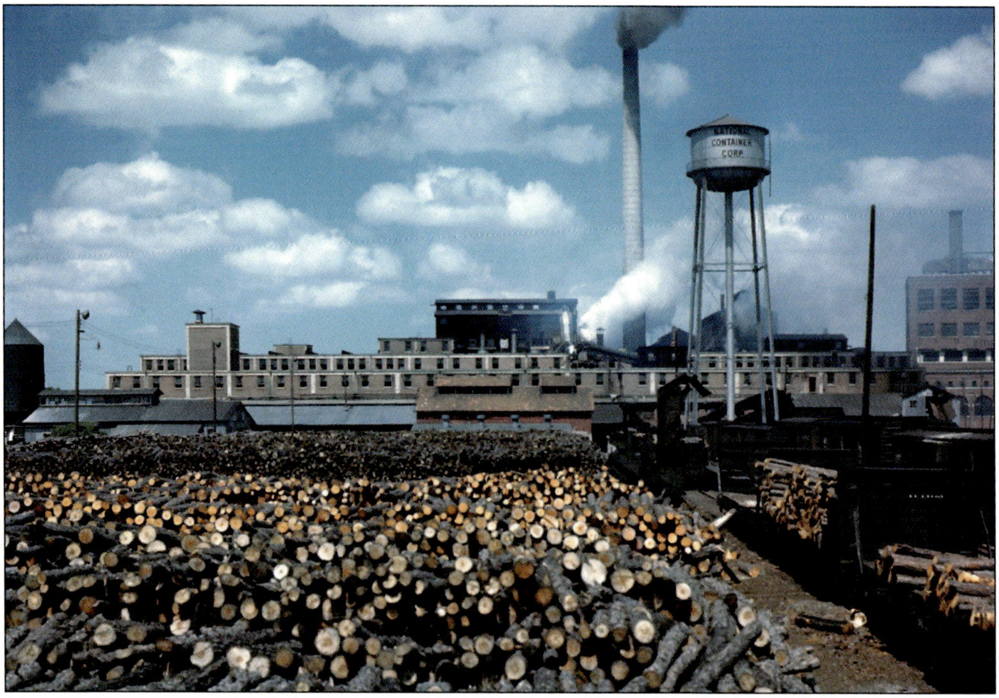

This is an early-1950s view of the National Container Corporation's paper mill along the St. Johns River. The mill was established in 1938 by Sam Kipnis, a Russian Jewish immigrant. National Container had become America's third-largest box maker by the time it was purchased by Owens-Illinois in 1956. Under court order to divest, Owens-Illinois sold the Tallyrand mill to Alton Box Board Company in 1965. The facility annually produced 355,000 tons of linerboard, the outer paper layer used to make boxes. In 1981, Jefferson Smurfit completed its takeover of the Alton Box. The merger of Jefferson Smurfit and Stone Container in 1998 would be the mill's downfall. The Jacksonville containerboard mill, along with mills in Circleville, Ohio; Alton, Illinois; and Port Wentworth, Georgia, were indefinitely shut down by the end of 1998. The mill that produced the rancid smell that once blanketed the urban core, earning Jacksonville the nickname "Armpit of Florida," was no more. (Courtesy of the State Archives of Florida.)

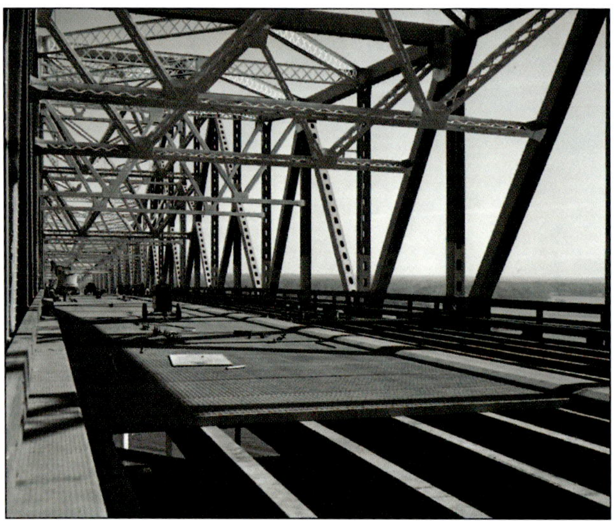

The Mathews Bridge, under construction in 1952, was dedicated to Judge John E. Mathews, who had advocated building the bridge since the early 1930s. The completion of the steel cantilever-truss structure opened the door to suburban growth in Jacksonville. It measures 7,382 feet long and consists of six main panels and 59 approach spans. Originally silver, the bridge was painted maroon in honor of the city's US Football League franchise, the Jacksonville Bulls, in 1984. (Courtesy of the State Archives of Florida.)

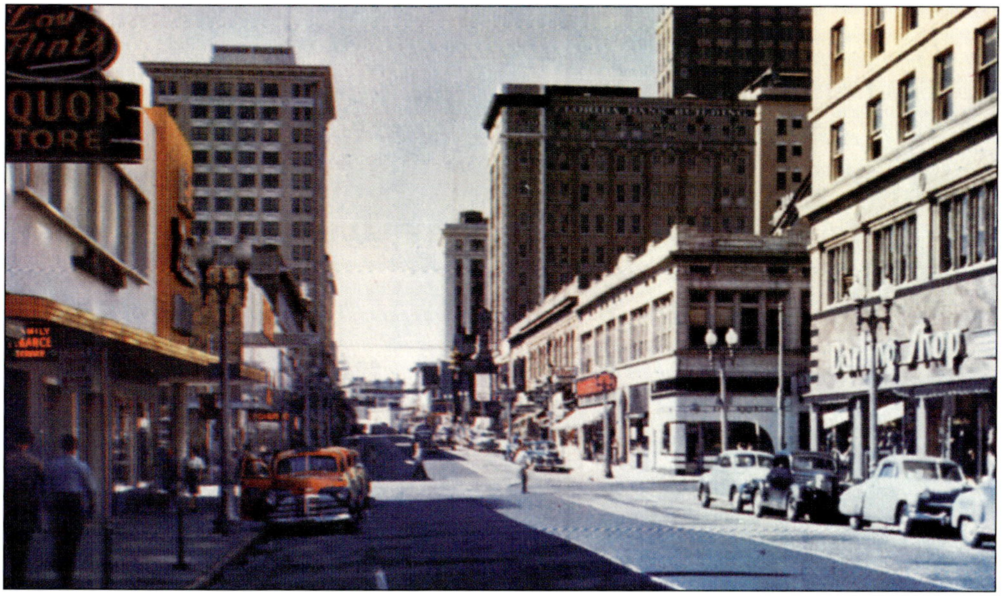

The Heard National Bank building (left) dominates the 1950s Forsyth Street skyline in the distance. Founded by J.J. Heard in 1911, the 15-story building was the city's tallest until the 1926 opening of the Barnett Bank building (right). Demolished in 1982, two of the building's columns were erected in front of the Times-Union Center for the Performing Arts as a memorial to Patricia Austin, wife of Mayor Ed Austin. (Courtesy of the Jacksonville Public Library Special Collections Department.)

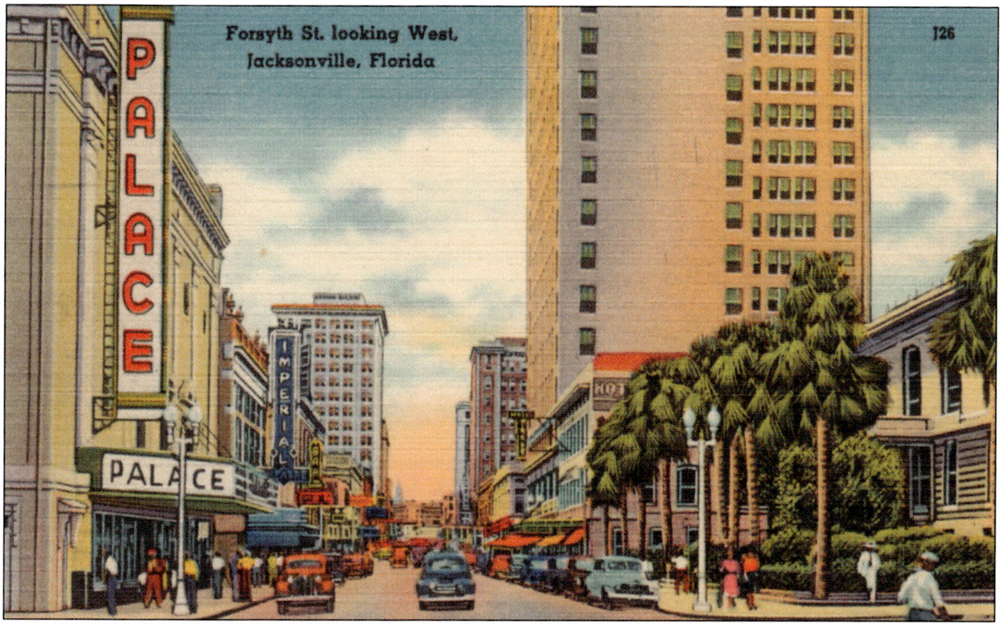

During the first half of the 20th century, Forsyth Street developed into Jacksonville's version of Manhattan's Great White Way. Nicknamed in honor of New York City's show district, this downtown entertainment area was a brightly-lit portion of Forsyth Street west of Newnan Street, once home to as many as 12 theatres within compact walking distance. Theatres included the Florida, Palace, Imperial, Rialto, Savoy, Grand, Roxy, Arcade, and the Majestic. (Courtesy of the Jacksonville Public Library Special Collections Department.)

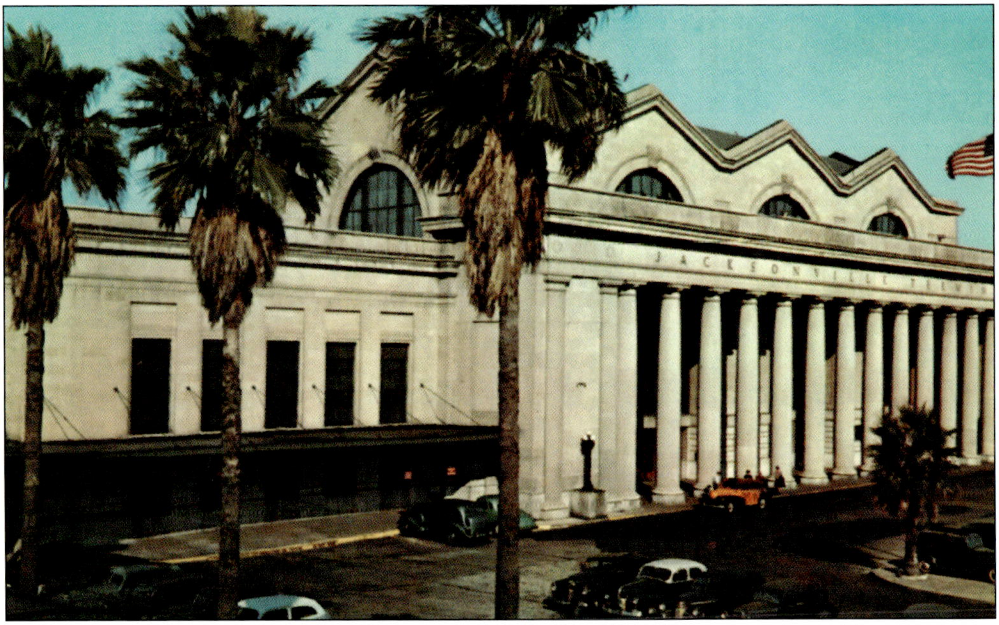

During its heyday, the Jacksonville Terminal was the official gateway to worldwide visitors entering Jacksonville and Florida. When it was completed in 1919, the terminal was the largest passenger railroad station south of Washington, DC, handling the heavy traffic of the Atlantic Coast Line, Seaboard Air Line, Florida East Coast, Southern, and Georgia-Southern and Florida Railroads. Traffic peaked in 1944, when nearly 40,000 trains passed through the terminal, carrying nearly 10 million passengers. (Courtesy of the Jacksonville Public Library Special Collections Department.)

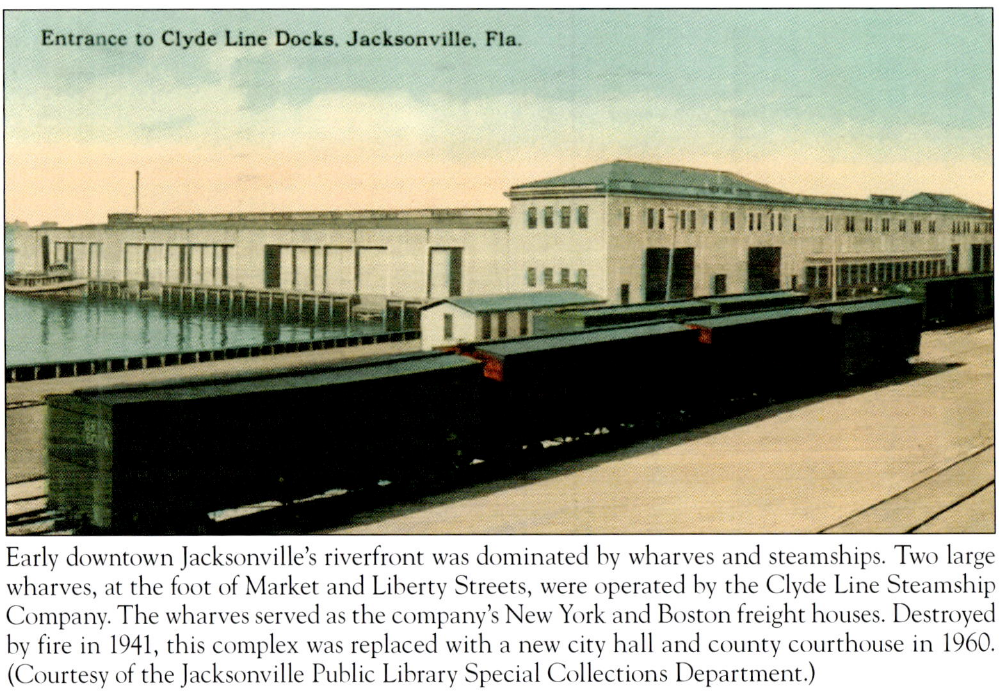

Early downtown Jacksonville's riverfront was dominated by wharves and steamships. Two large wharves, at the foot of Market and Liberty Streets, were operated by the Clyde Line Steamship Company. The wharves served as the company's New York and Boston freight houses. Destroyed by fire in 1941, this complex was replaced with a new city hall and county courthouse in 1960. (Courtesy of the Jacksonville Public Library Special Collections Department.)

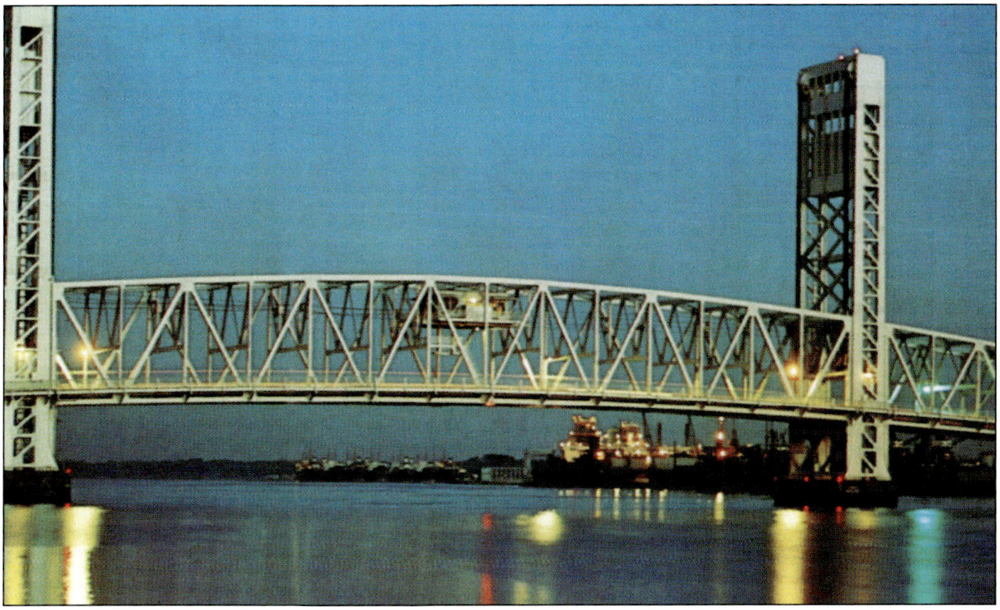

World War I and II resulted in Jacksonville becoming a major shipbuilding center. Gibbs Gas Engine Company's shipyard was originally established in 1908 by George Williams Gibbs. During World War II, the shipyard built minesweepers, covered lighters, submarine chasers, and tugboats for the US Navy and barges and sea skiffs for the US Army. Interstate 95's Overland Bridge was originally built over rail yards leading to the shipyard. (Courtesy of the Jacksonville Public Library Special Collections Department.)

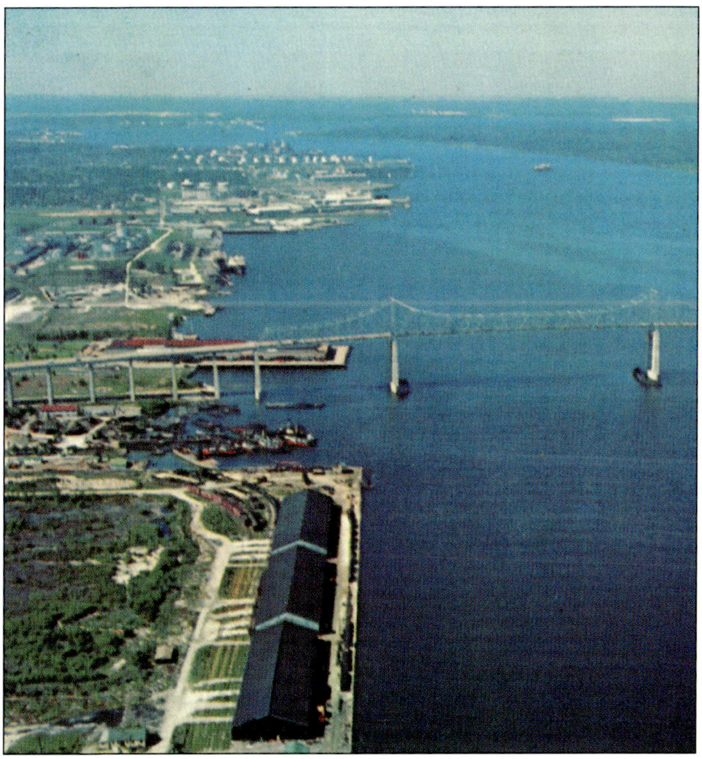

Commodores Point Terminal Corporation is one of the oldest private shipping terminals in operation along the city's industrial waterfront. When initially developed in 1915, Commodores Point's wharves and docks were home to the country's largest naval stores yard. A century later, Commodores Point contains downtown Jacksonville's last operating shipyard, North Florida Shipyards, Inc. (Courtesy of the Jacksonville Public Library Special Collections Department.)

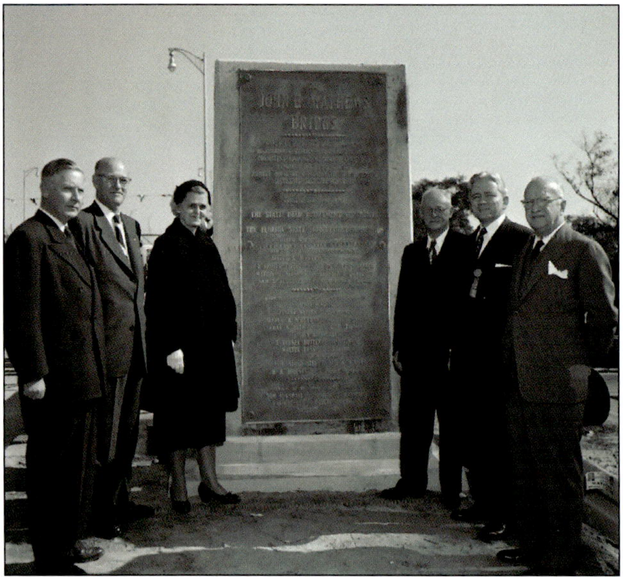

Gov. Fuller Warren (second from right) is standing with Florida Supreme Court justice John Elie Mathews (third from right) in a group portrait by the monument during the John E. Mathews Bridge dedication ceremony in 1953. The 1950s forever changed the landscape of Jacksonville. A compact and dense city for the first century of its existence, the groundwork was established for the urban environment that exists today via bridge and highway construction, urban renewal, rapid suburban growth, and Mayor Haydon Burns's Jacksonville Story. (Courtesy of State Archives of Florida.)

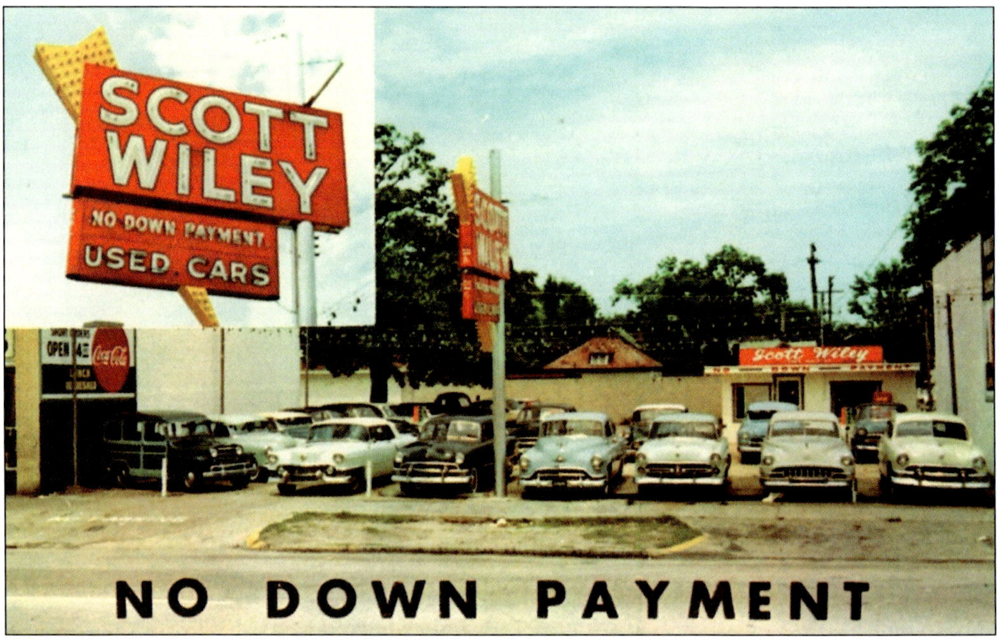

Pictured here is Scott Wiley's used car lot at 1425 North Main Street. Automobile rows developed in numerous cities in the mid-20th century as car companies sought to create districts where the sale and repair of cars could become an easy urban shopping experience. Springfield's Main Street was Jacksonville's first major auto row. Major dealerships on Main Street included Claude Nolan Cadillac, Downtown Chevrolet, Brumos Porsche, and Massey Motors. (Courtesy of the Jacksonville Public Library Special Collections Department.)

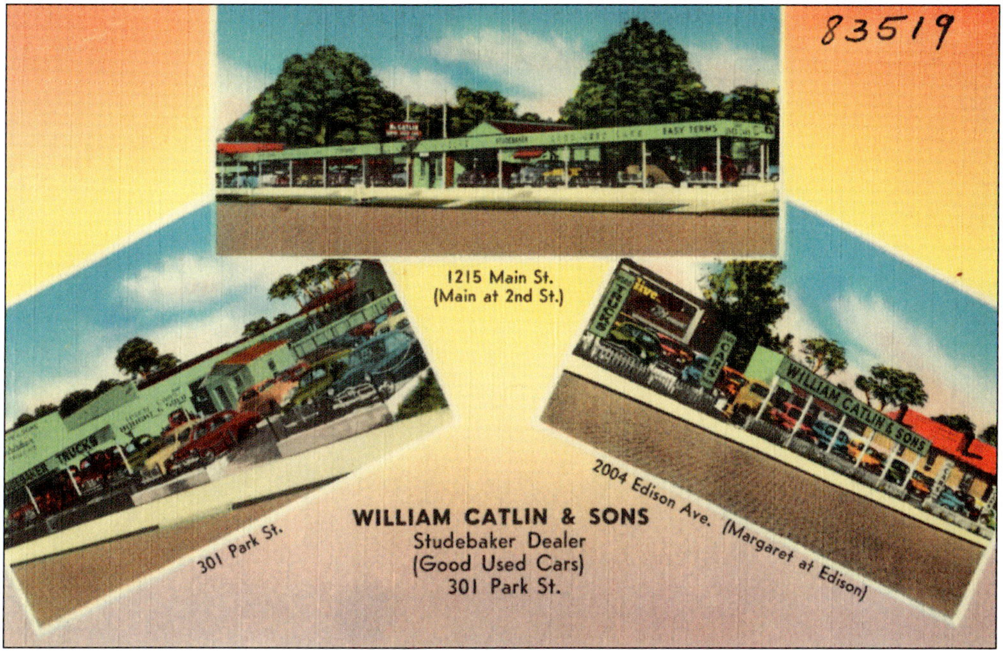

In 1917, William Catlin, a real estate broker in Richmond, Virginia, moved his family to Jacksonville, Florida. He took a sales job with Burts and Williamson, a Studebaker dealer in Jacksonville, and within six months became sales manager. In 1919, Catlin became the first exclusive used-car dealer in Florida. Still in operation, William Catlin and Son is now the second-oldest truck-accessory store in America. (Courtesy of Boston Public Library.)

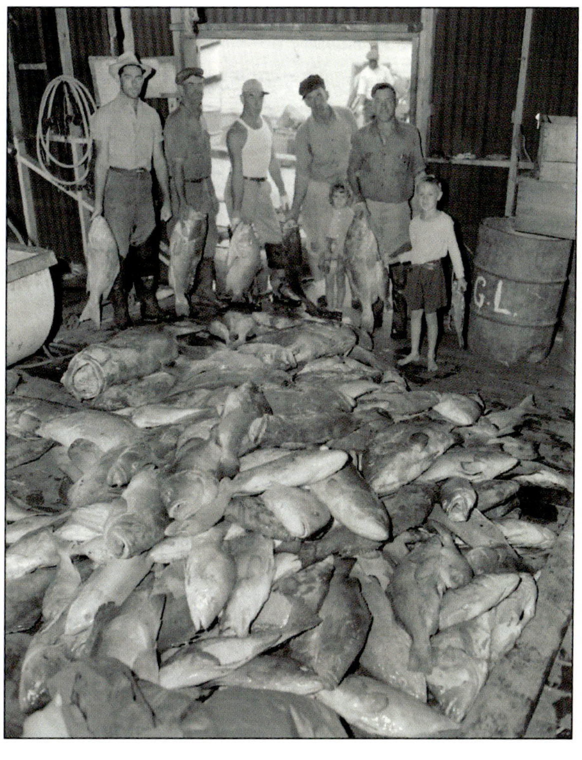

Commercial fishermen pose with their catch in Mayport. Located at the mouth of the St. John's River, Mayport derives its name from the French name for the river, the River of May. A historical coastal community designated as a "Florida working waterfront" by the State of Florida Waterfronts Florida Program, Mayport is well known for its commercial fishing industry, seafood markets, and restaurants. (Courtesy of the State Archives of Florida.)

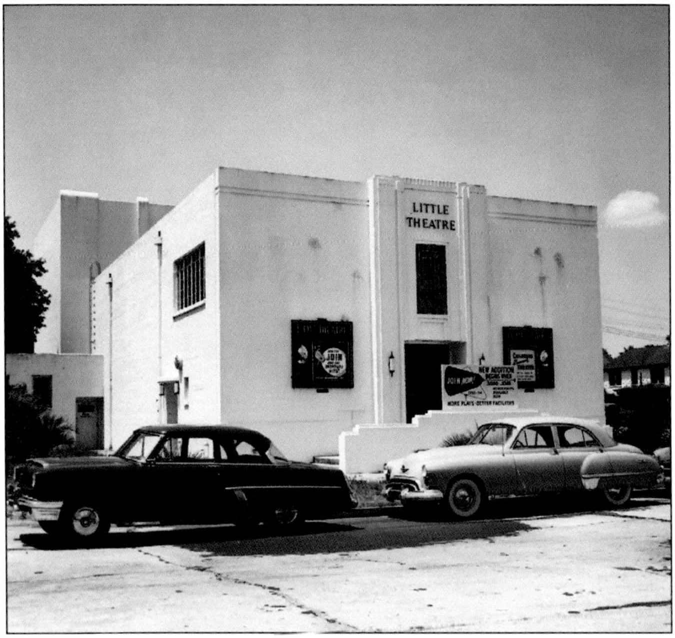

Pictured here in 1953, San Marco Square's Little Theatre is the home of one of the oldest continually producing community theatres in the country, Theatre Jacksonville. With local cigar magnate Carl Swisher as a major benefactor, a new building for the theatre was constructed in San Marco Square in 1927. At the time, San Marco Square had been conceived as a retail, dining, and entertainment destination along the South Jacksonville Municipal Railway streetcar line. (Courtesy of the State Archives of Florida.)

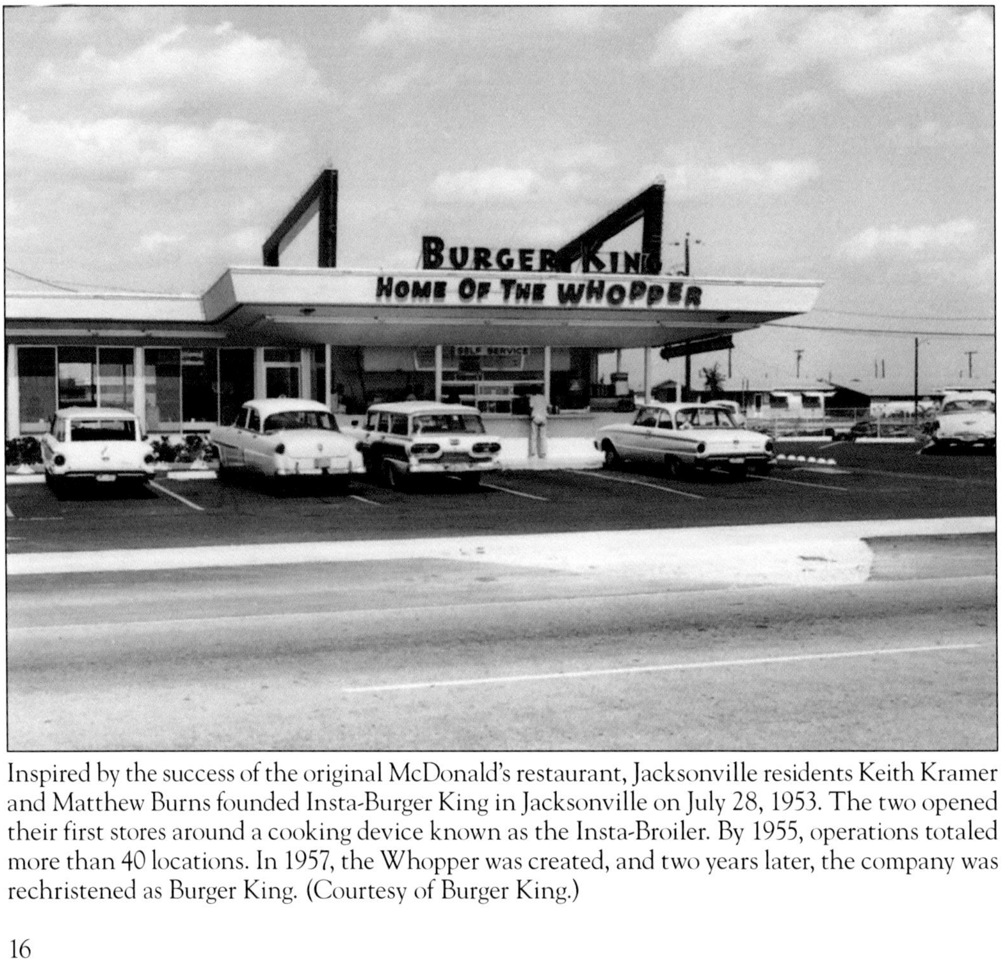

Inspired by the success of the original McDonald's restaurant, Jacksonville residents Keith Kramer and Matthew Burns founded Insta-Burger King in Jacksonville on July 28, 1953. The two opened their first stores around a cooking device known as the Insta-Broiler. By 1955, operations totaled more than 40 locations. In 1957, the Whopper was created, and two years later, the company was rechristened as Burger King. (Courtesy of Burger King.)

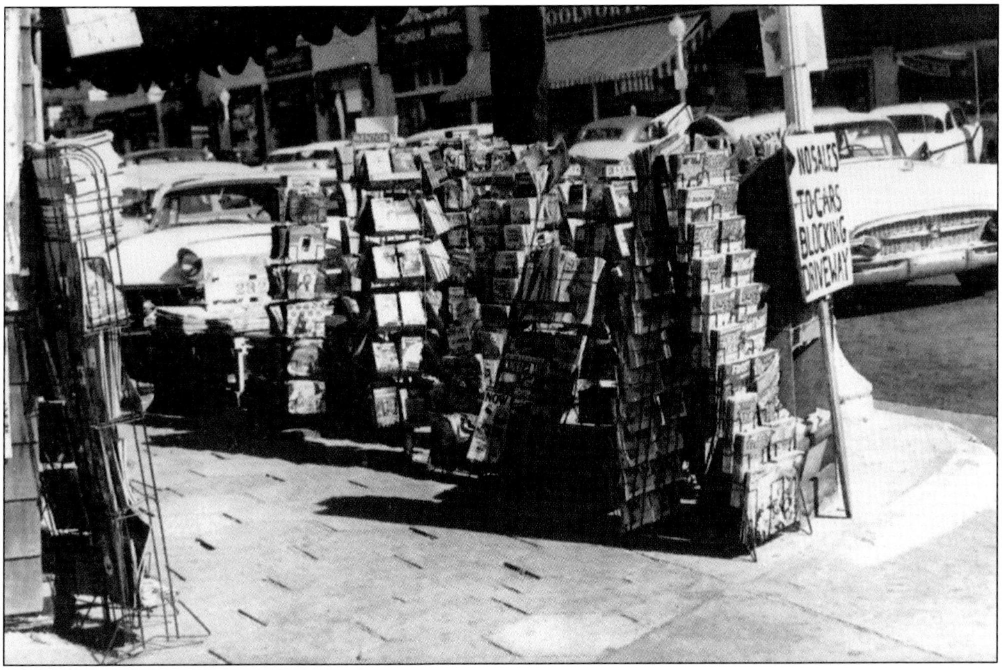

Jacksonville's last true newsstand was on Park Street, shown here on November 13, 1954. Before the age of the Internet, a day in Riverside's Five Points was not complete without a stop at the Five Points News Center. Established by brothers Roy and William Reeves in 1946 with a stock of $50 in magazines, by the 1980s the newsstand carried more than 1,000 books, magazines, and newspapers. (Courtesy of Whiteway Corner.)

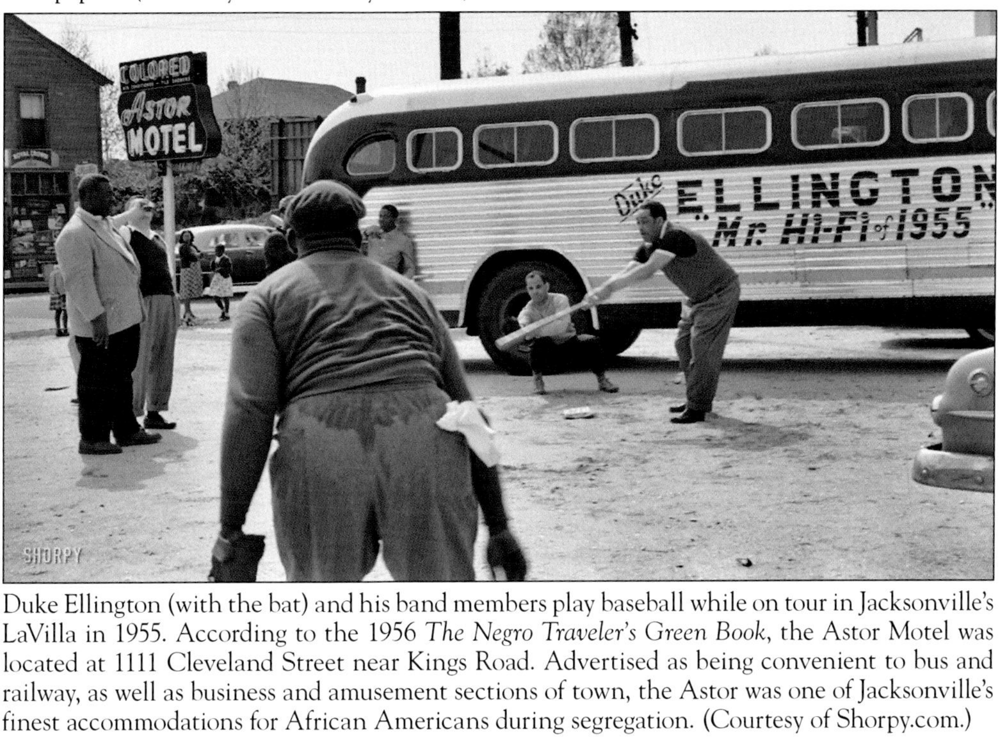

Duke Ellington (with the bat) and his band members play baseball while on tour in Jacksonville's LaVilla in 1955. According to the 1956 *The Negro Traveler's Green Book*, the Astor Motel was located at 1111 Cleveland Street near Kings Road. Advertised as being convenient to bus and railway, as well as business and amusement sections of town, the Astor was one of Jacksonville's finest accommodations for African Americans during segregation. (Courtesy of Shorpy.com.)

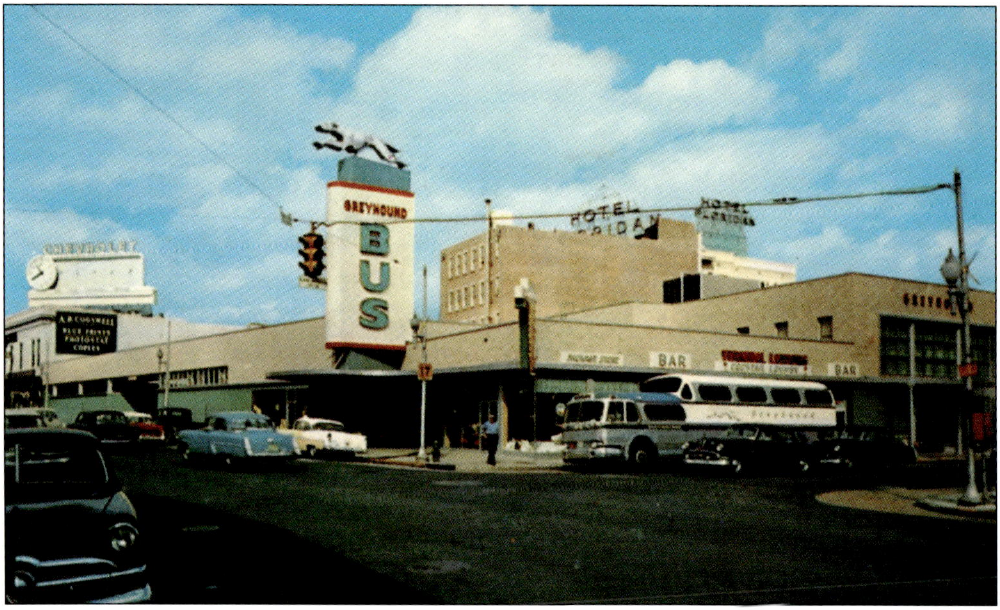

In 1956, a new, state-of-the-art Greyhound bus terminal opened at the corner of West Bay and North Pearl Streets. This station replaced downtown's Union bus station on the corner of West Bay and Hogan Streets. The Union station was torn down to build the downtown Sears store that opened in 1959 and closed in 1981, replaced by the Regency Square Mall location. (Courtesy of the Jacksonville Public Library Special Collections Department.)

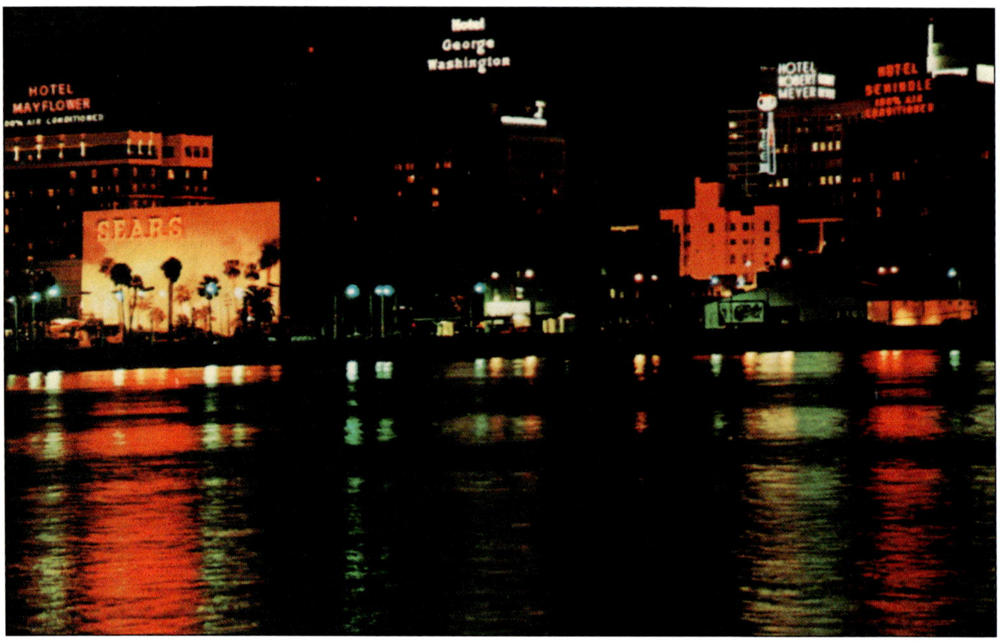

The George Washington Hotel dominates the Northbank night skyline. In 1927, the hotel's owner announced a $1,000 prize for the first flier to conquer the Atlantic. His hope was that the winner would come to Jacksonville to collect. His wish came true, when Charles Lindbergh accomplished the feat less than a month later, coming to the hotel to collect the pot on May 16, 1927. (Courtesy of the Jacksonville Public Library Special Collections Department.)

The heart of Florida's first major city was simultaneously home to one of the largest theatre districts in the South and an African American cultural district in LaVilla, whose vibrancy provided the genesis for the Harlem Renaissance. Visitors and tourists came from all over the world to visit the city's beautiful and unforgettable charm, creating an environment for several grand hotels that defined the downtown experience. Hotel magnate Robert Kloeppel's Hotel Mayflower featured the "South's Finest Roof Garden." It was advertised as one of Jacksonville's finest with every known convenience in first-class hotel operations: television, radio, private bath with tub and shower in every room, an excellent coffee shop, and a unique tavern and bar. Built in 1912 at the corner of Bay and Julia Streets, the hotel featured 250 rooms. (Courtesy of the Jacksonville Public Library Special Collections Department.)

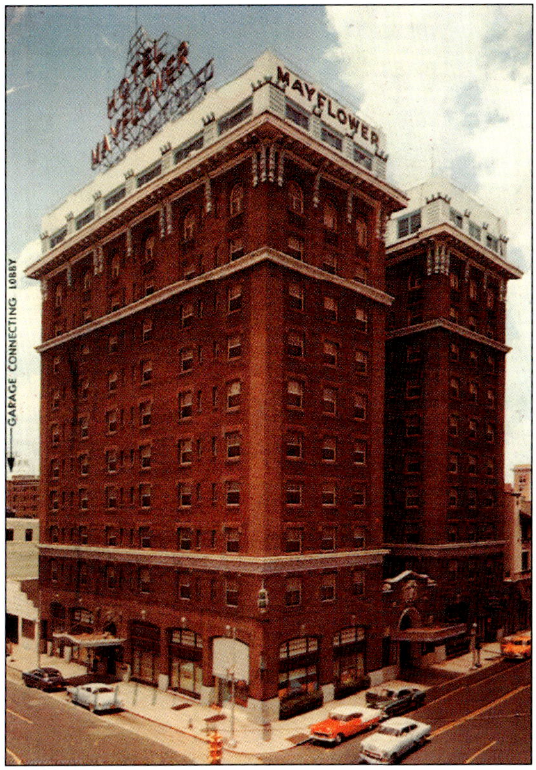

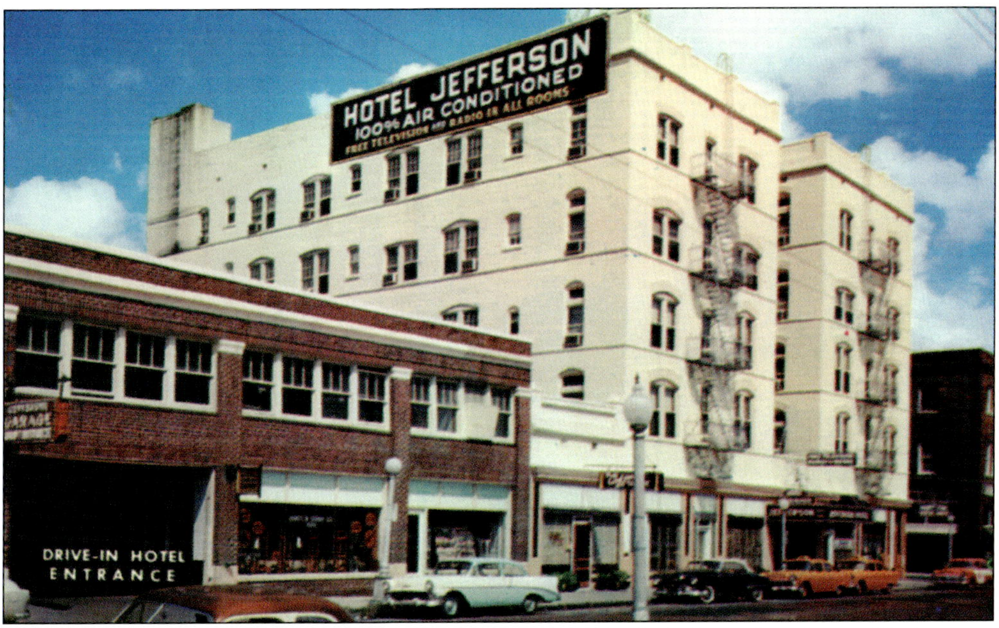

Local hotelier magnate Robert Kloeppel owned and operated both the legendary George Washington and Hotel Jefferson in downtown Jacksonville. Located at 905 West Adams Street in LaVilla, the 125-room Hotel Jefferson offered "Family Plan" rates and a coffee shop and cocktail lounge within walking distance of the Jacksonville Terminal passenger rail station. (Courtesy of the Jacksonville Public Library Special Collections Department.)

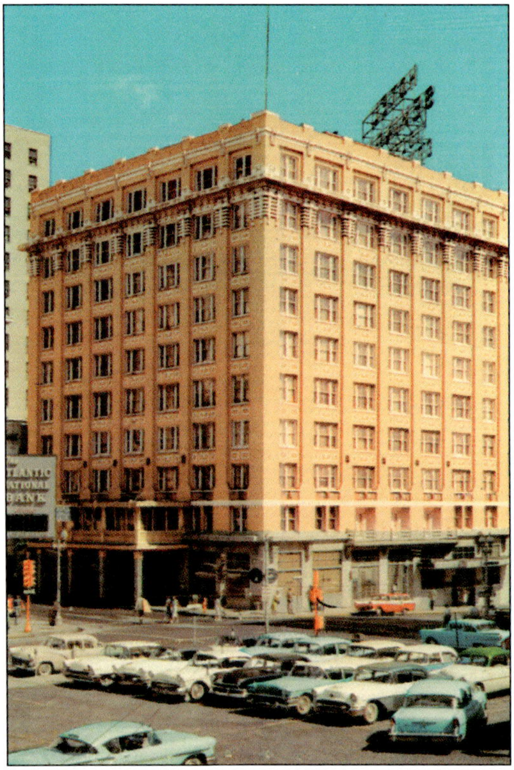

When it opened on January 1, 1910, the 10-story Hotel Seminole was advertised as Jacksonville's first fireproof hotel. Located on West Forsyth Street, the 250-room elegant Prairie School structure was designed by noted Jacksonville architect Henry J. Klutho. During the first half of the 20th century, it was known for its popular dining and meeting facilities. (Courtesy of the Jacksonville Public Library Special Collections Department.)

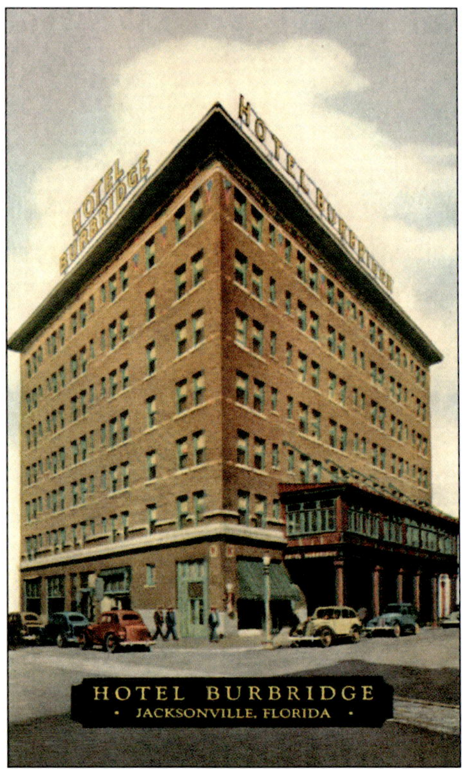

Located at West Forsyth and Clay Streets, the 150-room Hotel Burbridge featured large, airy rooms and elegant furnishings with rates from $2 per day. A garage on-site offered parking for 50¢ per day. Its coffee shop and grill was known for serving good food at popular prices. Original owner Gustav Muller also owned a pre-Prohibition liquor, Chattanooga beer, and Schlitz beer distribution company on West Beaver Street in LaVilla. (Courtesy of the Jacksonville Public Library Special Collections Department.)

One of the few buildings to survive the Great Fire of 1901, Hotel Aragon had become one of the city's oldest continuously operating hotels by the mid-20th century. Coined "A Good Hotel in A Good Town," advertisements described the Aragon as the warmest spot in the winter, the coolest spot in the summer, and offering the finest beach in the world only a 20-minute drive from its front door. Air-cooled and refined with moderate rates, the hotel included garage service and had a Krystal hamburger restaurant on the first floor. Located at 230 West Forsyth Street, the six-story, 230-room hotel was in the epicenter of what could have been described as Jacksonville's hotel row. The majority of the city's largest hotels were within a three-block radius of West Forsyth and Julia Streets. (Courtesy of the Jacksonville Public Library Special Collections Department.)

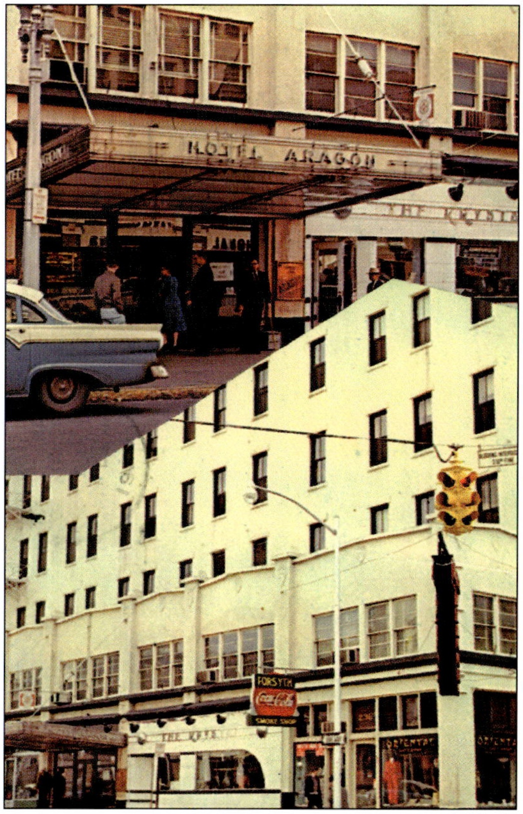

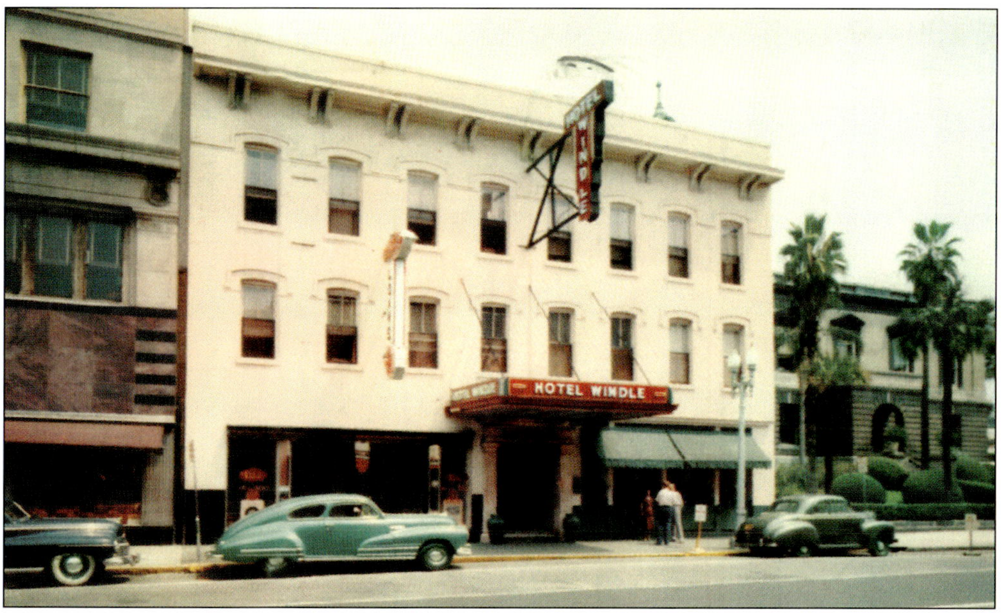

The Hotel Windle, at 17 East Forsyth Street, was one of the first hotels of any size rebuilt after being destroyed by the Great Fire of 1901. In the heart of the city's vibrant theatre district, it was advertised as being clean, air-cooled with the best of service, homelike, and comfortable, with a coffee shop. (Courtesy of the Jacksonville Public Library Special Collections Department.)

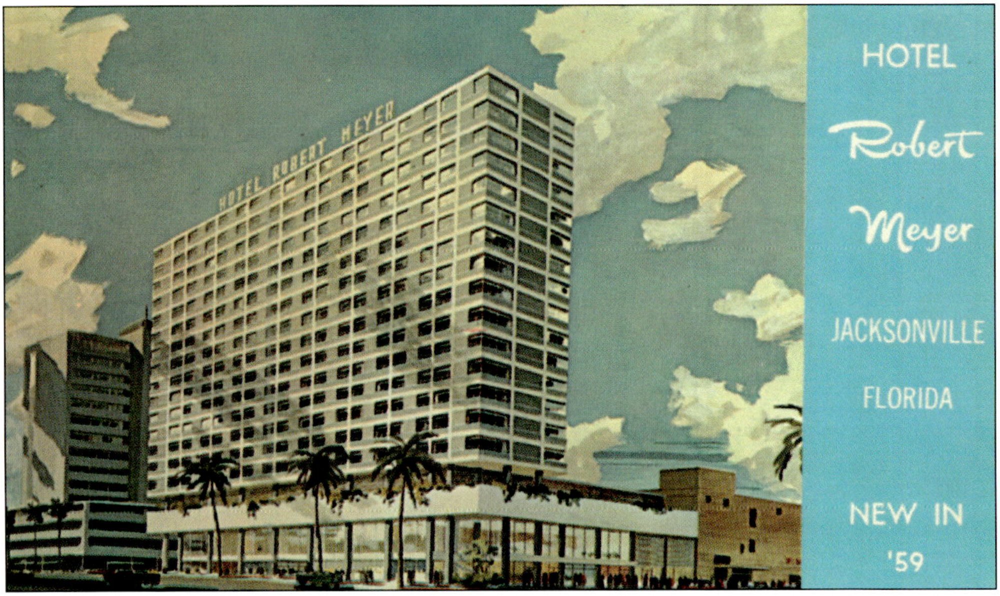

Standing 21 stories tall, the $6-million Robert Meyer Hotel instantly became Florida's largest hotel when it opened on March 22, 1959. The brainchild of Jack Meyer of Alabama, a former World War II Flying Tigers squadron pilot, the hotel featured 563 rooms, a block-long marble lobby and tropical garden, a jewelry store, a rooftop pool, a cabana deck, three restaurants, a cocktail lounge, and a two-level, 190-space underground parking garage. (Courtesy of the Jacksonville Public Library Special Collections Department.)

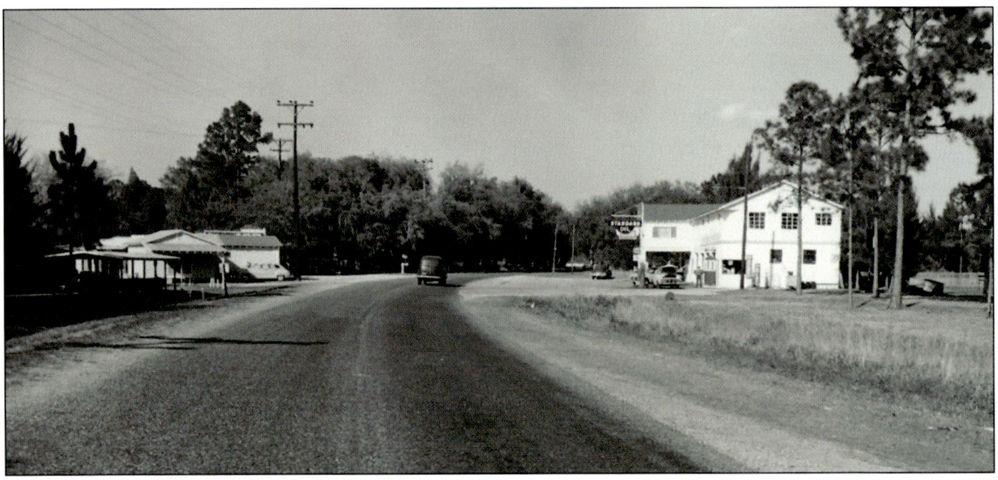

State Road (SR) 13, also known as San Jose Boulevard and seen here in 1956, was maintained by the Florida Department of Transportation. SR 13 is a 32.3-mile thoroughfare that was established in 1945. It runs north from SR 16 near Green Cove Springs to the east shore of the St. Johns River in downtown Jacksonville. It is a major north-south conduit serving Mandarin, the southernmost community in Duval County. Named after the Mandarin orange around 1830, Mandarin was incorporated in 1841, and by 1881, its population had grown to 1,200. Several freezes during the 1890s brought an end to Mandarin's citrus production, and the community fell in decline during the early 20th century. Mandarin's fortunes changed with the 1971 opening of the Buckman Bridge. Despite being engulfed by growth, parts of Old Mandarin still retain a rural charm. (Courtesy of the State Archives of Florida.)

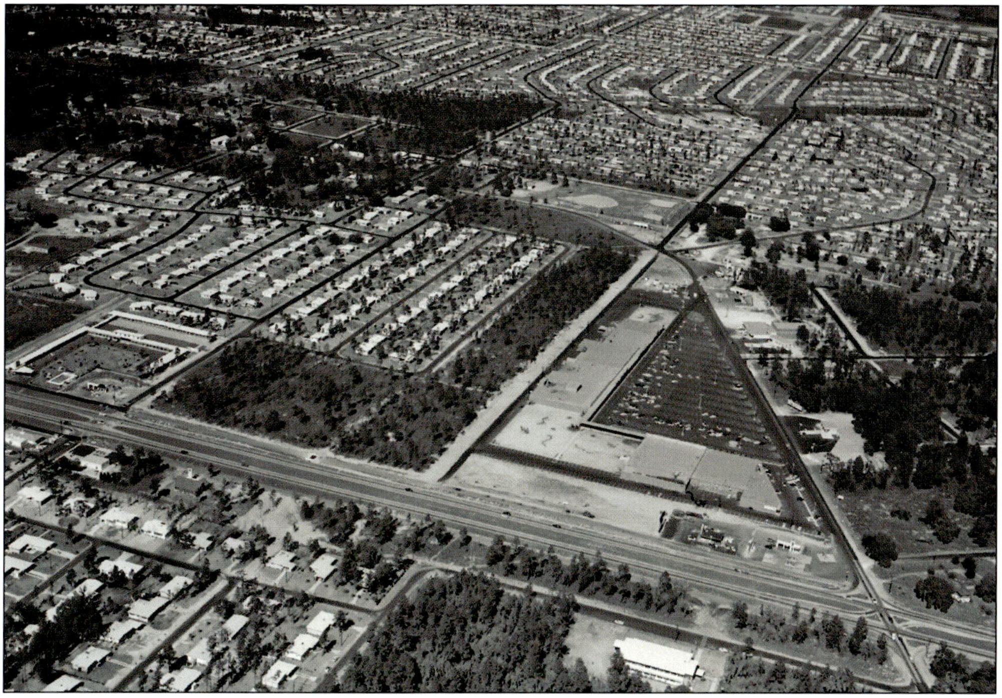

Arlington Plaza shopping center, shown here in 1957, is located near Arlington Road and Arlington Expressway. Previously cut off from downtown by the St. Johns River, Arlington was sparsely inhabited prior to the 1953 completion of the Mathews Bridge, which opened the area up to development. By 1961, over 50,000 people had made the neighborhood their new home. Over the next two decades, Arlington became the fastest-growing section of Jacksonville. (Courtesy of State Archives of Florida.)

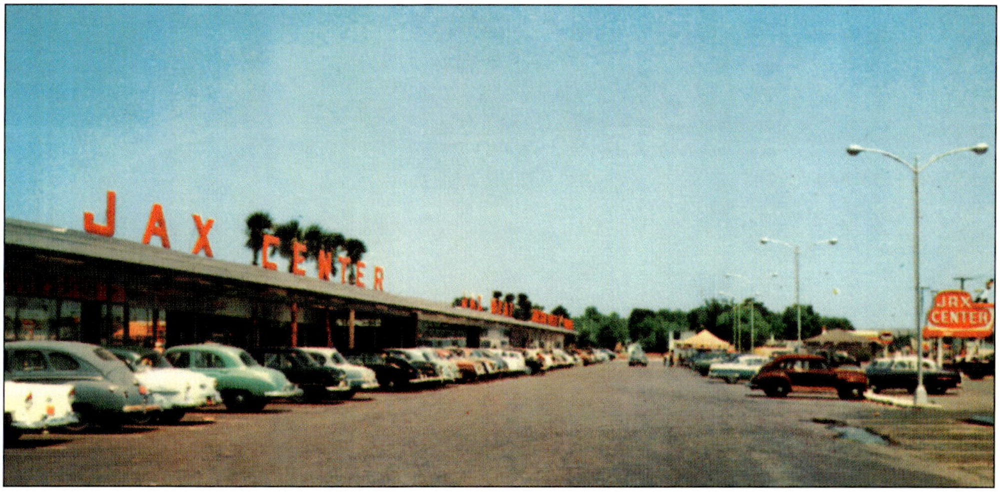

The construction of expressways, rapid growth of suburbs, and automobile ownership led to a change in retail design. By the 1950s, pedestrian-scale neighborhood shopping districts began to be replaced with strip malls. The Jax Center shopping center at Forty-eighth and Main Streets was one of the city's first. Completed in 1956, it offered 50,000 square feet of open-air shopping and 300 parking spaces adjacent to a large J.M. Fields store. (Courtesy of the Jacksonville Public Library Special Collections Department.)

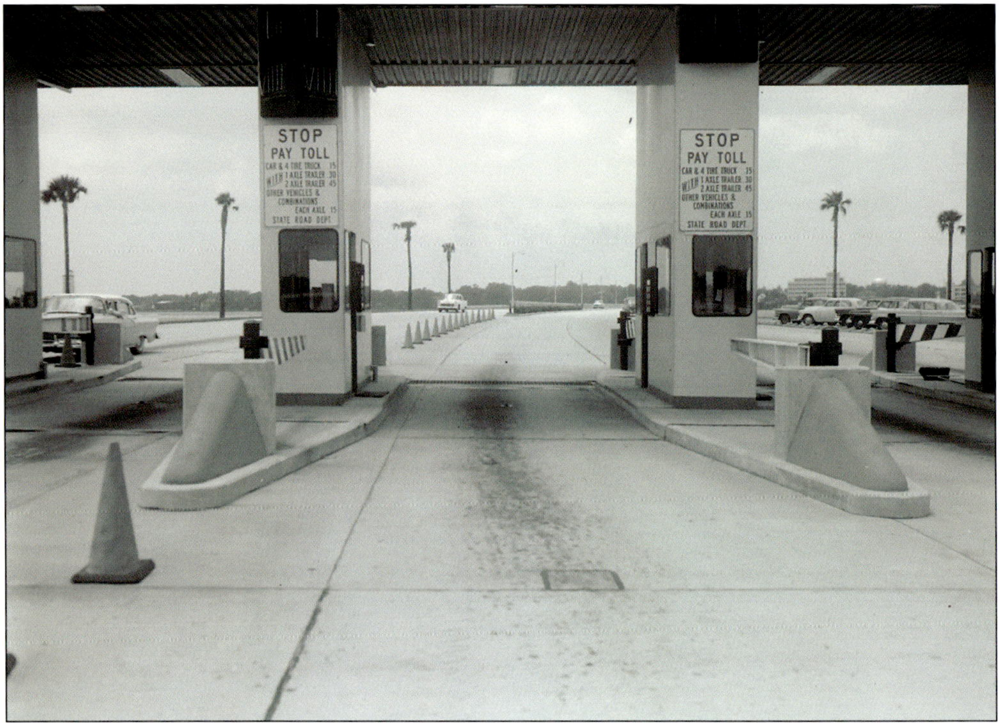

Tolls on the Fuller Warren Bridge (shown here in 1957), Trout River, Mathews and Hart Bridges, and J. Turner Butler Boulevard provided funding for the Jacksonville Transportation Authority's (JTA) road and bridge projects since the establishment of the state agency in 1955. In 1988, JTA removed its toll booths in exchange for receiving a voter-approved transportation sales surtax of 0.5 percent on taxable sales in Duval County. (Courtesy of the State Archives of Florida.)

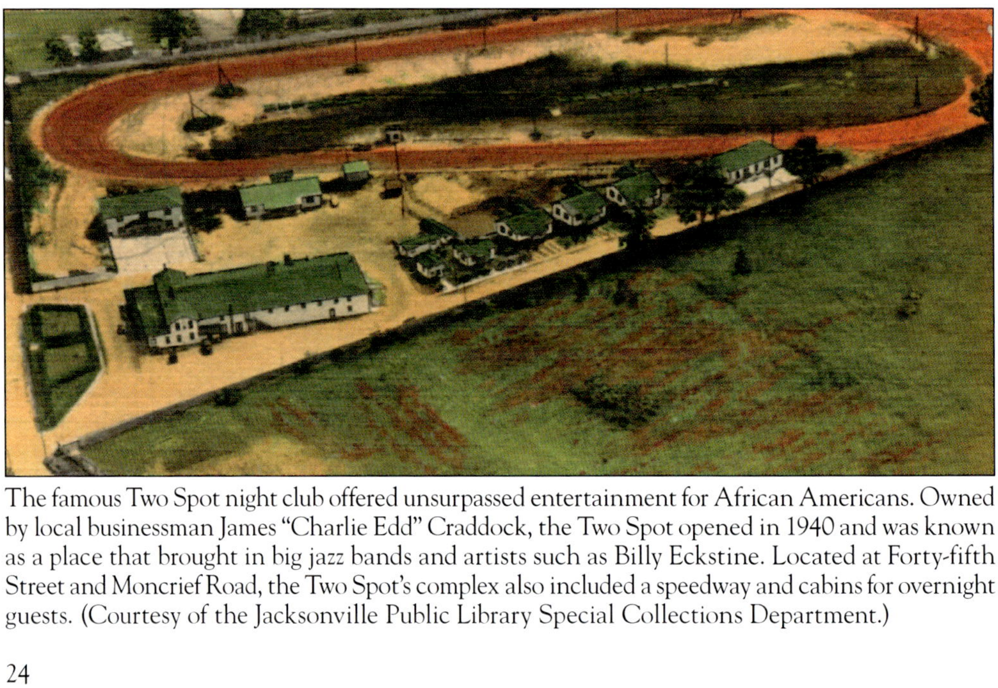

The famous Two Spot night club offered unsurpassed entertainment for African Americans. Owned by local businessman James "Charlie Edd" Craddock, the Two Spot opened in 1940 and was known as a place that brought in big jazz bands and artists such as Billy Eckstine. Located at Forty-fifth Street and Moncrief Road, the Two Spot's complex also included a speedway and cabins for overnight guests. (Courtesy of the Jacksonville Public Library Special Collections Department.)

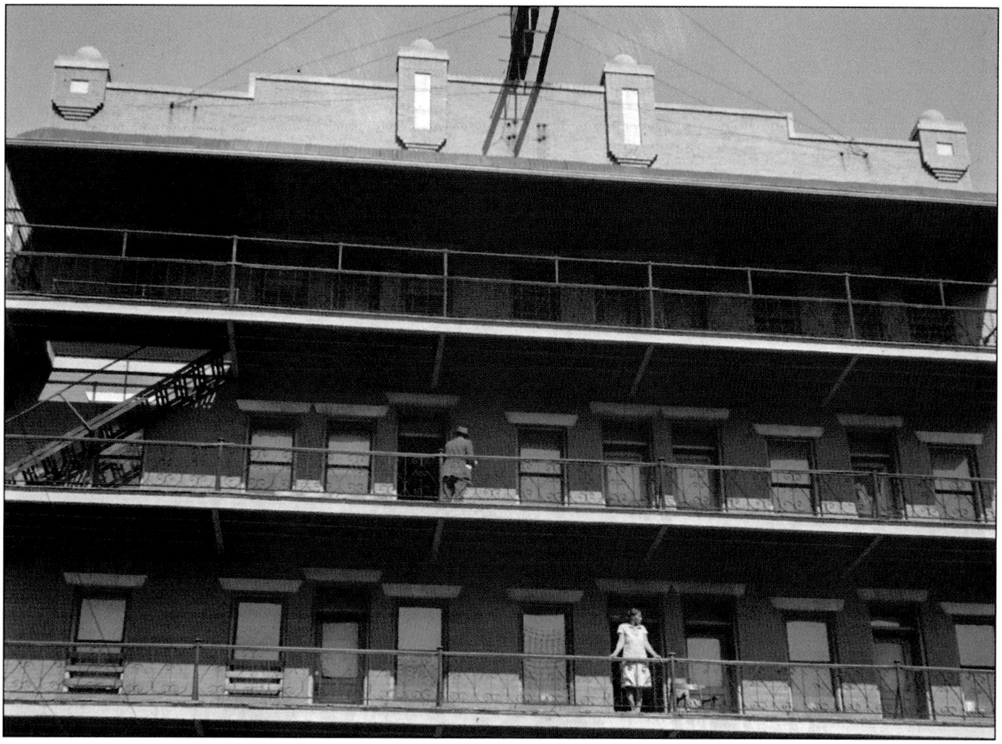

During the late 19th and early 20th centuries, LaVilla was the city's railroad hub, primary red-light district, and center of African American life and culture in northeast Florida. In 1943, when LaVilla was still in its heyday, the area around Ashley Street's Knights of Pythias Building drew crowds. African American patrons made treks to establishments such as the Strand Theater, Frolic Theater, Lenape Bar, Hollywood Music Store, Hotel Charlie Edd, and Green Front Hotel. Ashley Street's vibrant music and entertainment scene emerged as an important stop on what was known as the "Chitlin Circuit" for black entertainers. Along with the Ritz Theatre, the Knights of Pythias Hall hosted numerous famous performers. The building also featured upper-level apartments. In 1957, the Knights of Pythias Building was demolished for a project that never came to fruition. During the 1990s, much of this section of LaVilla was redeveloped into the LaVilla School of the Arts. (Courtesy of the Library of Congress.)

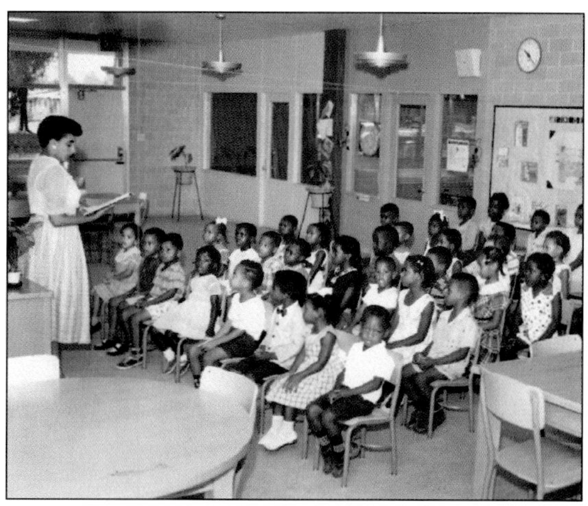

Shown here is a view inside Mary McLeod Bethune Elementary School in 1958. For several decades, the elementary school served as a stronghold for Jacksonville's Moncrief community; however, it was an example of racial inequality in Jacksonville during the mid-20th century. Prior to becoming a public school for African Americans, the property was utilized as a dumping ground for contaminated incinerator ash leading up to the civil-rights era. (Courtesy of the Jacksonville Public Library Special Collections Department.)

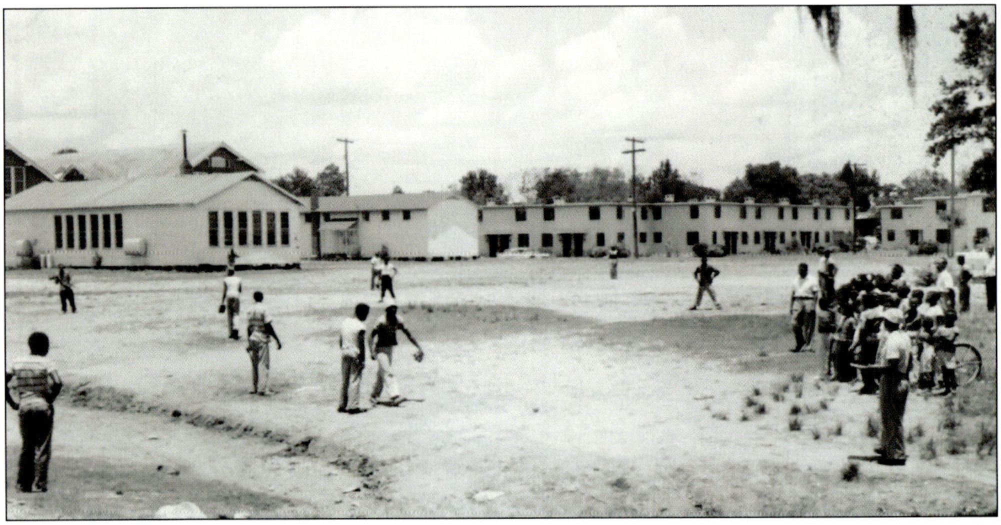

Youth enjoyed the recreational fields at Isaiah Blocker Junior High School, as shown here in 1958. During this era, Rutledge Henry Pearson was an American history teacher at Isaiah Blocker. Pearson was the president of the local NAACP branch and advisor to the NAACP Youth Council. He then became president of the Florida State Conference of NAACP and a member of the board of directors for the national NAACP. (Courtesy of the Jacksonville Public Library Special Collections Department.)

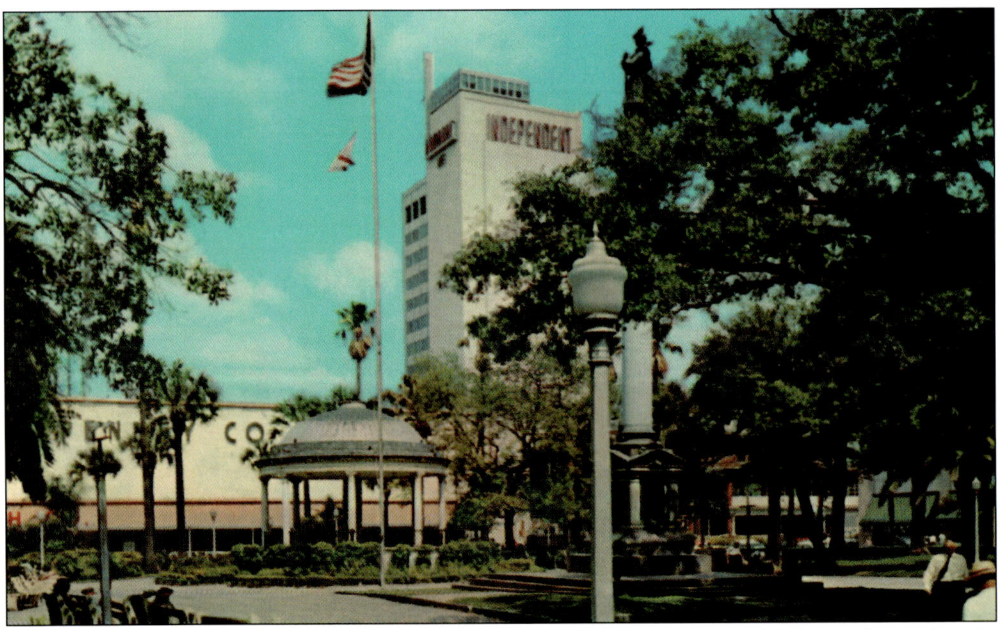

The building at 233 West Duval Street towered above Hemming Park, shown here shortly after its completion in 1955. Stretching 260 feet into the air, the 162,000-square-foot, 19-story tower was constructed to serve as the headquarters for the Independent Life and Accident Insurance Company. The modern reinforced-concrete building's interior is dominated by the use of granite, limestone, and marble finishes. (Courtesy of the Jacksonville Public Library Special Collections Department.)

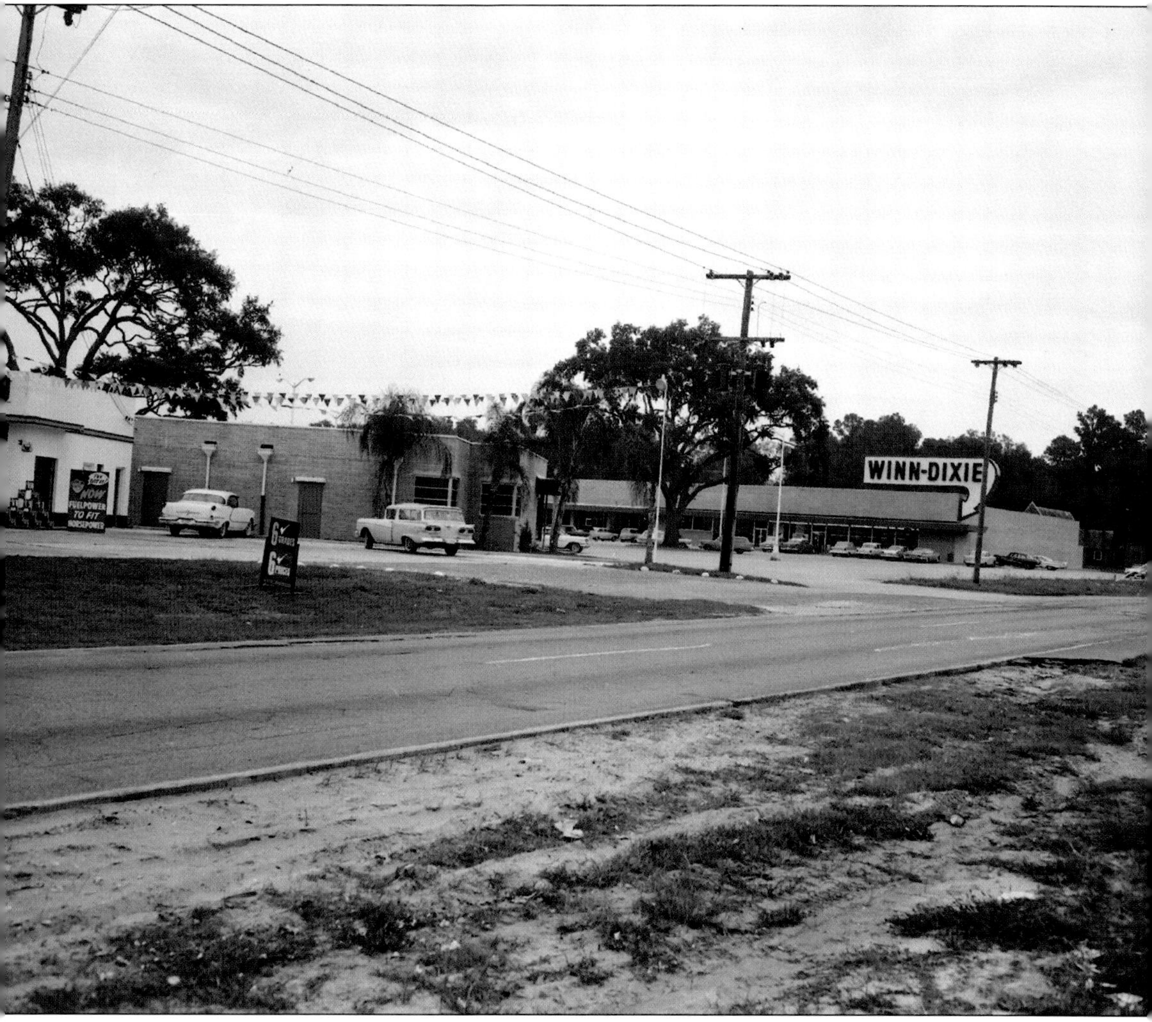

This 1959 image looks south along San Jose Boulevard, near Lone Grove Road (rebranded as University Boulevard with the opening of Jacksonville University) and the Lakewood Shopping Center. Lakewood is one of several Jacksonville neighborhoods that sprang to life during the 1950s. The Lakewood subdivision and shopping area was developed by Walter Crabtree. It is characterized by midcentury shopping plazas and a number of streets named after colleges such as Clemson, Cornell, Fordham, and Emory. Winn-Dixie supermarket has anchored the Lakewood Shopping Center since its opening in 1959. Other early tenants of the shopping center included Lakewood Pharmacy, Dipper Dan's ice cream, Dobb's Restaurant, French Novelty, McCrory's 5 & 10, Worman's Bakery, and Toy Parade. Tracing its roots back to 1925, Winn-Dixie has been headquartered in Jacksonville since the 1944 merger of the Winn & Lovett grocery chain. On December 19, 2011, Winn-Dixie was sold to BI-LO Holdings for $560 million. Based in Jacksonville, the new company operates close to 700 stores in eight southeastern states, employing over 63,000 people. (Courtesy of the State Archives of Florida.)

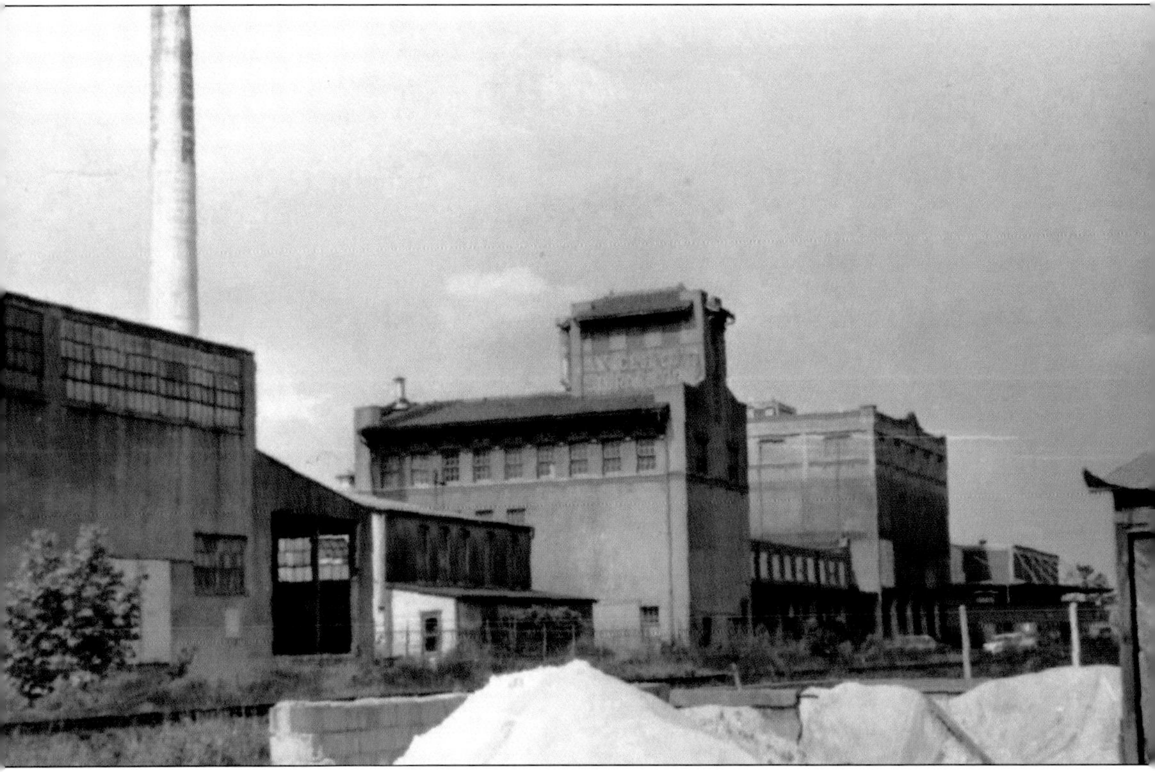

America reigned as the industrial powerhouse of the world by the 1950s, and Jacksonville was Florida's industrial center; however, the city's economy began to change in the decade following the end of World War II. The Jax Brewing Company was one longtime local manufacturer that would not survive this decade. The last brewery to open in the country before Prohibition, Jax Beer had grown to become one of Jacksonville's largest industrial employers at the time the Volstead Act was enacted. In the decades following the passage of the 21st Amendment, the Durkeeville brewery's "Jax Beer, The Drink of Friendship" became one of the most popular drinks in the Southeast. Shortly after World War II, the company created the concept of the six-pack; however, they say all good things must come to an end. In 1956, unable to compete with national brands when it came to absorbing the cost of aluminum cans, the brewery ceased operations. (Courtesy of Ernie Oest via Bob Kay and Beercanhistory.com.)

Two

1960s
Jacksonville Consolidation

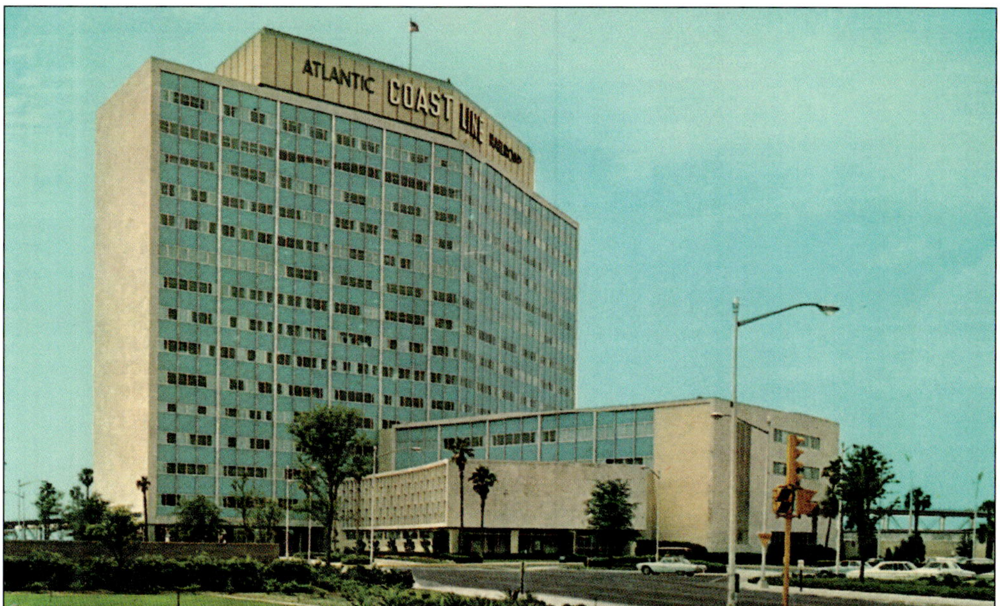

The 17-story Atlantic Coast Line (ACL) headquarters building was the centerpiece of Mayor Haydon Burns's downtown revitalization efforts when it opened in 1960. The ACL was founded in 1900 and announced its departure from Wilmington, North Carolina, in 1955. Jacksonville was selected from three candidate cities, the other two being Savannah, Georgia, and Charleston, South Carolina. The ACL merged with the Seaboard Air Line Railroad (SAL) in 1967, becoming the Seaboard Coast Line Railroad. (Courtesy of the Jacksonville Public Library Special Collections Department.)

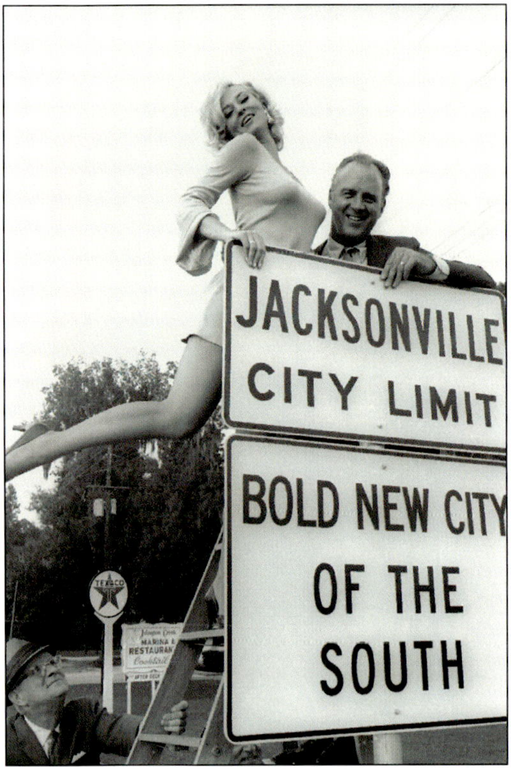

Mayor Hans Tanzler poses with actress Lee Meredith. In 1968, Jacksonville became known as the "Bold New City of the South" after its merger with Duval County. Over time, this photograph has become an icon for Jacksonville's consolidation, which transformed the city into the largest in the continental United States by land area. Elected mayor in 1967, Tanzler won two more terms before an unsuccessful run for governor in 1979. In 1968, Meredith was a popular 30-year-old actress in town for a performance at the Alhambra Dinner Theatre. Hoping to encourage media to cover the city-limits sign event, Tanzler's administration arranged for Meredith to attend. According to the *Florida Times-Union*, Tanzler was quoted, "Jack wanted her to put up the sign and me to hold the ladder. I didn't just fall off the turnip truck. If I do that, it's going to be immediately assumed I had advantages a lot of people would like to have. So I said, I'll get up there and she can hand it to me." (Courtesy of the Jacksonville Historic Society.)

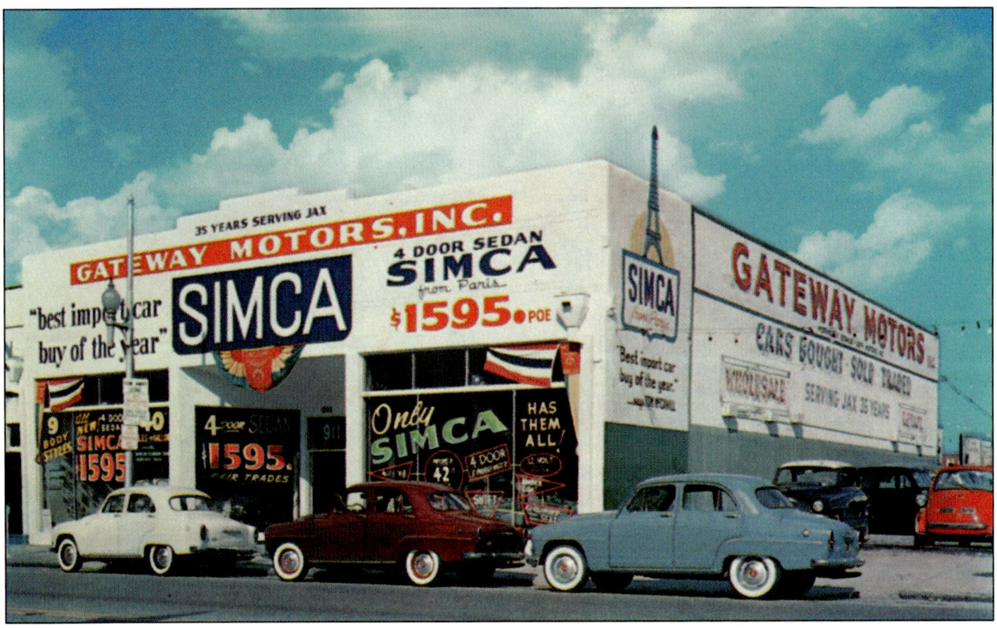

Gateway Motors, at 911 North Main Street, was an exclusive Simca dealer in 1960. During most of its postwar activity, Simca was one of the biggest automobile manufacturers in France. A few years later, Gateway Motors was razed to make way for the Heart of Jacksonville Motor Hotel. At the time, the mid-century Moderne hotel boasted one of the best skyline views of Jacksonville. (Courtesy of the Jacksonville Public Library Special Collections Department.)

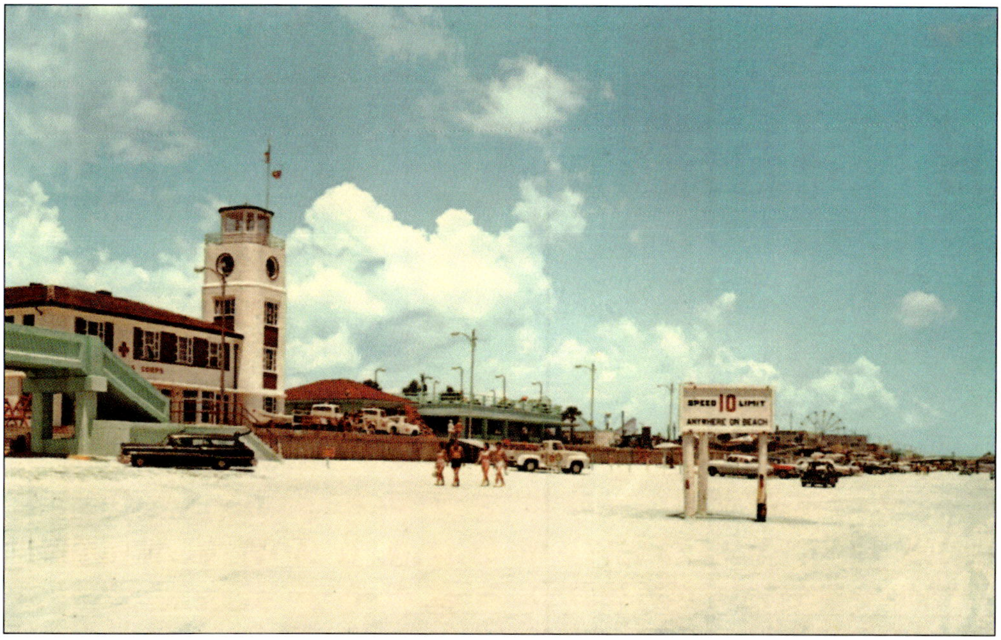

The Art Deco–style American Red Cross Volunteer Lifesaving Corps building was completed in 1946. The American Red Cross Volunteer Lifesaving Corps have operated out of this Jacksonville Beach site since 1913, making it the oldest and only operating volunteer lifesaving corps in the world. (Courtesy of the Jacksonville Public Library Special Collections Department.)

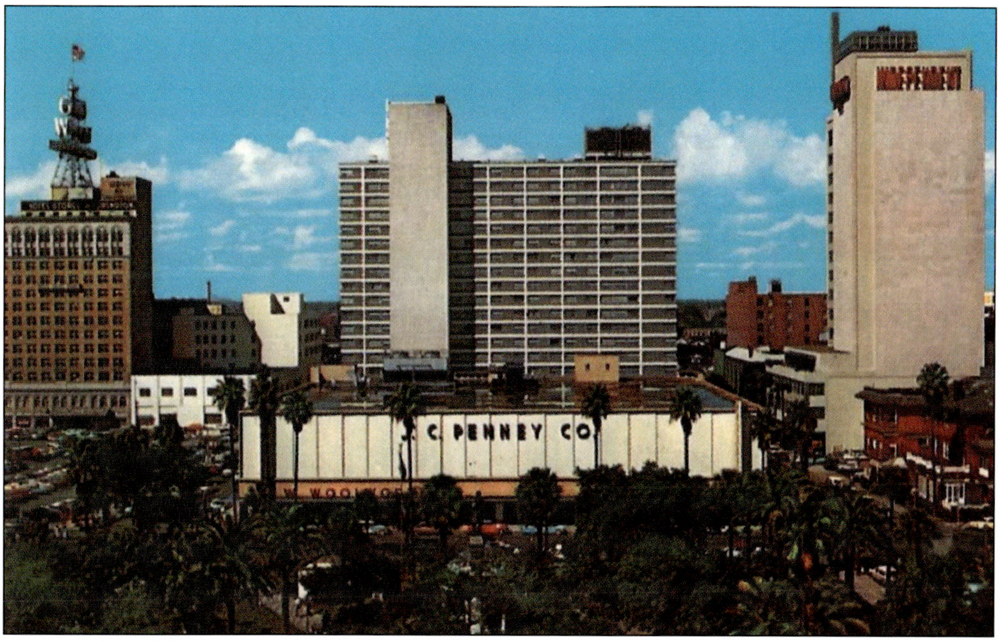

Long anchored by the Cohen Brothers' flagship department store, Hemming Plaza evolved into downtown's retail epicenter with the 1955 opening of J.C. Penney and F.W. Woolworth on the former Hotel Windsor site. F.W. Woolworth shared a common wall with the 90,000-square-foot, three-story J.C. Penney store, allowing shoppers to walk from one to the other without going outside. (Courtesy of the Jacksonville Public Library Special Collections Department.)

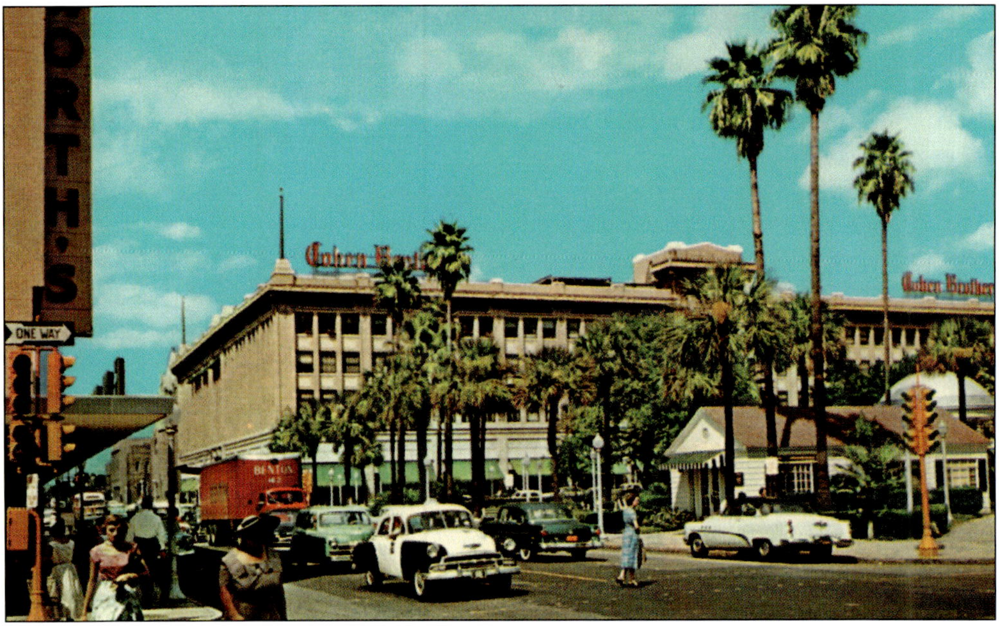

The F.W. Woolworth lunch counter, at the intersection of North Hogan Street and West Monroe Street, was the site of an NAACP Youth Council demonstration on August 13, 1960. That day, the youth were attacked by segregationists with axe handles. The event, now known as Axe Handle Saturday, became a turning point in the city's history. (Courtesy of the Jacksonville Public Library Special Collections Department.)

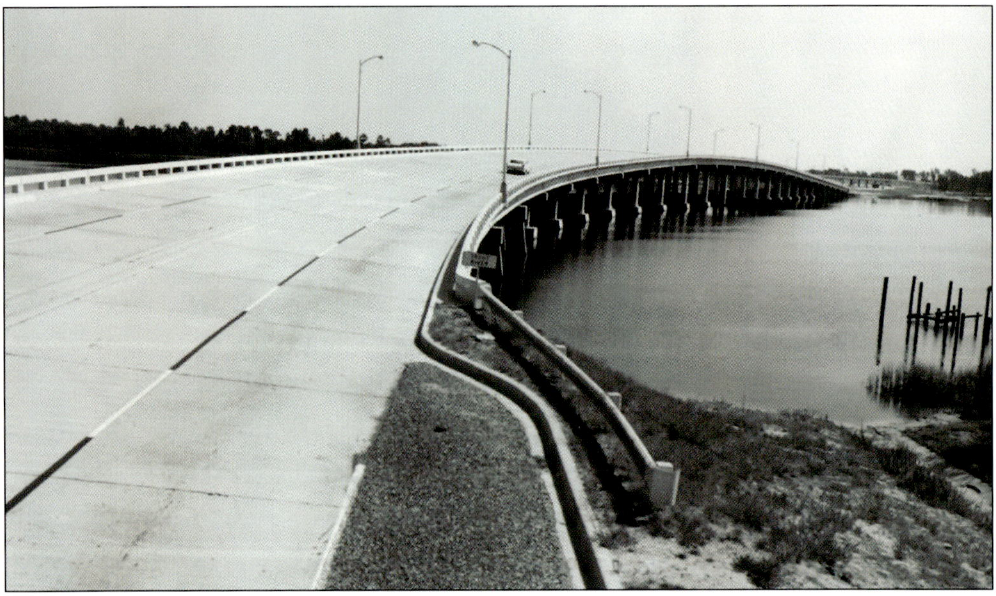

Interstate 95 was initially signed in 1959, and the first section to be opened to traffic was in Jacksonville in 1960. Pictured here on June 3, 1960, the Trout River Bridge was the northern terminus of the new Jacksonville Expressway. The selection of the initial 18-mile expressway system's routes was determined by avoiding areas deemed most valuable and used as a tool to eliminate neighborhoods political leaders had viewed as blight. (Courtesy of the State Archives of Florida.)

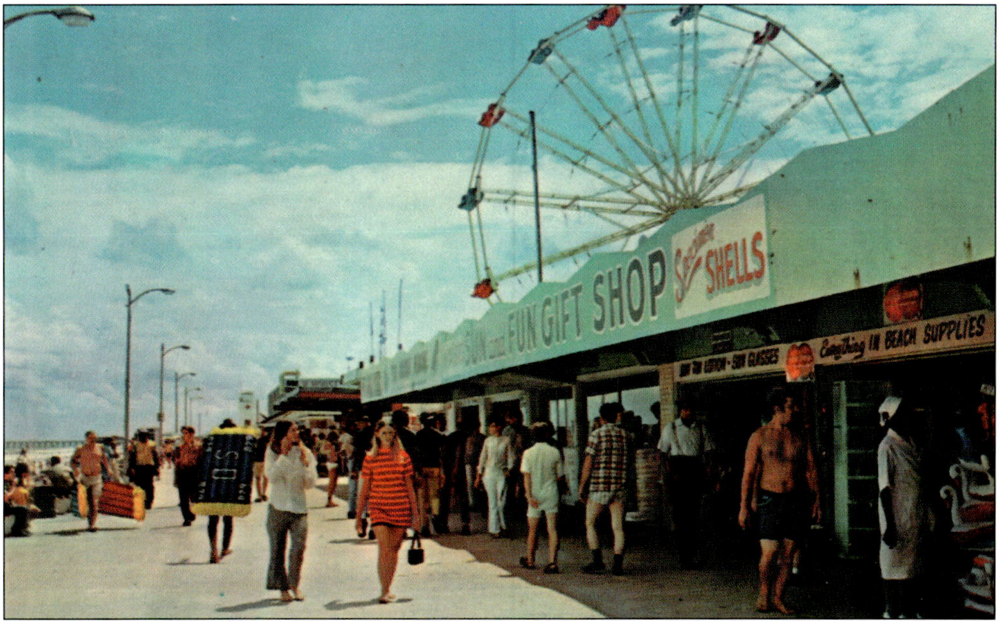

A diverse crowd enjoys the shops and entertainment along the Jacksonville Beach on a warm summer day. Seeking to avoid the racial disturbances and demonstrations that had taken place in Jacksonville and St. Augustine, the City of Jacksonville Beach desegregated its public accommodations before the passage of the Civil Rights Act of July 4, 1964. (Courtesy of the Jacksonville Public Library Special Collections Department.)

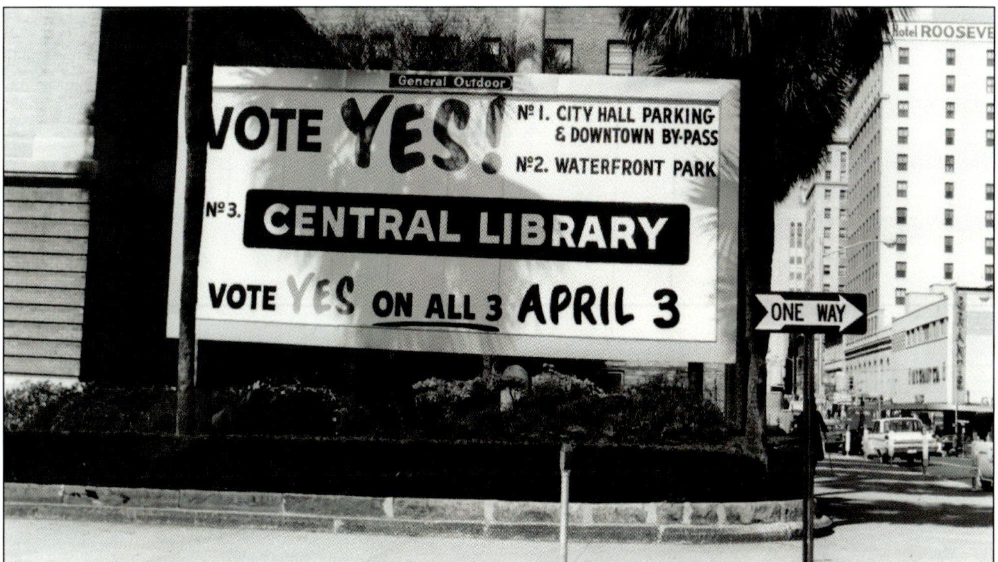

This is an image of a bond election–campaign billboard, located on the site of the proposed Haydon Burns Library. The billboard, approved on April 3, 1962, was one of three such billboards sponsored by Citizens for Progress, a group that handled promotion for civic improvements. The buildings in the background, the old city hall and Windle Hotel, were soon demolished to make way for the new public library. (Courtesy of the Jacksonville Public Library Special Collections Department.)

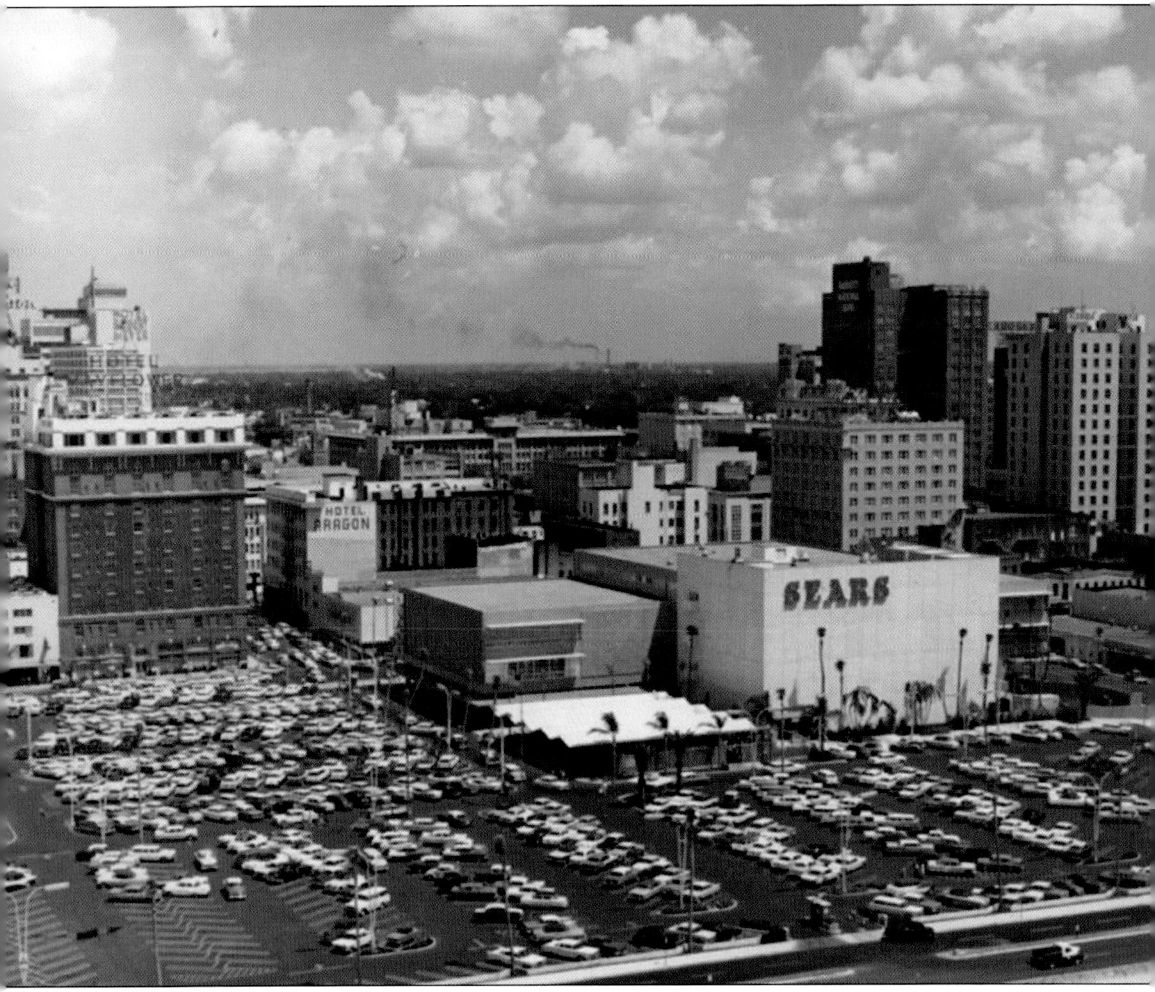

Downtown's Sears was envisioned to be the best. It was the chain's largest in the South, measuring 260,000 square feet spread out over four levels and a basement. Over 40,000 people turned out for its grand opening in June 1959. Called the "Cadillac Store," its unique features included the largest automobile-accessory department in the nation. It was also the first department store to have a sit-down restaurant with waiter service instead of cafeteria style, the last Sears store built with more than two floors, and the first urban department store to have a surface parking lot of its own. Employing 1,100 people, to some degree the store operated as a mini-mall. By 1972, the Cadillac store had become the chain's leading location in volume of sales in its 13-state southeastern territory; however, the large store was also one of the chain's most expensive to operate and maintain. In 1981, Sears relocated from its waterfront downtown location to Regency Square Mall. (Courtesy of the Jacksonville Public Library Special Collections Department.)

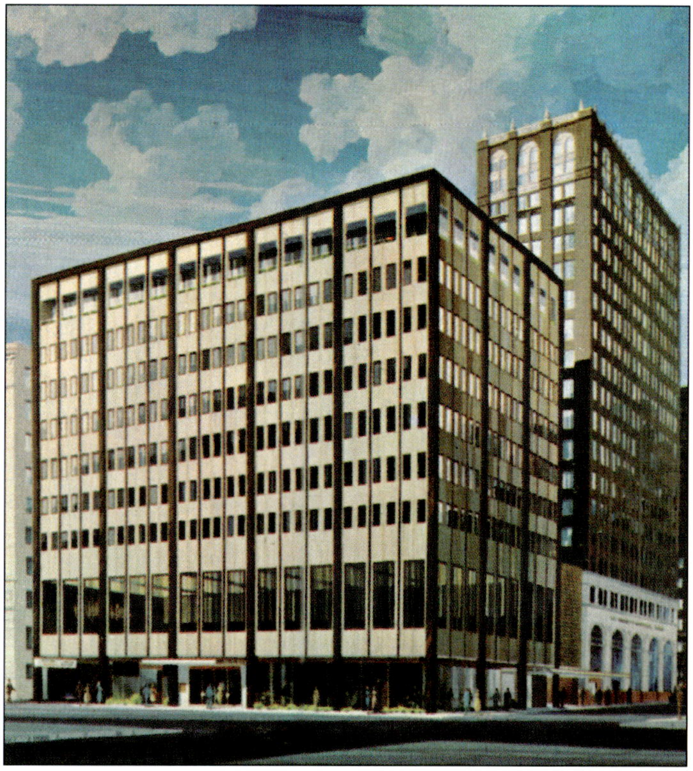

Pictured here is a rendering of 100 North Laura Street, which became the headquarters of Barnett Bank when completed in 1962. Founded in 1877, the institution grew to become Florida's largest commercial bank and a Fortune 500 company by 1995, with over 600 branches, $3.10 billion in revenue, and 6,800 local employees. In 1997, Barnett was acquired by NationsBank. A year later, NationsBank acquired BankAmerica to become Bank of America. In 2004, Jacksonville Bank moved its headquarters into the building. (Courtesy of the Jacksonville Public Library Special Collections Department.)

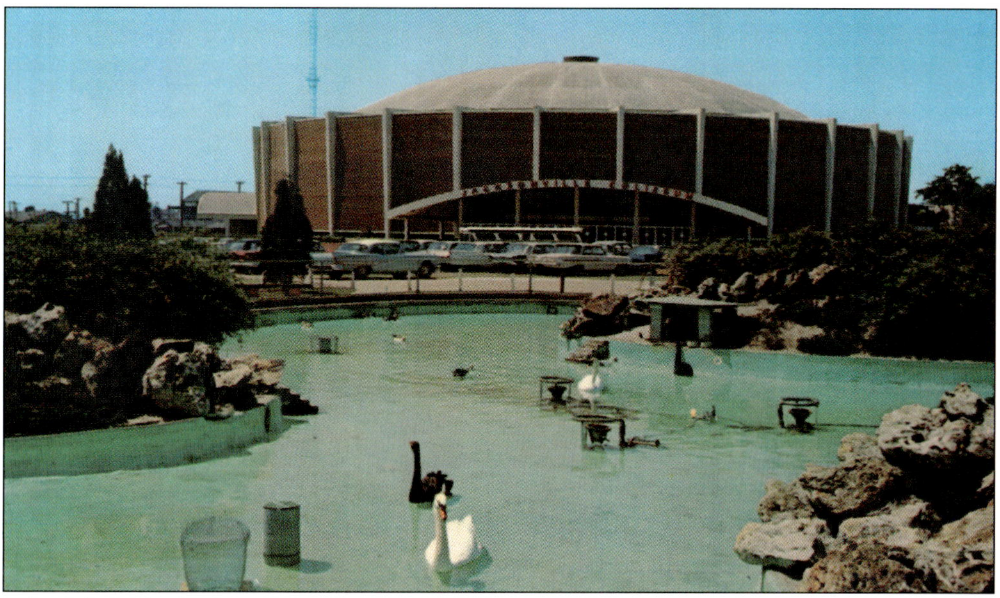

When the Jacksonville Coliseum was dedicated on November 24, 1963, it provided the city with a 10,276-seat arena for indoor professional sports, high school graduations, concerts, circuses, and other events. Concerts and shows during its 43-year history include Rush, Bob Dylan, Duran Duran, Billy Joel, Bon Jovi, Frank Sinatra, Jimi Hendrix, Elvis Presley, the Smashing Pumpkins, David Bowie, Bruce Springsteen, Led Zeppelin, Lynyrd Skynyrd, Journey, AC/DC, Deep Purple, Def Leppard, and Iron Maiden. (Courtesy of the Jacksonville Public Library Special Collections Department.)

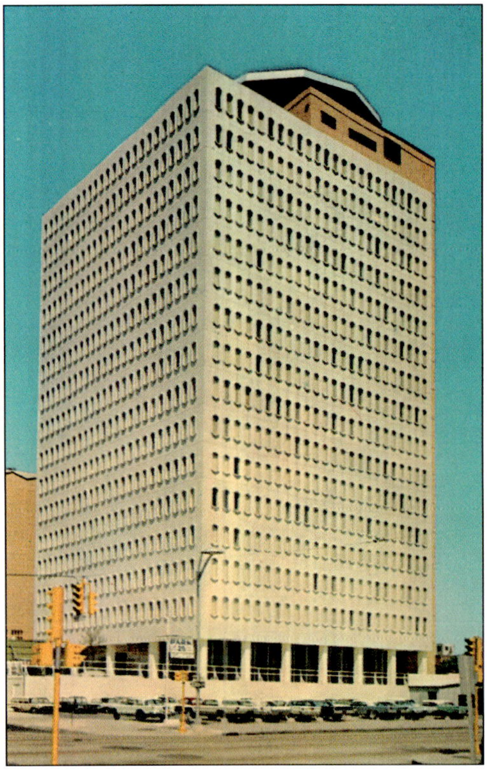

Completed at a cost of $12 million in 1963, the Universal Marion Building was the crown jewel of the downtown center. At the time, the 19-story tower was the second tallest in the city and included the Embers, the world's largest revolving restaurant, which rotated 360 degrees every 90 minutes. The complex also included a six-story, 180,000-square-foot J.B. Ivey & Company department store. The downtown Jacksonville store was the first major department store to be constructed in a metropolitan US downtown location in 30 years. Anticipating growth, the store's foundation was designed to accommodate two additional floors as needed. The complex's largest tenant, Universal Marion, was founded by Louis Elwood Wolfson, a Wall Street financier and eventual owner of Affirmed, the 1978 American Triple Crown winner. The firm cofinanced the production of Mel Brooks' first movie *The Producers*, which won an Academy Award. It also funded Woody Allen's movie *Take the Money and Run*. (Courtesy of the Jacksonville Public Library Special Collections Department.)

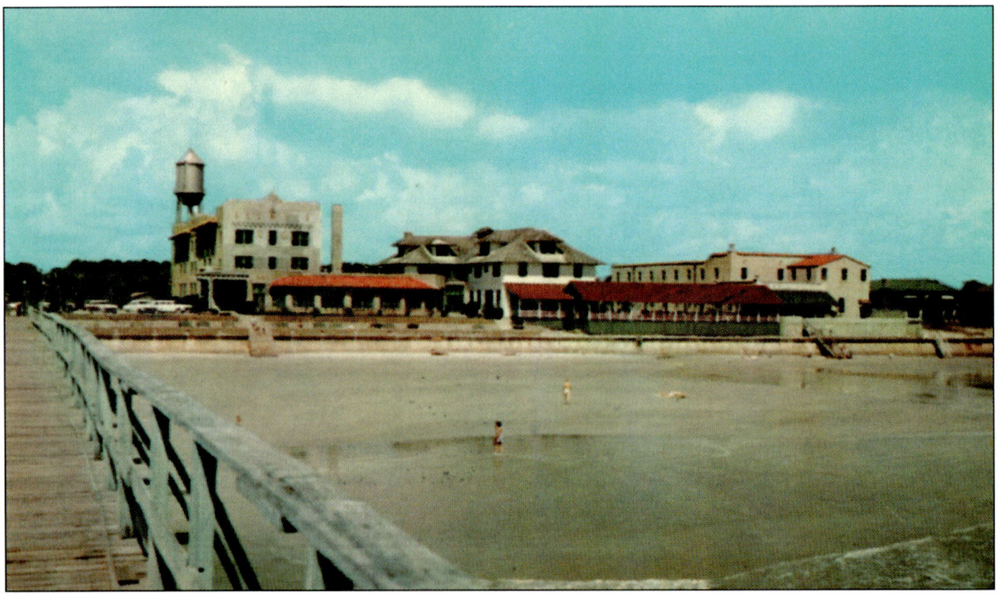

The 50-room Atlantic Beach Hotel was built in 1925 by W.H. Adams Sr. on the former site of Henry Flagler's massive six-story, 200-room Continental Hotel. The City of Atlantic Beach constructed the adjacent concrete bulkhead in 1933 and 1934. In 1964, Hurricane Dora would devastate the hotel and adjacent fishing pier. Although the hotel was rebuilt, the site has since been redeveloped into the Cloister Condominiums. (Courtesy of the Jacksonville Public Library Special Collections Department.)

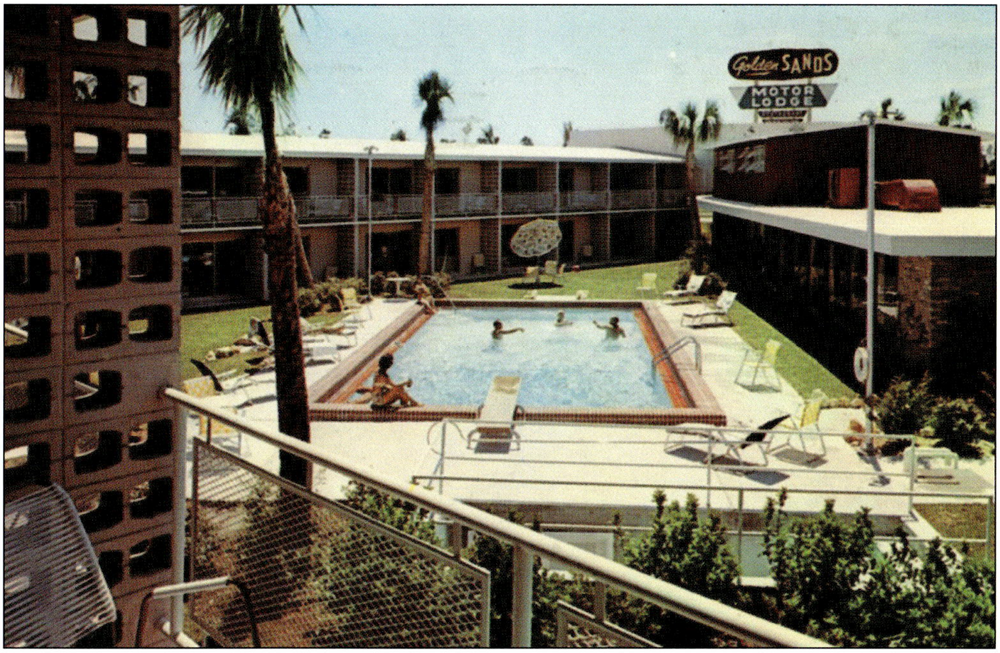

This is a 1964 postcard of the Golden Sands Motor Lodge at the junction of Philips Highway and Expressway By-Pass Route 8, some 10 miles south of downtown. As the country's highway system began to develop, long-distance road journeys became more common, and the need for inexpensive, easily accessible overnight accommodations close to major routes led to the growth of the motor lodge. (Courtesy of the Jacksonville Public Library Special Collections Department.)

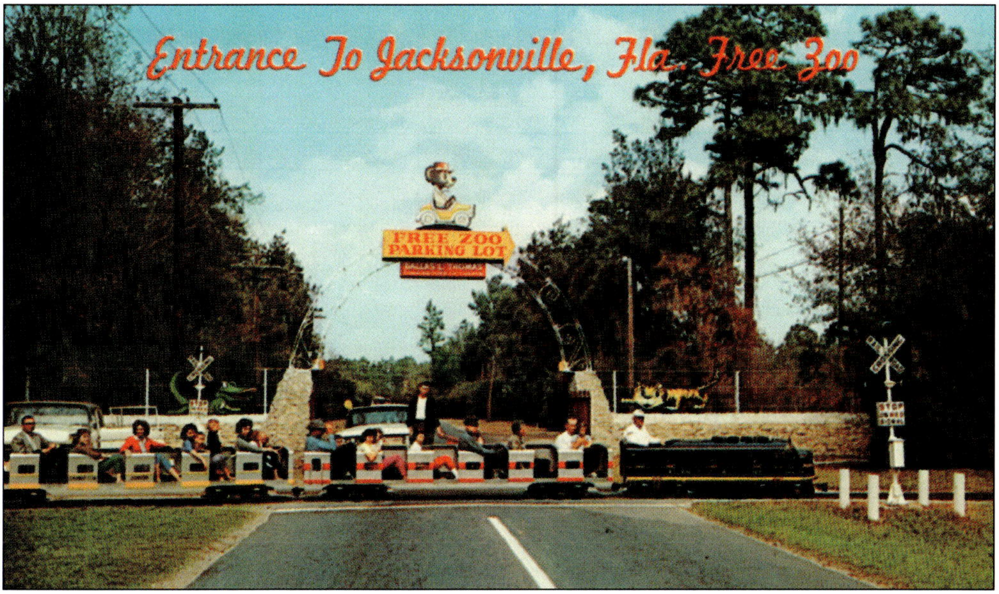

The entrance to the Jacksonville Free Zoo is blocked by the passenger-carrying zoo train. The zoo originally opened as the Municipal Zoo in Springfield Park on May 12, 1914. The first animal on exhibit was a red deer fawn. Now known as the Jacksonville Zoo and Gardens, the zoo is considered one of the city's premiere attractions, drawing over 800,000 paying visitors annually. (Courtesy of the Jacksonville Public Library Special Collections Department.)

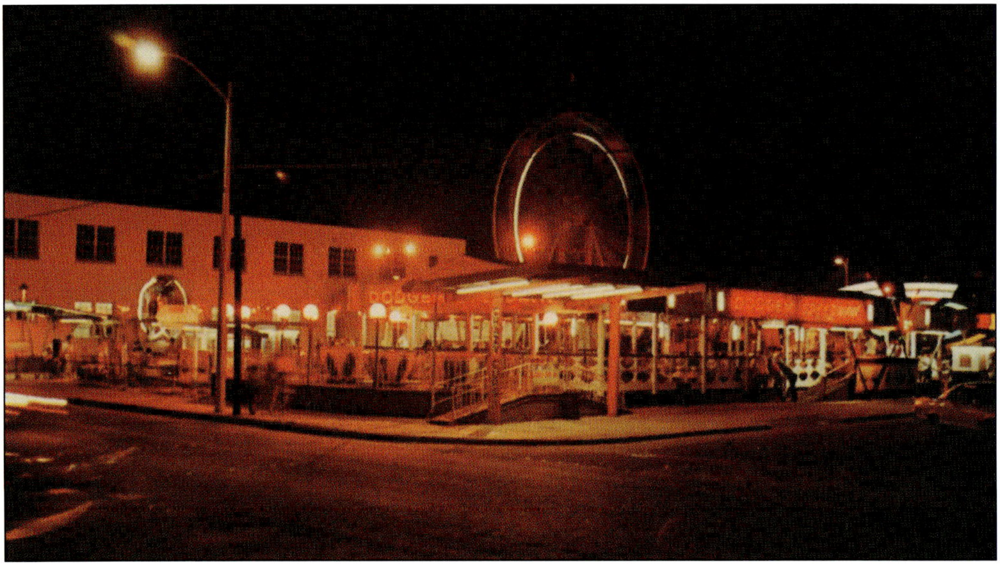

Pictured here is the intersection of First Street North and Second Avenue North in Jacksonville Beach. Once known as Little Coney Island, Jacksonville Beach had a vibrant amusement park scene that consisted of roller coasters, Ferris wheels, bumper cars, Tilt-A-Whirls, penny arcades, a fishing pier, and a half-mile-long boardwalk. A direct hit by Hurricane Donna in 1964 led to the downfall of Jacksonville Beach's amusement-park scene. (Courtesy of the State Archives of Florida.)

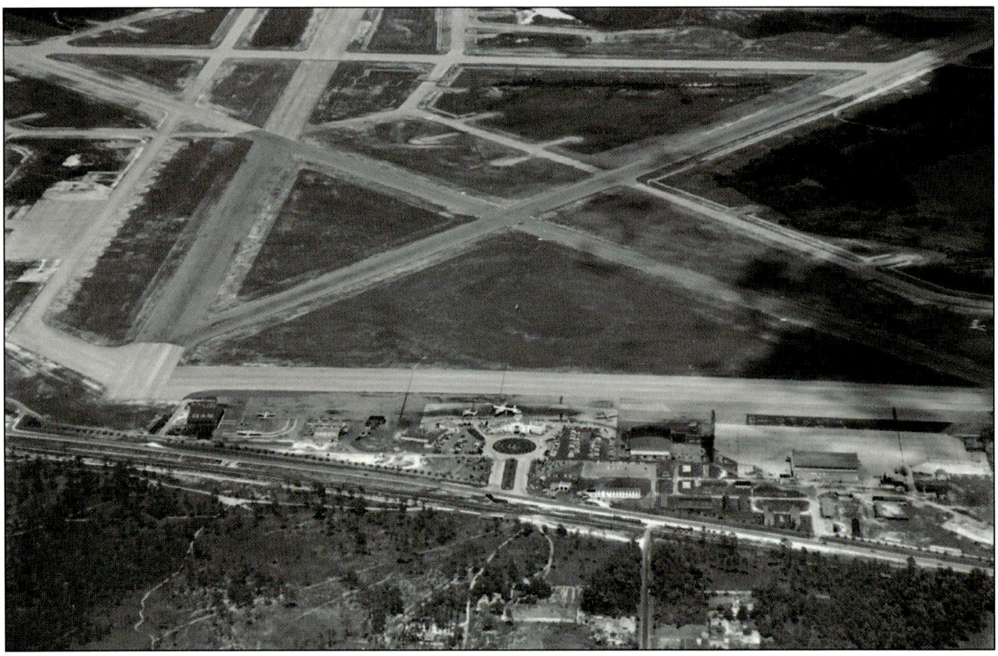

Before airlines like JetBlue, Spirit, and Southwest hit the scene, there was National Airlines. National was the first airline to introduce domestic jet service in the United States. It was based at Jacksonville's Imeson Field until the late 1950s. In 1965, taxpayers approved a $9-million bond for a larger airport. After the opening of Jacksonville International Airport, Imeson was abandoned and converted into Imeson International Industrial Park in 1970. (Courtesy of State Archives of Florida.)

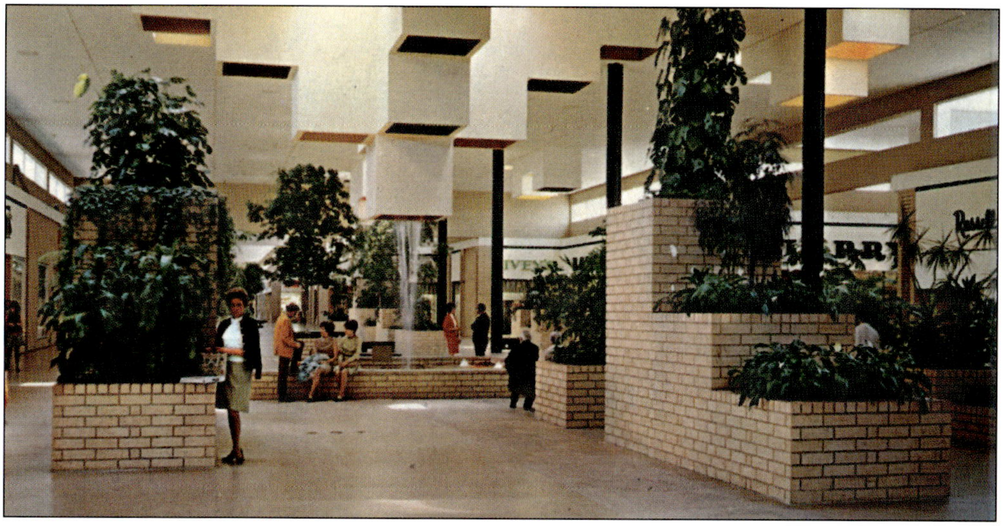

Built on the site of Humphrey's Gold, a titanium strip mine, Martin Stein's Regency Square Mall was one of the nation's largest and most modern enclosed-mall shopping centers when it opened its doors to 25,000 shoppers on March 1, 1967. Grand-opening ceremonies were held at 9:45 a.m. at the mall's main arcade, which was blocked by a golden chain that was opened by the Steins. Mayor Louis Ritter, county commissioner Bob Harris, and W. Ashley Verlander of the Jacksonville Area Chamber of Commerce took part in the opening ceremonies. Considered one of the country's most successful malls, Regency expanded to include Montgomery Ward and Sears in 1981. Relocating to Regency from downtown, Sears store manager Benard Datz would go on to say, "The day of the big downtown department stores is gone until we get more people living downtown." (Courtesy of the State Archives of Florida.)

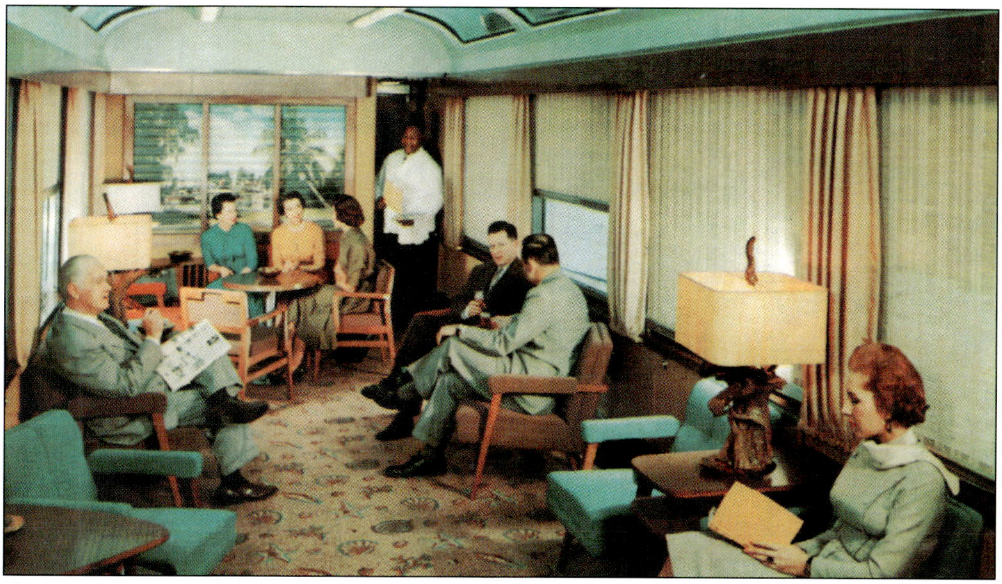

Here is a scene inside the *Silver Meteor* passenger train's Sun Lounge. The Seaboard Air Line Railroad (SAL) introduced the *Silver Meteor* on February 2, 1939. Running between New York and Florida, it was the first diesel-powered streamliner in Florida. The best timing for Amtrak's *Silver Meteor* between Miami and New York City was 27 hours in 2008; SAL's first edition took 25 hours in 1939. (Courtesy of the Jacksonville Public Library Special Collections Department.)

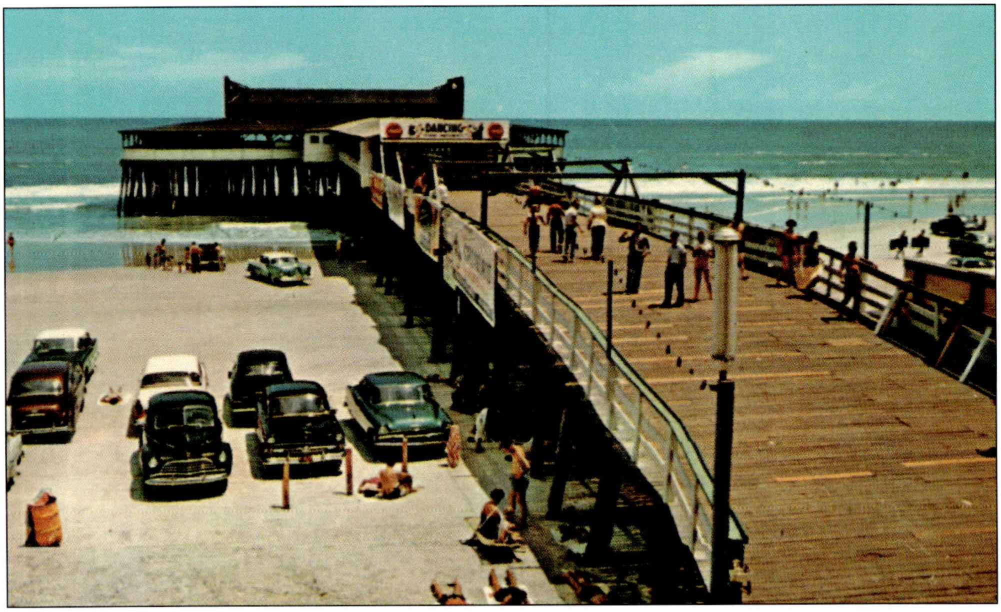

Spending time at Shad's Pier was a favorite pastime for many Jacksonville Beach residents and visitors. Constructed in 1922, the pier was located between Second Avenue North and Third Avenue North. Shad's Pier was largely destroyed by fire in 1961. A year before its destruction, a new pier opened at the foot of Sixth Avenue South. (Courtesy of the Jacksonville Public Library Special Collections Department.)

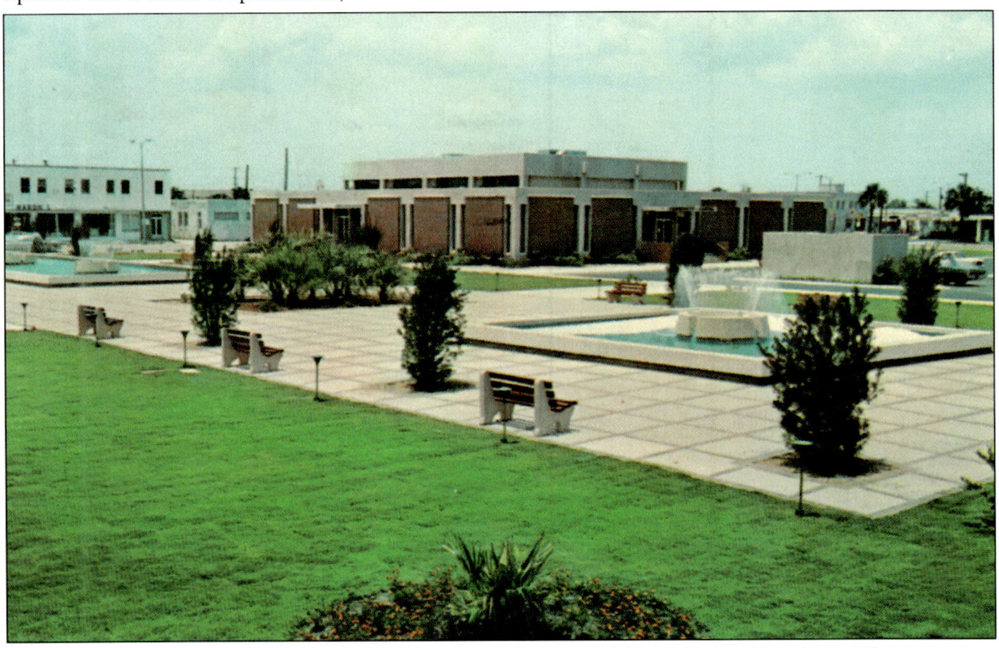

The Jacksonville Beach Library and Community Center, at Third Street North and First Avenue North, is pictured here in 1967. The adjacent block had been the site of the Ocean View amusement park since August 1926. Ocean View included a large roller coaster in imitation of New York's Coney Island coasters. On March 9, 1961, a fire destroyed most of the amusement park. (Courtesy of the Jacksonville Public Library Special Collections Department.)

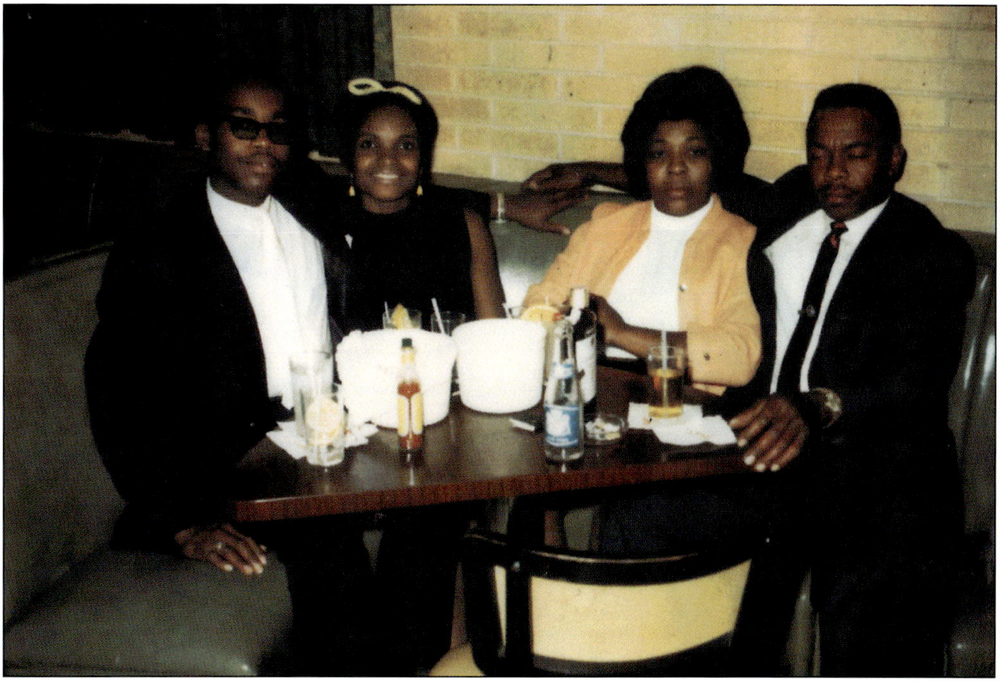

This is the interior of the Edgewood Lounge in 1969. Before the completion of Interstate 295, Edgewood Avenue served as the bypass around the west side of the city. As the Northwest and Westside areas of Jacksonville exploded with rapid population growth during the 1960s, Edgewood Avenue emerged to become a major commercial thoroughfare for residents. (Courtesy of Edwin and Erma Davis Jr.)

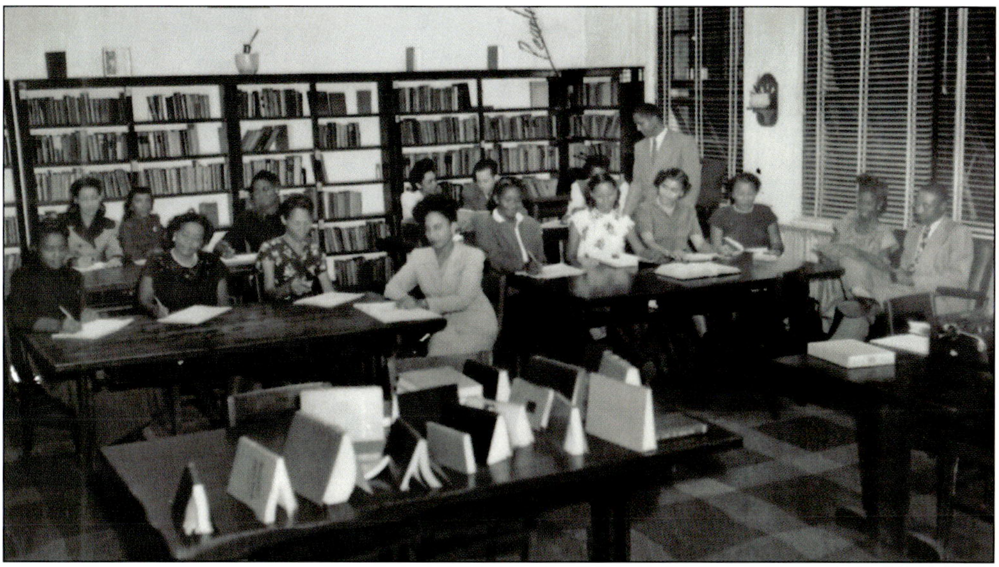

Wilder Park was the city's largest public space for the African American community during segregation. Donated by the descendants of Charles B. Wilder, the 30-acre park included a track, baseball diamond, community center, and branch library (pictured). Located at the intersection of Third and Lee Streets, the Wilder Park Library was the Jacksonville Public Library's first branch location. (Courtesy of the Jacksonville Public Library Special Collections Department.)

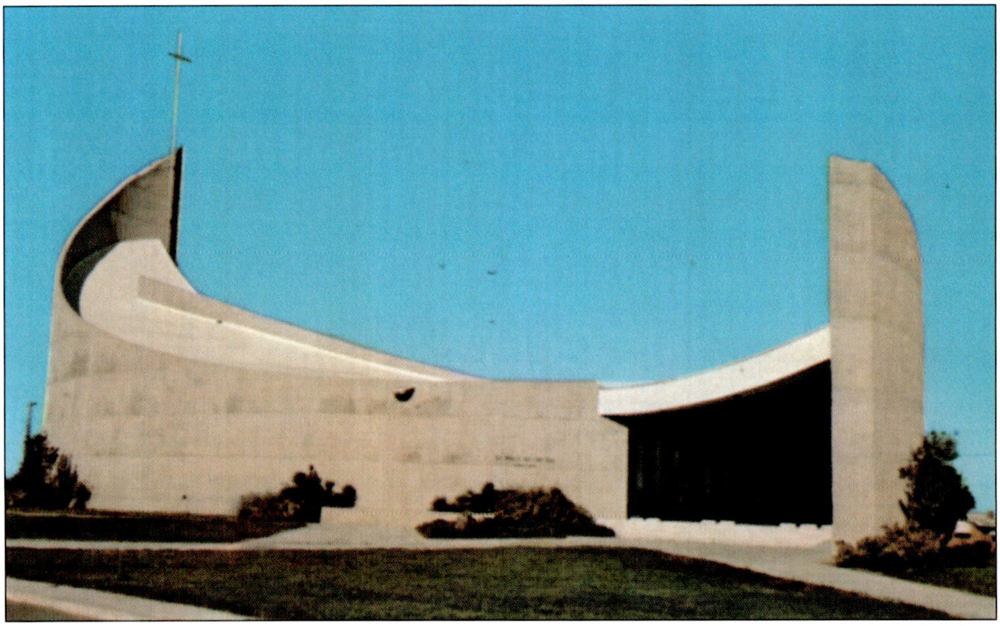

Dating back to 1887, St. Paul's by-the-Sea Episcopal Church is the first church to be established in the Jacksonville Beaches. In 1967, the congregation dedicated its current building. The large, modern coquina-concrete structure was included on the American Institute of Architects' Florida chapter's list "Florida Architecture: 100 Years, 100 Places" on April 18, 2012. (Courtesy of the Jacksonville Public Library Special Collections Department.)

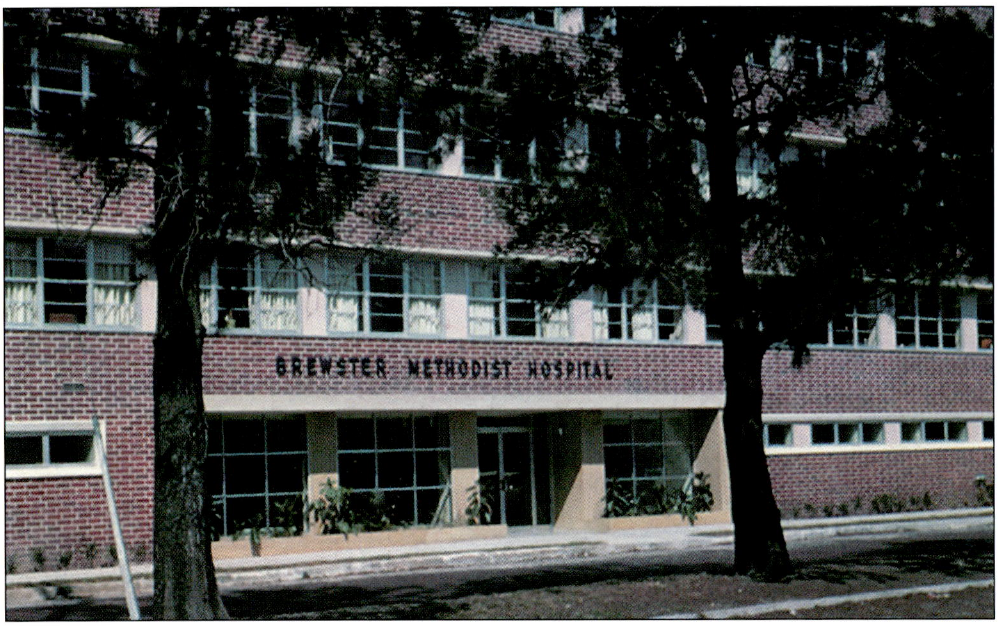

Brewster Methodist Hospital was established in 1967 after the closing of Brewster Hospital. Brewster, Jacksonville's first hospital for African Americans, dating back to 1901, shut its doors in 1966 after the passage of the 1964 Civil Rights Act opened the city's other health-care facilities to African Americans. Brewster Methodist's Springfield medical campus is now a part of UF Health Jacksonville. (Courtesy of UF Health Jacksonville.)

Three

1970s
The New Bold City of the South

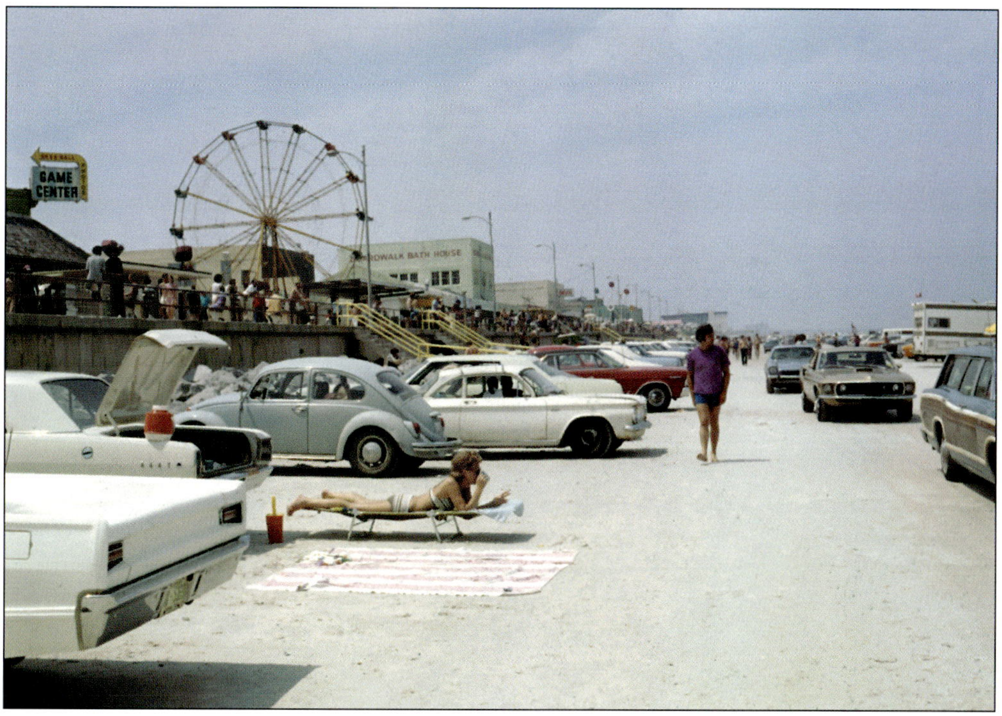

An automobile-filled Jacksonville Beach scene in May 1973 is pictured here. In 1968, when most residents of Duval County voted to approve consolidation between the county and the city of Jacksonville, Jacksonville Beach, together with Atlantic Beach, Neptune Beach, and the Westside community of Baldwin, voted to retain their own municipal governments. As such, they are not part of the city of Jacksonville but receive county-level services from Jacksonville and vote for Jacksonville's mayor and city council. (Courtesy of the State Archives of Florida.)

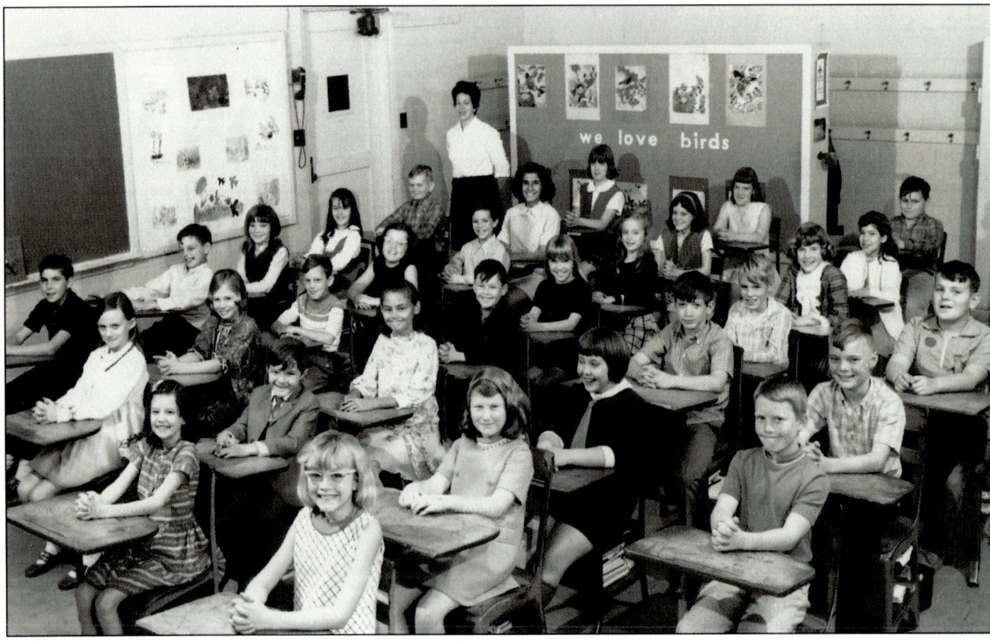

Shown here is Jane S. Coffey's fourth-grade class at Ramona Elementary School during the 1969–1970 school year. Located at 5540 Ramona Boulevard, the school opened in 1951 as a result of rapid suburban growth. Additional Westside growth was fueled with the opening of nearby Normandy Mall in 1963. Developed by the Edward J. DeBartolo Corporation, the 427,000-square-foot mall was the first fully enclosed mall in Jacksonville. (Courtesy of the Jacksonville Public Library Special Collections Department.)

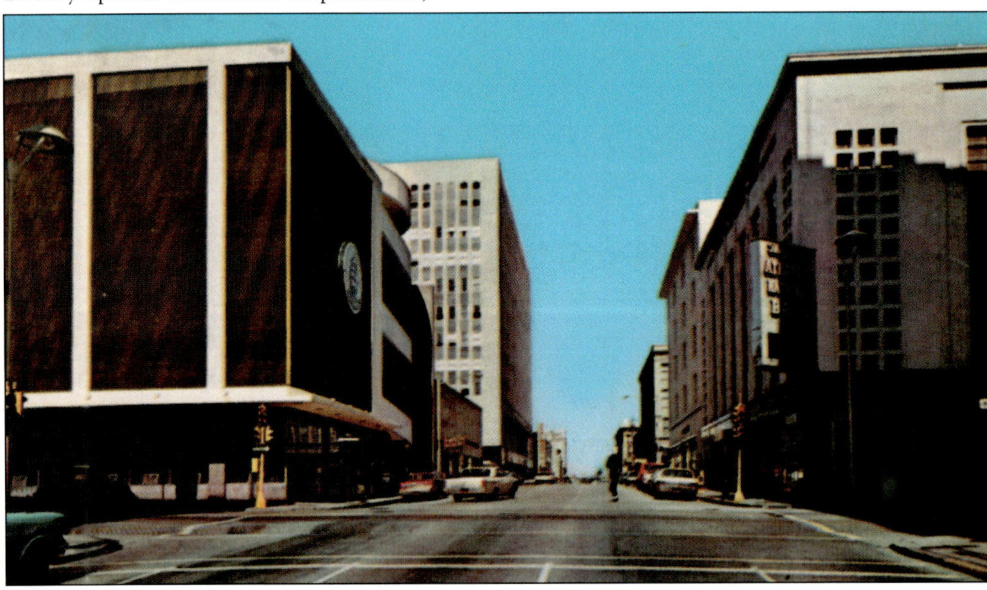

Atlantic National Bank dominates the intersection of North Hogan and West Forsyth Streets in 1970. The bank was founded by Edward W. Lane, railroad magnate Thomas P. Denham, and Fred W. Hoyt in 1903. By 1976, the Jacksonville-based bank had grown to include assets of $3.9 billion. In 1985, it merged with First Union of Charlotte, North Carolina. (Courtesy of the Jacksonville Public Library Special Collections Department.)

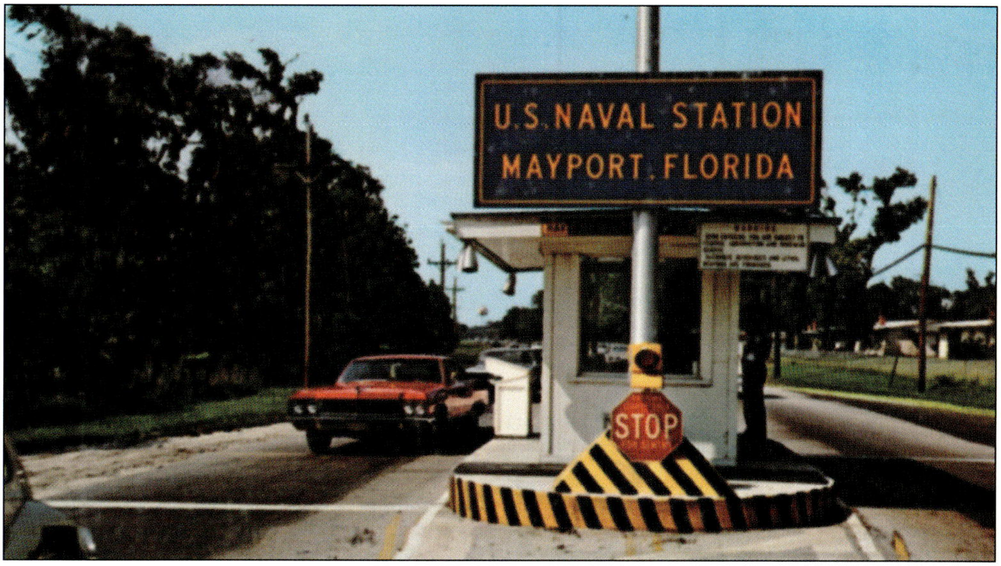

Since its commissioning in December 1942, Naval Station Mayport has grown to become the third-largest fleet concentration area in the United States. Mayport's operational composition is unique, with a busy harbor capable of accommodating 34 ships and an 8,000-foot-long runway capable of handling any aircraft in the Department of Defense inventory. (Courtesy of the Jacksonville Public Library Special Collections Department.)

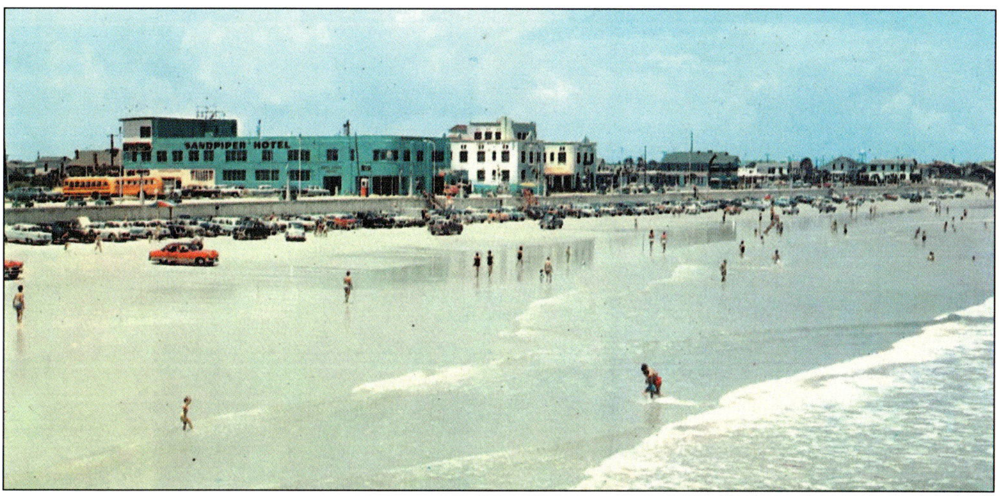

The Sandpiper Hotel, near the intersection of Fifth Avenue North and North First Street, and the Casa Marina Hotels dominate the boardwalk in the background. This 1970s Jacksonville Beach scene is almost unrecognizable in the 21st century. Today, the seawalls are buried under sand, and driving on the beach was outlawed in 1979, ending a 73-year-old tradition that began in 1906. (Courtesy of Boston Public Library.)

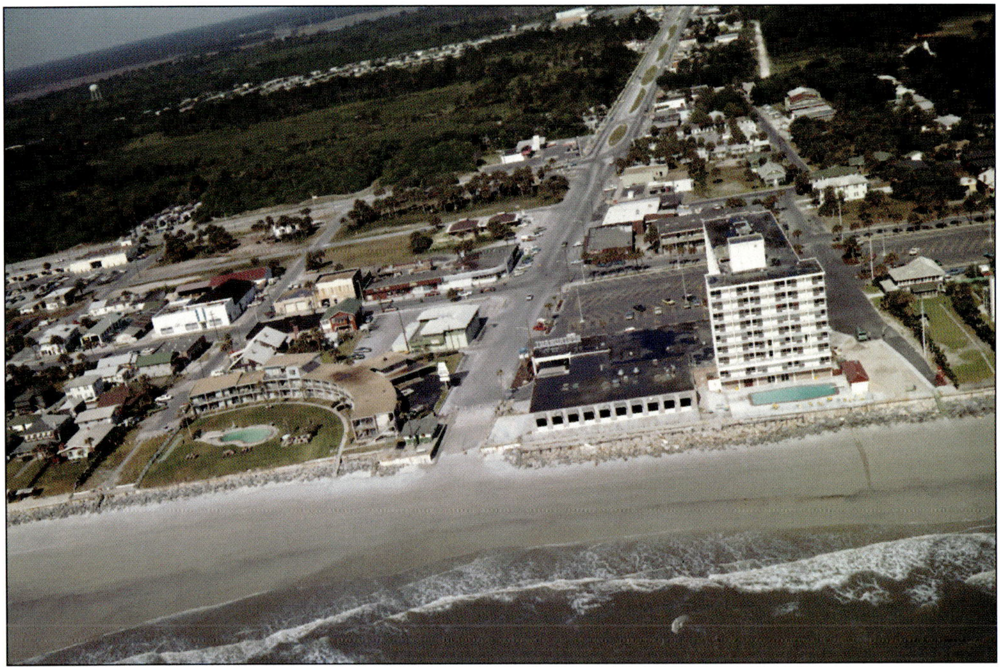

Atlantic Boulevard serves as the boundary between the cities of Atlantic and Neptune Beach. Originally a resort community developed around Henry Flagler's Continental Hotel, Atlantic Beach was incorporated in 1925. In 1931, a tax revolt resulted in Neptune Beach seceding from neighboring Jacksonville Beach. What is now known as the Beaches Town Center developed near a small train station that originally served as Neptune Beach's first city hall. (Courtesy of the State Archives of Florida.)

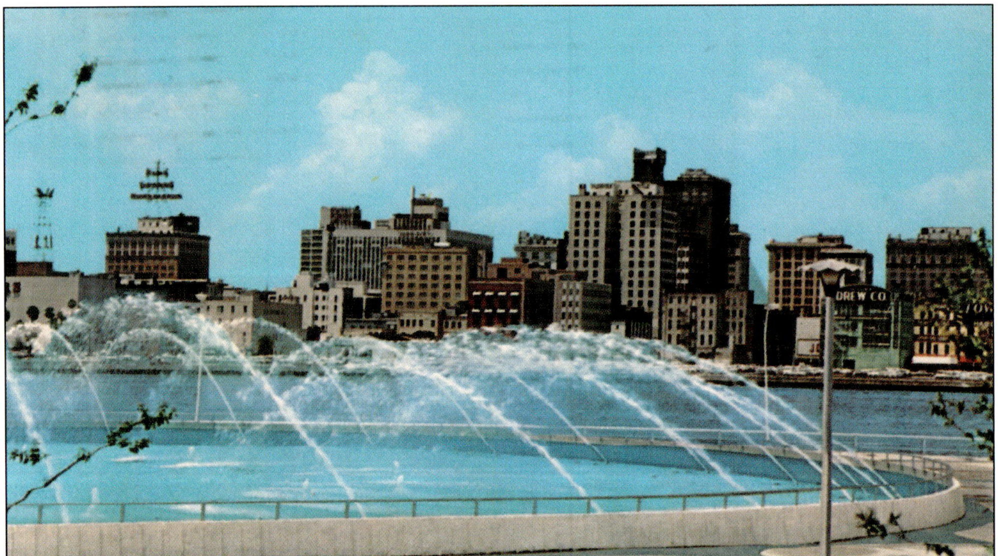

Downtown Jacksonville's Northbank skyline is visible from the Southbank's Friendship Fountain in 1971. When the Fountain of Friendship opened in 1965, it was the world's largest and tallest fountain, capable of spraying 17,000 gallons of water a minute to a height of 120 feet. (Courtesy of the Jacksonville Public Library Special Collections Department.)

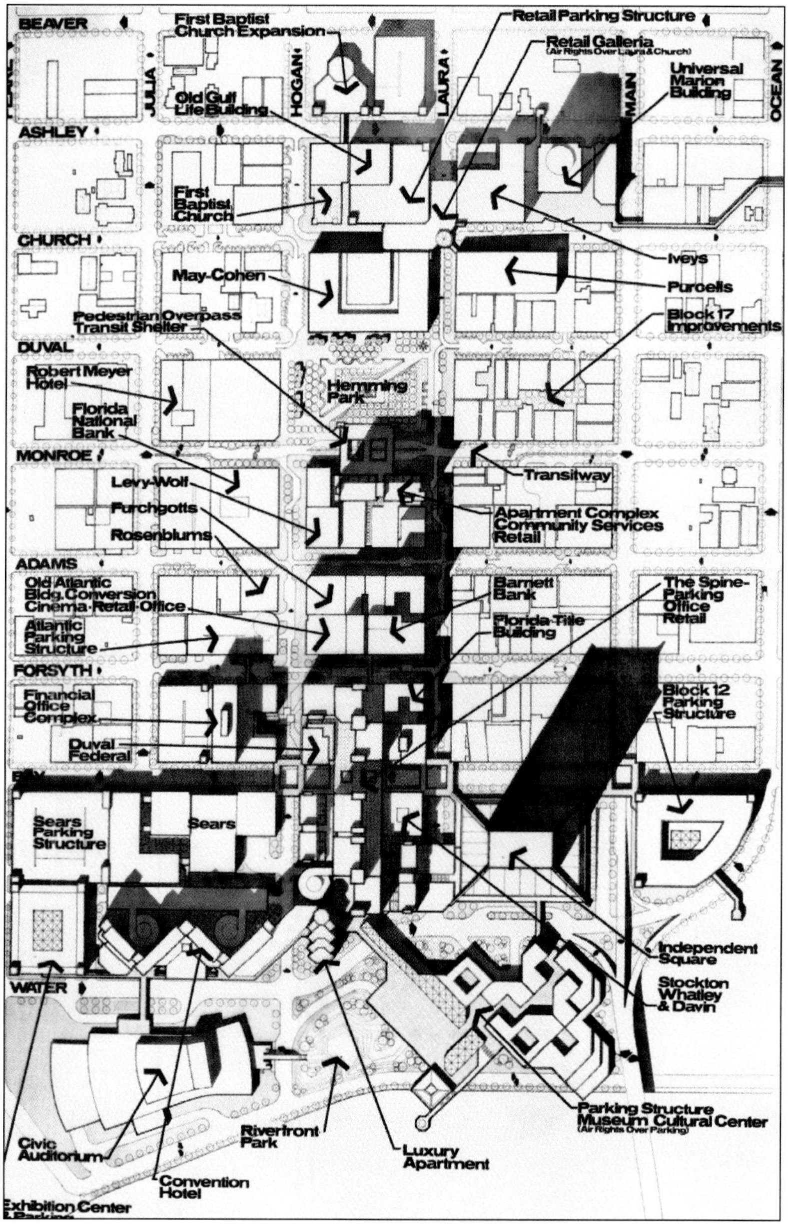

A pedestrian street or pedestrian mall is a street where pedestrian traffic is given partial or total priority over all other kinds of traffic. It is a limited form of an automobile-free zone. Under the Downtown Development Authority's 1971 Downtown Master Plan, Hogan Street between Duval and Bay Streets, Laura Street between Church and Bay Streets, and Duval/Monroe Streets between Hogan and Laura Streets would have been converted into pedestrian use only. Designed by Baltimore, Maryland–based consultant RTKL, the 1971 Downtown Master Plan evolved around three major features: the first was a vehicular and pedestrian public circulation system, the second was focusing on concentrated and mixed-use land activities, and the third was to create a new landmark symbolizing the revitalization of downtown. The RTKL plan was legally adopted on January 12, 1971, by the Jacksonville City Council. (Courtesy of the Jacksonville Public Library Special Collections Department.)

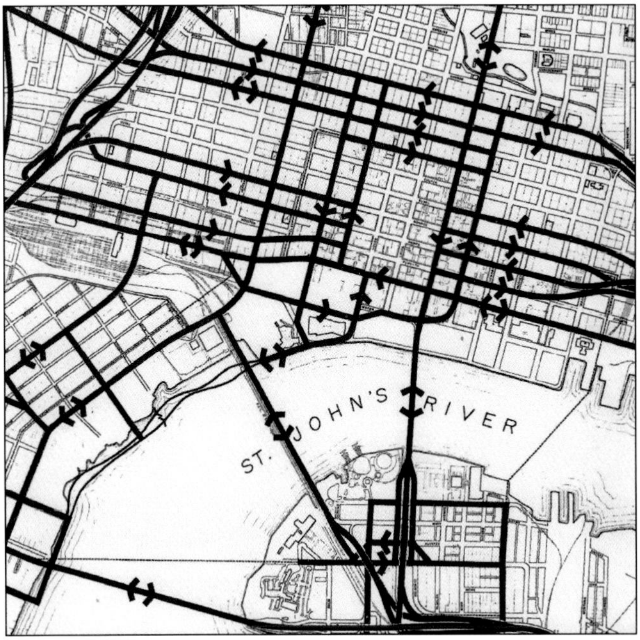

The creation of a loop network of one-way streets surrounding the proposed downtown pedestrian mall was an essential part of the 1971 plan. The loop system consisted of converting Water, Ocean, Beaver, and Pearl Streets into a one-way outer loop while turning Main, Ashley, Julia, and Bay Streets into the inner loop. Parking garages and surface lots containing at least 5,000 spaces would then be constructed along the loop streets. (Courtesy of the Jacksonville Public Library Special Collections Department.)

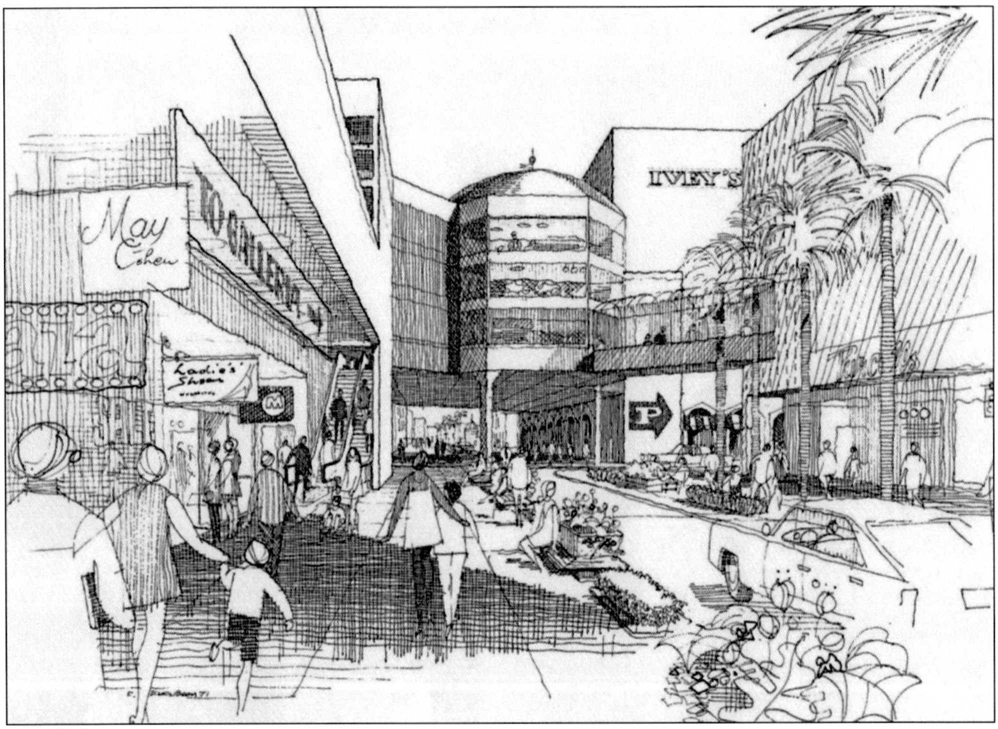

Believing that downtown revitalization would be most effective by transforming the core into a mall-like environment to help rejuvenate retail sales suffering from the competition of new suburban malls, planners proposed an enclosed vertical retail galleria mall, connecting May-Cohens, Ivey's, and Purcell's department stores with a multilevel parking garage above Church and Laura Streets. Although intended to be completed by 1974, the mall development was never initiated. (Courtesy of the Jacksonville Public Library Special Collections Department.)

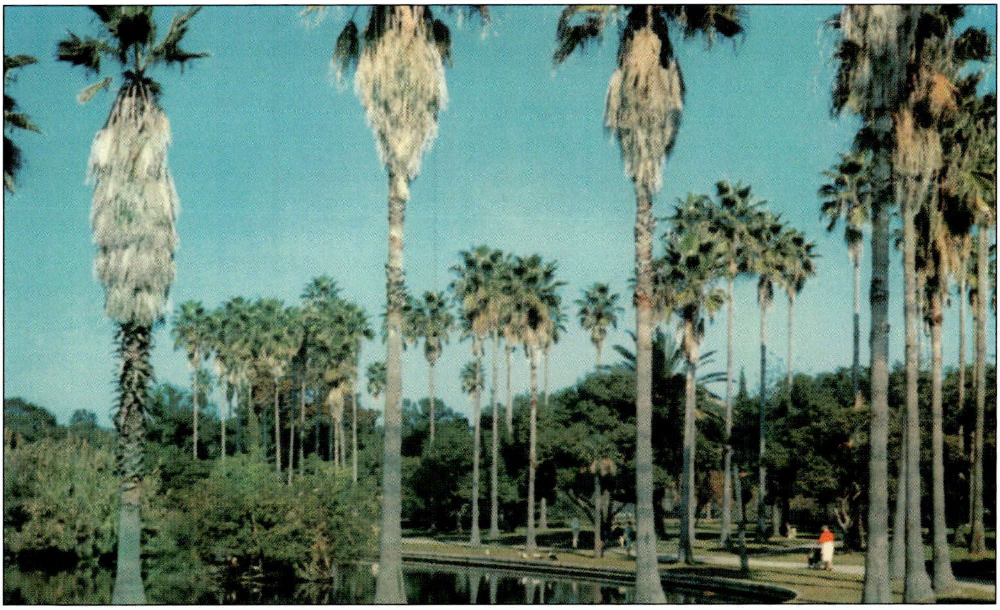

Jacksonville is home to one of the largest urban park systems in the country. Dating back to 1907, Confederate Park is one of the city's oldest. First named Dignan Park, the United Confederate Veterans selected the park as the site for their annual reunion in 1914. Five months after the reunion of an estimated 8,000 former Confederate soldiers, the city renamed the park. (Courtesy of the Jacksonville Public Library Special Collections Department.)

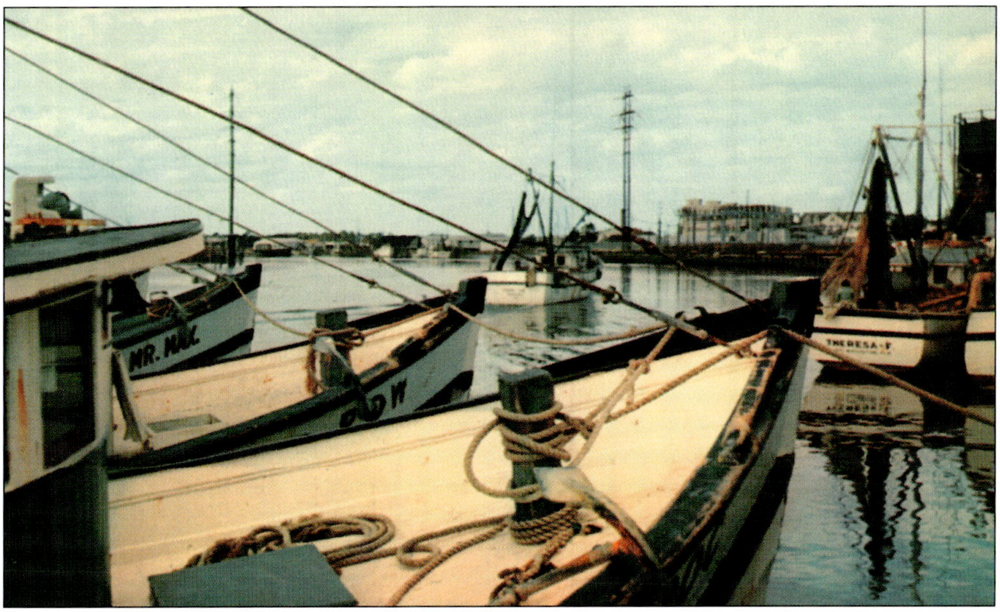

A number of shrimp trawlers lined up along the St. Johns River. Commercial shrimping is a landmark industry for northeast Florida. White and brown shrimp are the two primary species in the Jacksonville region. Shrimp harvested in the area are known for their size and sweetness. Typically, after wild shrimp are caught, shrimpers sell their harvest to a processor, which prepares them for consumption. The processor then sells the product to a grocery store or restaurant. (Courtesy of the Jacksonville Public Library Special Collections Department.)

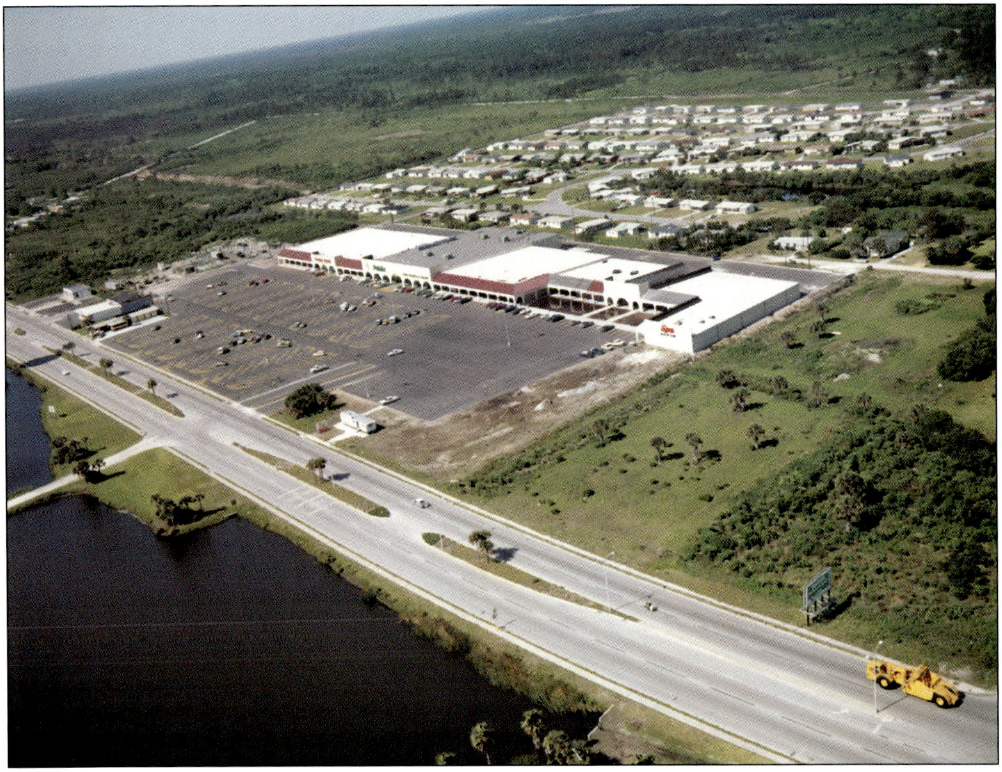

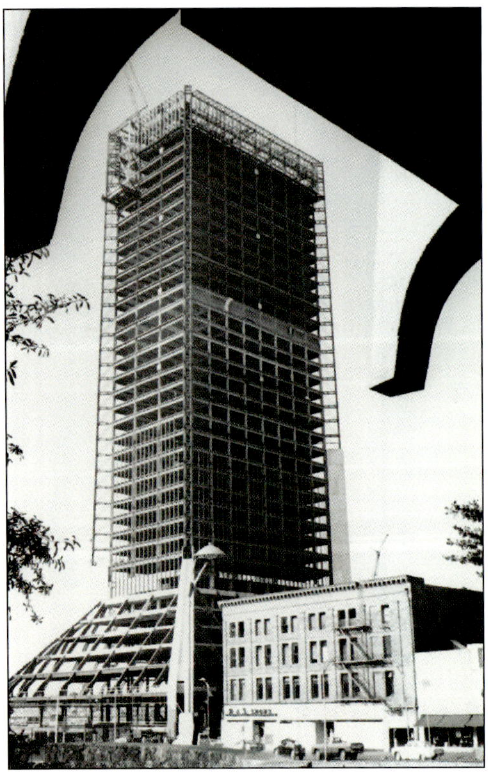

This is an aerial view of Pablo Plaza at 1822 South Third Street in 1972. In 1940, Jacksonville Beach was a sparsely populated community with a population of 3,566. By 1970, the city's population had increased to 12,779. Original tenants of the 153,800-square-foot shopping center included Publix, Excerd Drugs, Merle Norman, Radio Shack, Lynra's Bazaar and All-American Spa. (Courtesy of the State Archives of Florida.)

Designed by KBJ Architects, the distinctive Independent Life Building became an instant landmark for the city after its completion in 1974. Show here is a view of its construction from Haydon Burns Library in 1973. The 535-foot-high, 37-floor structure held the title of the tallest building in Florida until 1981, when One Tampa City Center was completed. (Courtesy of the Jacksonville Public Library Special Collections Department.)

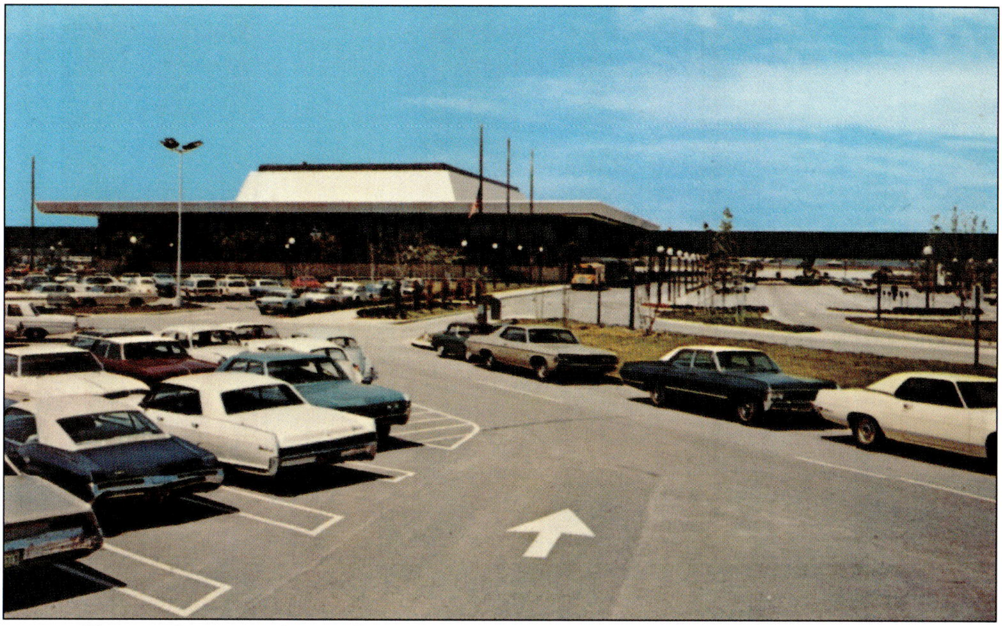

Pictured here is the new Jacksonville International Airport in 1972. Located about 18 miles north of downtown, the airport is known as being one of the cheapest to fly out of in the country. With two runways and an estimated five million annual passengers, the airport is served by a number of airlines. Its construction started in the mid-1960s and was completed in 1968. Dedicated on September 1, 1968, as a replacement to the nearby old Imeson Airport, which had become too small for jet-powered aircraft, Jacksonville's new airport soon began offering a range of domestic flights. By the 1980s, and now known officially as Jacksonville International Airport (JAX), passenger levels had reached more than two million each year, prompting the need for a series of major improvements. Boeing jet-powered aircraft soon became a major fixture, and cargo flights rose sharply. Particularly notable was the year 1990, when a new terminal building opened, costing in excess of $100 million. (Courtesy of the State Archives of Florida.)

The entrance to Englewood's Ramada Inn South at 5624 Cagle Road is shown here shortly after the hotel's opening in 1973. Englewood is a Southside neighborhood that rapidly came to life in the decade following the end of World War II. Fueled by the expansion of Interstate 95 between Jacksonville and Daytona Beach in 1960, Englewood's University Boulevard corridor transformed from rural dairy pastures into a busy commercial thoroughfare. Along with the Philips Highway corridor neighborhoods of North St. Augustine, Spring Park, and Pine Forest, Englewood has been called the "Squeeze Box" by locals. (Courtesy of the State Archives of Florida.)

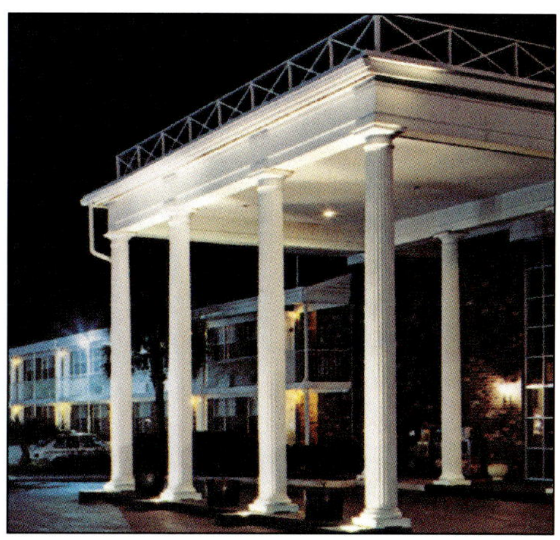

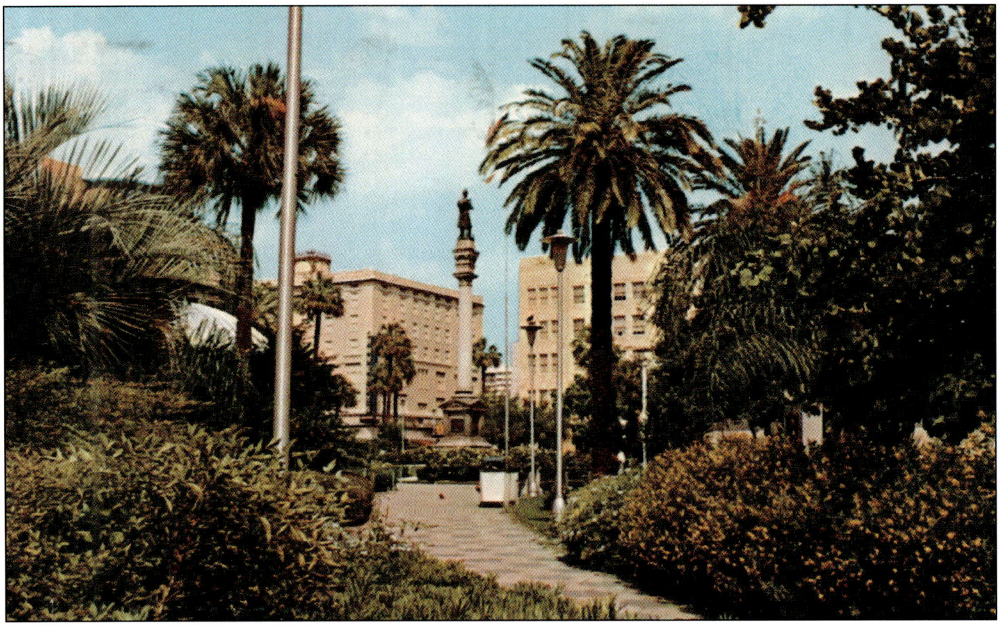

This is a tropical scene in Hemming Park looking toward the park's Confederate Soldier monument in 1973. Created in 1857, the park was the first and is the oldest park in the city. First known as City Park, it was renamed in 1899 in honor of Civil War veteran Charles C. Hemming after he installed the 62-foot-tall Confederate monument in the park in 1898. (Courtesy of the Jacksonville Public Library Special Collections Department.)

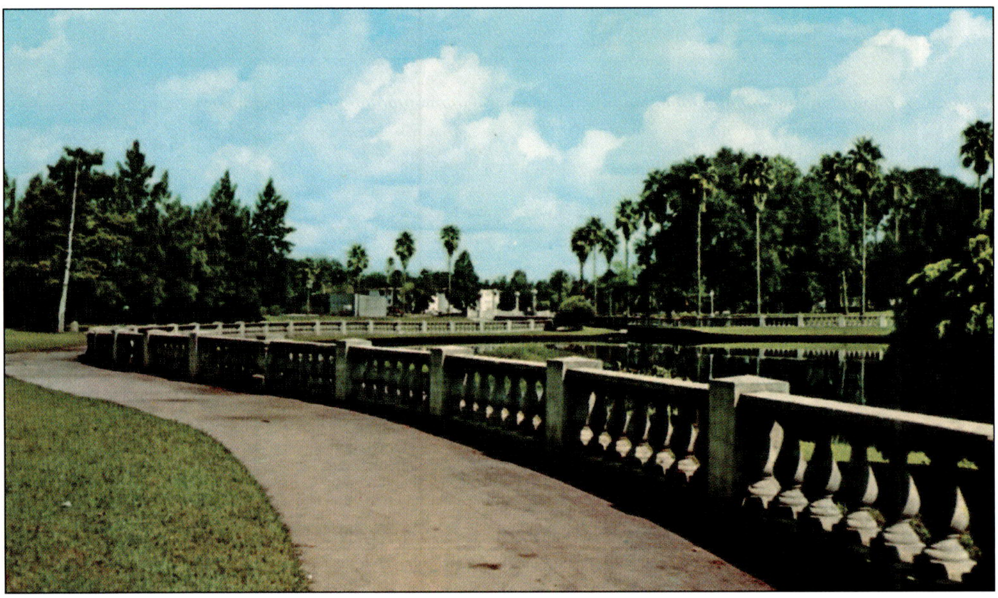

This is a view of the pristine, well-maintained Hogans Creek Promenade in Springfield. The promenade was the aesthetic centerpiece of Henry J. Klutho's Hogans Creek Improvement Project in 1929. Intended to prevent flooding, the creek channelization project added bulkheads, ornamental footbridges, 10,000 square yards of sidewalks, decorative balustrades, and light fixtures, transforming the park into one of the city's most scenic promenades. (Courtesy of the Jacksonville Public Library Special Collections Department.)

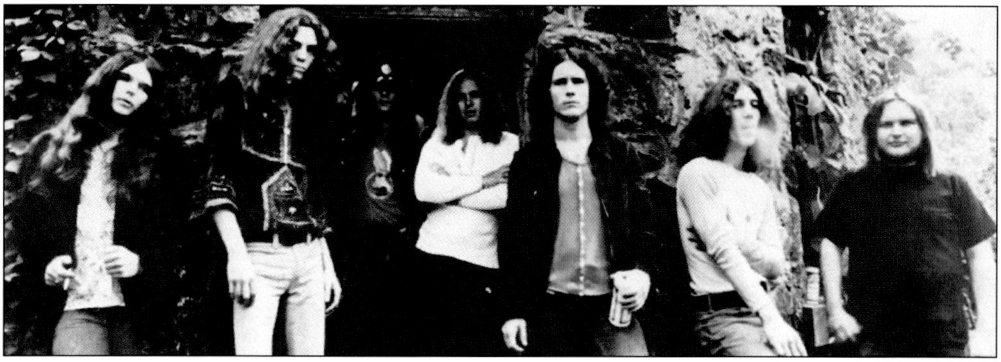

Pictured here is Lynyrd Skynyrd in 1973. Lynyrd Skynyrd is one of several Jacksonville-native rock bands known for popularizing the Southern hard-rock genre during the 1970s. In 1969, teenage friends Ronnie Van Zant, Allen Collins, and Gary Rossington named their band in a mocking tribute to Robert E. Lee High School's Leonard Skinner. A physical education teacher, Skinner was known for strictly enforcing the school's policy against boys having long hair. Southern rock is a subgenre developed from rock and roll, country music, and blues. Other popular rock bands affiliated with Jacksonville include the Allman Brothers Band, .38 Special, Rossington Collins Band, and Blackfoot.

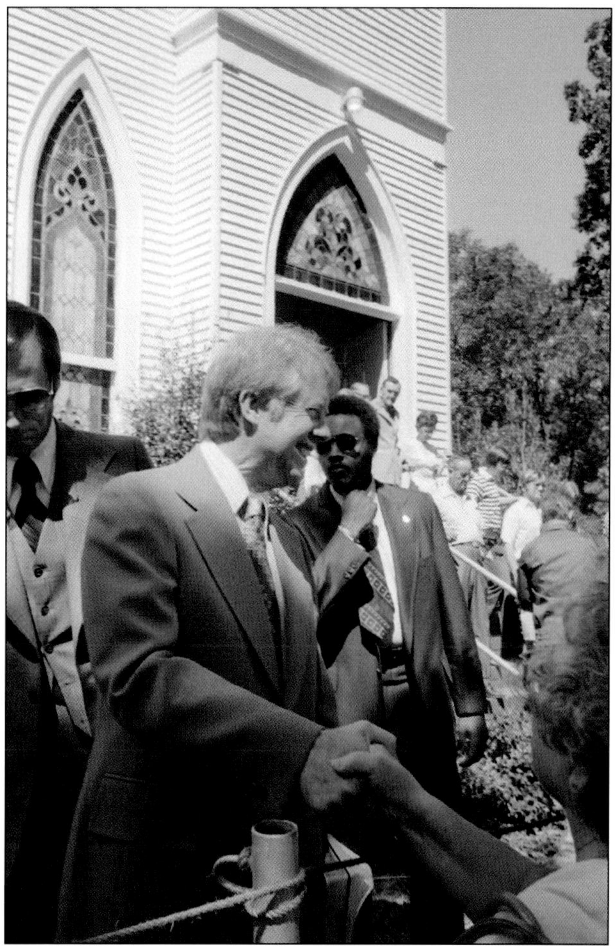

Presidential candidate Jimmy Carter shakes hands after leaving a Jacksonville church on September 10, 1976. During his Jacksonville campaign trip, Carter attended a reception at the Thunderbird Hotel and stopped by Regency Square Mall to address a huge crowd. A few months later, Carter defeated incumbent president Gerald Ford to become the 39th president of the United States. (Courtesy of the Library of Congress.)

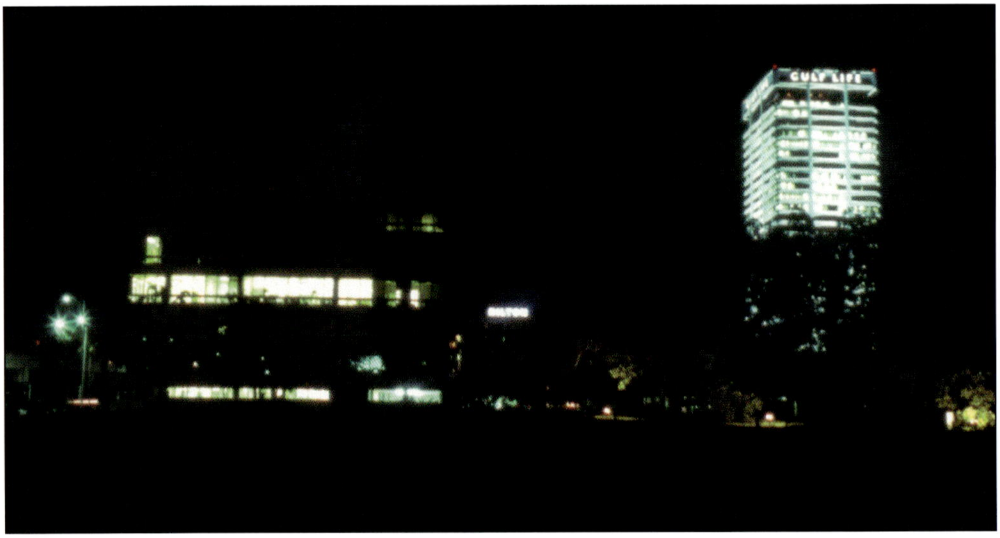

Pictured here is a June 1976 nighttime view of the Gulf Life Insurance Company building. When the 28-story, mid-century Moderne skyscraper was completed in 1966, it was the tallest precast, post-tensioned concrete structure in the world and the tallest building in Florida. The Gulf Life Insurance Company was founded as the Gulf Life & Accident Insurance Company in 1911. The company operated its headquarters out of the Gulf Life Tower until it was merged into American General Life of Houston in 1991. On April 18, 2012, the American Institute of Architects' Florida chapter placed the building on its list of "Florida Architecture: 100 Years, 100 Places" as the Riverplace Tower/Formerly Gulf Life Tower. (Courtesy of the State Archives of Florida.)

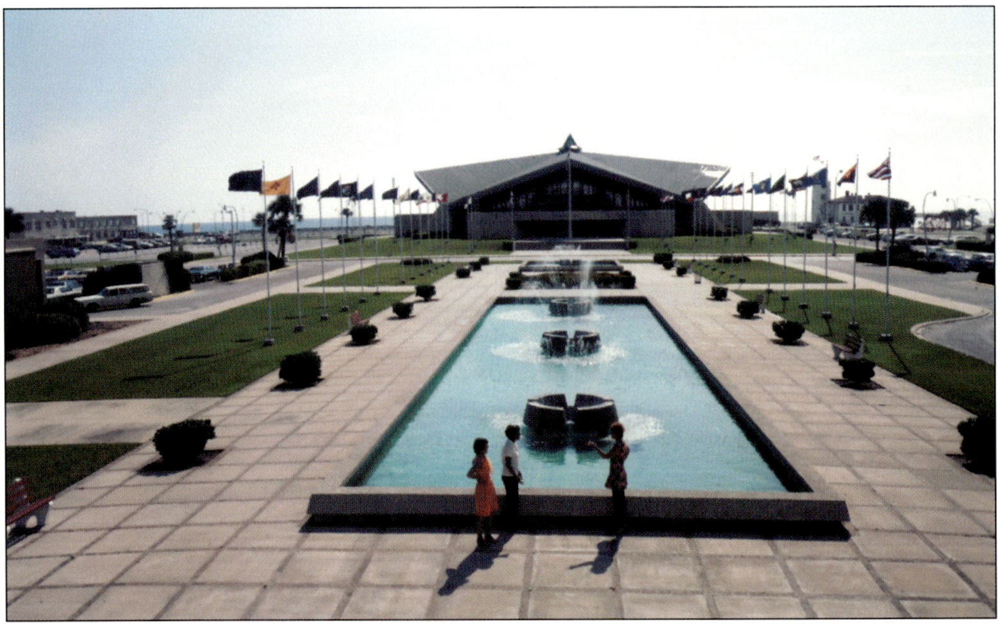

The Jacksonville Beach Auditorium's 13,655-square-foot main hall could seat as many as 1,600 guests on the main floor and an additional 400 in its balcony. The auditorium was constructed during the 1960s as a part of a redevelopment plan to breathe life back into downtown Jacksonville Beach, which had suffered from new tourist attractions in central and south Florida and Hurricane Dora. (Courtesy of the State Archives of Florida.)

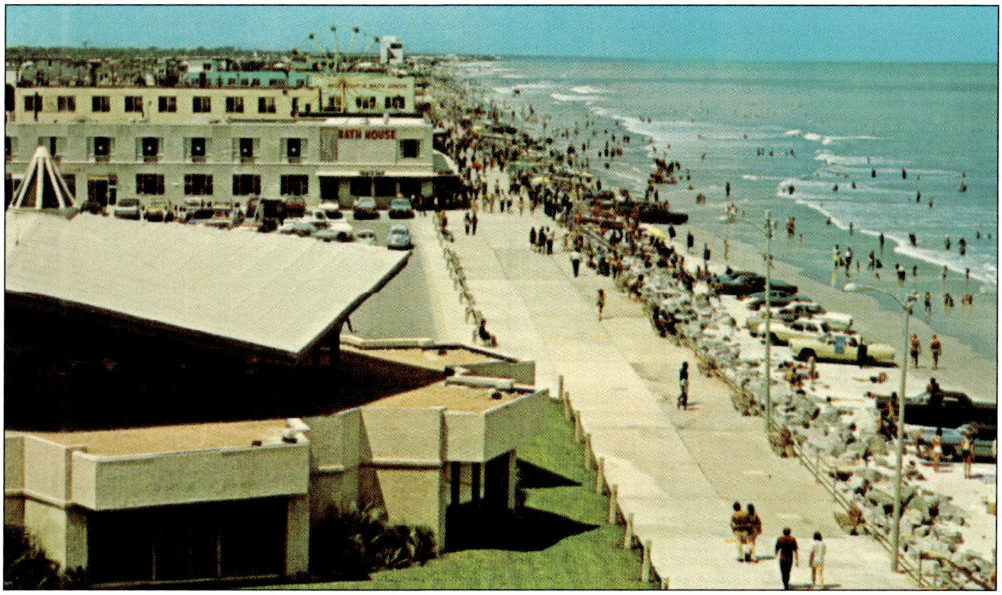

This view is looking north near the Jacksonville Beach City Auditorium along the Jacksonville Beach boardwalk in 1978. Also known as the Sea Walk, the boardwalk has been a fixture at Jacksonville Beach since the early 20th century. Initially constructed of wood, much of it was destroyed by fire in 1933. Later that decade, the Works Progress Administration (WPA) built a concrete seawall and boardwalk to replace the wooden structure. (Courtesy of the Jacksonville Public Library Special Collections Department.)

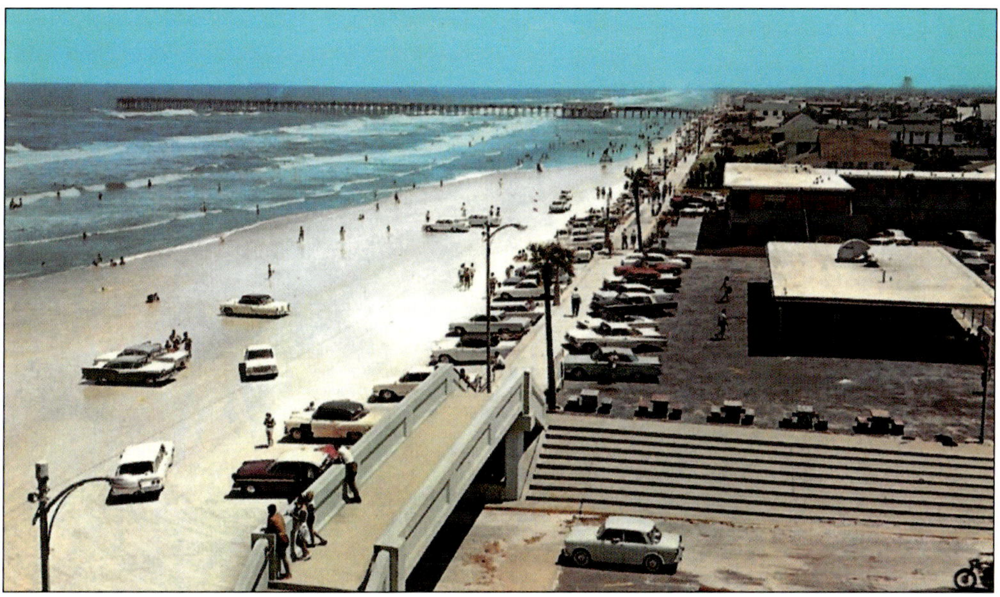

For more than 50 years, the Beach Boulevard pedestrian overpass was one of Jacksonville Beach's most photographed landmarks. The crossing was built to allow pedestrians to avoid automobile traffic when motorists were allowed to drive on the beach. Deemed a safety hazard in 1990, the landmark was removed because officials believed it was no longer needed since driving on the beach had already been banned. (Courtesy of the Jacksonville Public Library Special Collections Department.)

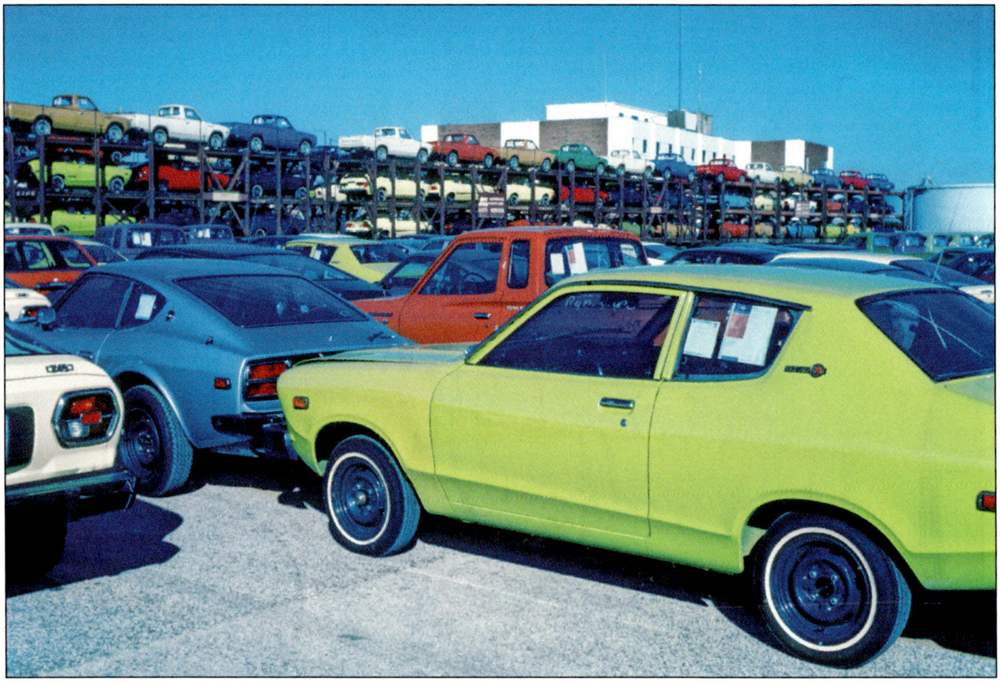

Jacksonville's port is one of the largest commercial cargo ports on the Atlantic coast and one of the busiest automobile import and export centers in the country. The Jacksonville Port Authority (JAXPORT) was created in 1963 by the Florida Legislature to progress, preserve, and promote the city's port facilities. JAXPORT replaced the city's municipal docks and terminals, which was established in 1915 along the St. Johns River between Eighth and Twenty-first Streets. (Courtesy of JAXPORT and MetroJacksonville.com.)

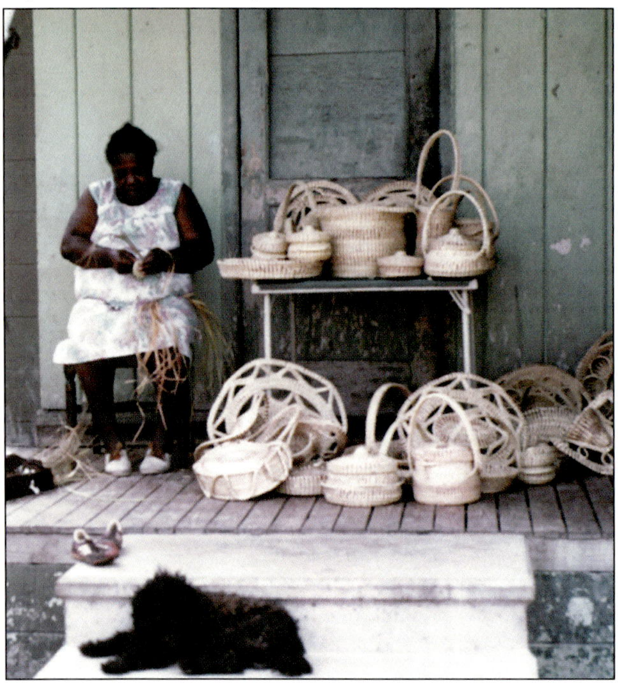

Lucille Jones makes a Gullah, or sweetgrass basket, on her porch in June 1979. Jacksonville is a part of the Gullah-Geechee Cultural Heritage Corridor that was designated by Congress in 2006. The Gullah/Geechee people are descendants of enslaved Africans from various ethnic groups of West and Central Africa. Stretching from Wilmington, North Carolina to northeast Florida, the people have retained many aspects of their African heritage due to the geographic barriers of the region's coastal landscape. (Courtesy of the State Archives of Florida.)

Four

1980s

The Billion-Dollar Decade

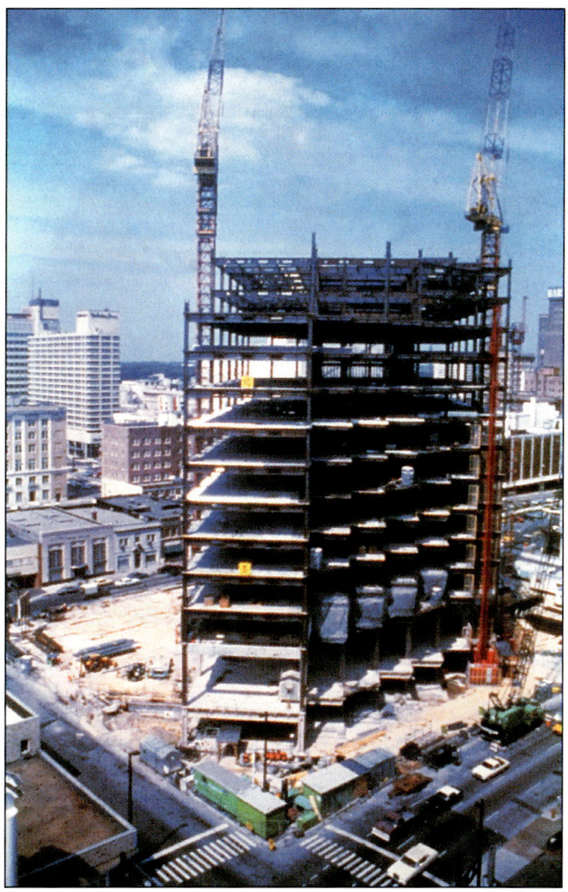

Pictured here in 1982 is the construction of the 447-foot-tall AT&T Tower. Completed in 1983, the building is the city's third tallest and the largest in terms of rentable square footage. While downtown retail declined during the 1980s, the era was known as the Billion-Dollar Decade due to the number of skyscrapers completed that reshaped the downtown skyline. Towers completed include Jax Center (American Heritage Life), AT&T, SunBank, Enterprise Center, and the Omni Hotel. (Courtesy of the State Archives of Florida.)

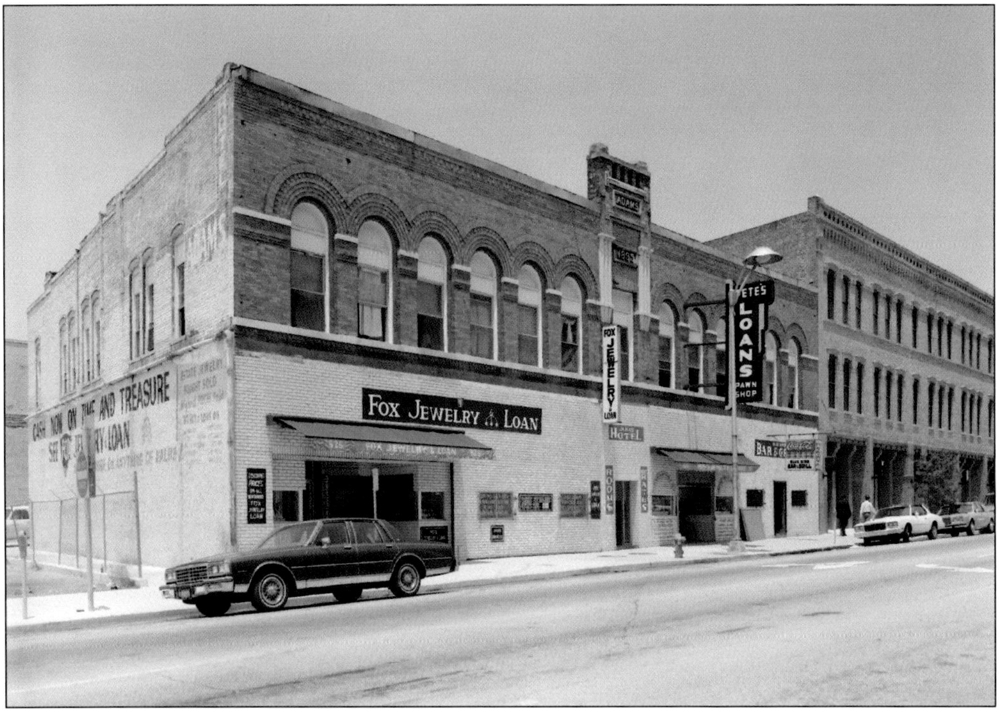

Pictured here are Fox Jewelry & Loan and the St. James Hotel in the Adams Building and the El Modelo Block during the 1980s. In business for over 85 years and still going, Fox Jewelry & Loan is one of downtown Jacksonville's oldest businesses. Both buildings are a part of a handful of 19th-century structures that predate the devastating Great Fire of 1901. A part of downtown's long lost Railroad Row district, the Adams Building was constructed in 1895 as a hotel catering to transients using the nearby railroad terminal. The El Modelo Block was constructed in 1886 and occupied by the El Modelo Cigar Factory. In 1893, José Martí, founder of the Cuban Revolutionary Party, gave a fiery speech at this location to build support for the liberation of his homeland. From 1915 to 1965, the building was a hotel, operating as the Plaza, the Hillsboro, the Southern, and the New York Hotel. (Courtesy of the Library of Congress.)

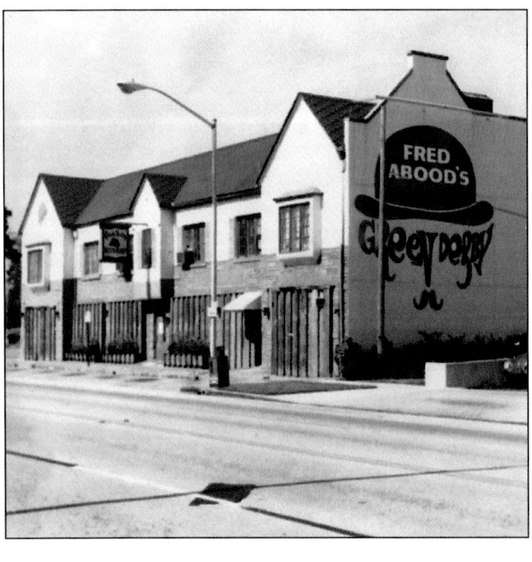

Located at the corner of Riverside Avenue and Roselle Street, the Green Derby was a Riverside fixture, hallowed ground for the sporting crowd when it dressed in a classy manner. Established after World War II by Van Fletcher, the eatery quickly became the preeminent restaurant and lounge in Jacksonville. After Van Fletcher's retirement, the Green Derby was acquired by Fred Abood, owner of the famed Steer Room steak house at the Jacksonville Farmers Market. According to a 1989 *Florida Times-Union* interview with Abood, "There is no mystery to the operation of a fine restaurant if the owner is qualified in quality food preparation." (Courtesy of Whiteway Corner.)

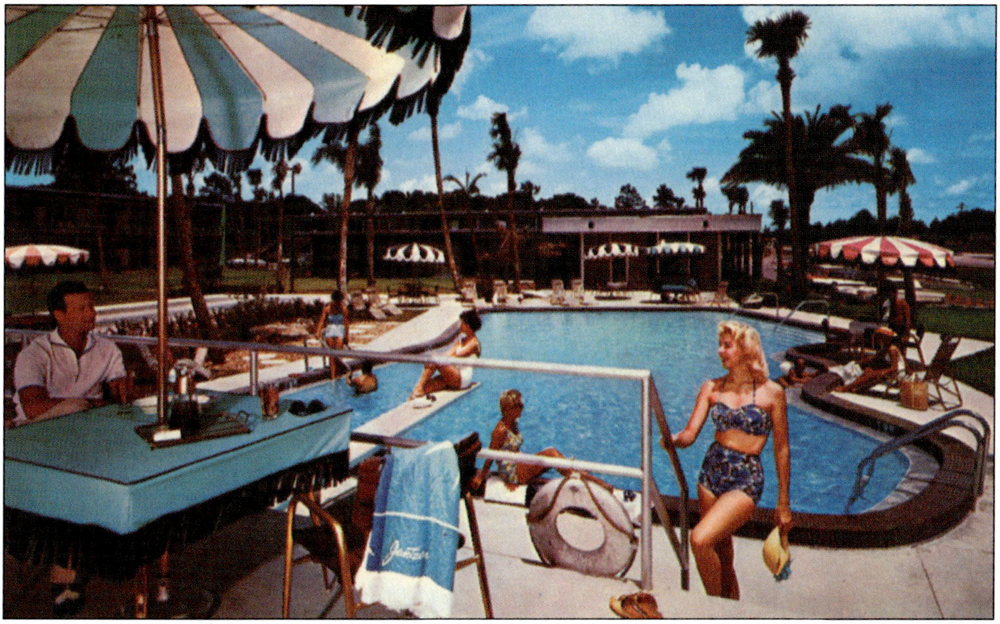

Shown sitting in the shade poolside, owner Albert Stein's Thunderbird Motor Hotel and Dinner Theatre, located at 5865 Arlington Expressway, was a major destination. The 270-room Thunderbird represented a carefree time after the war, when young families were in search of fun and entertainment. Anchored by the 1967 opening of Regency Square Mall, developed by Stein's brother Martin, by 1980 the Arlington Expressway had developed into a congested corridor lined with restaurants, office parks, shopping centers, gas stations, and hotels. (Courtesy of the Jacksonville Public Library Special Collections Department.)

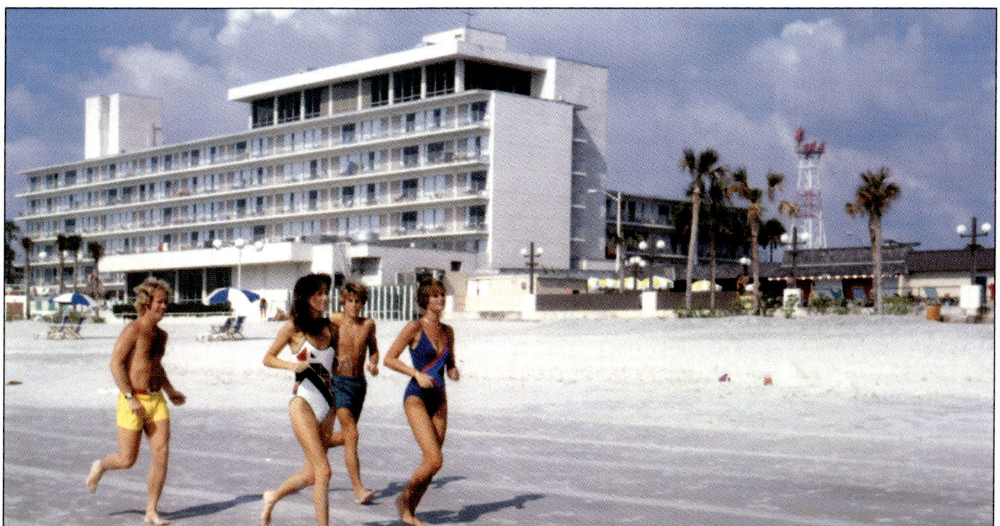

A group of joggers passes Jacksonville Beach's Holiday Inn Oceanfront in 1981. Built in 1970 and located at 1617 First Street North, the Holiday Inn was known for its giant mural of two blue whales swimming into the sunset. In 2006, the 150-room hotel underwent a $12-million renovation that resulted in its conversion to a Courtyard by Marriott. (Courtesy of Karl E. Holland and the State Archives of Florida.)

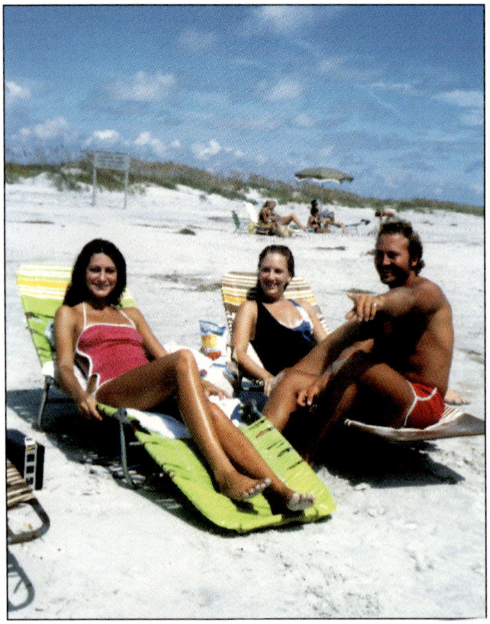

This group lying in the sun is enjoying the beach at Little Talbot Island in September 1980. For the nature-lover and the adventurer in everyone, this state park covers 2,500 acres of forests, dunes, and marshes. Little Talbot State Park is one of the few underdeveloped barrier islands in northeast Florida, making it home to myriad animals and trees and even more pretty sights to see. There is a lot to do at this state park, too. Tidal streams make a great place for anglers to practice their craft. Rivers and marshes provide lots of space for kayaking. There are also nature trails and approximately five miles worth of beaches that are the perfect place for a nice afternoon walk. Big Talbot Island State Park lies to the immediate north. Erosion on Big Talbot Island and sand deposition on Little Talbot have resulted in Little Talbot Island being the larger of the two Talbot Islands. (Courtesy of the State Archives of Florida.)

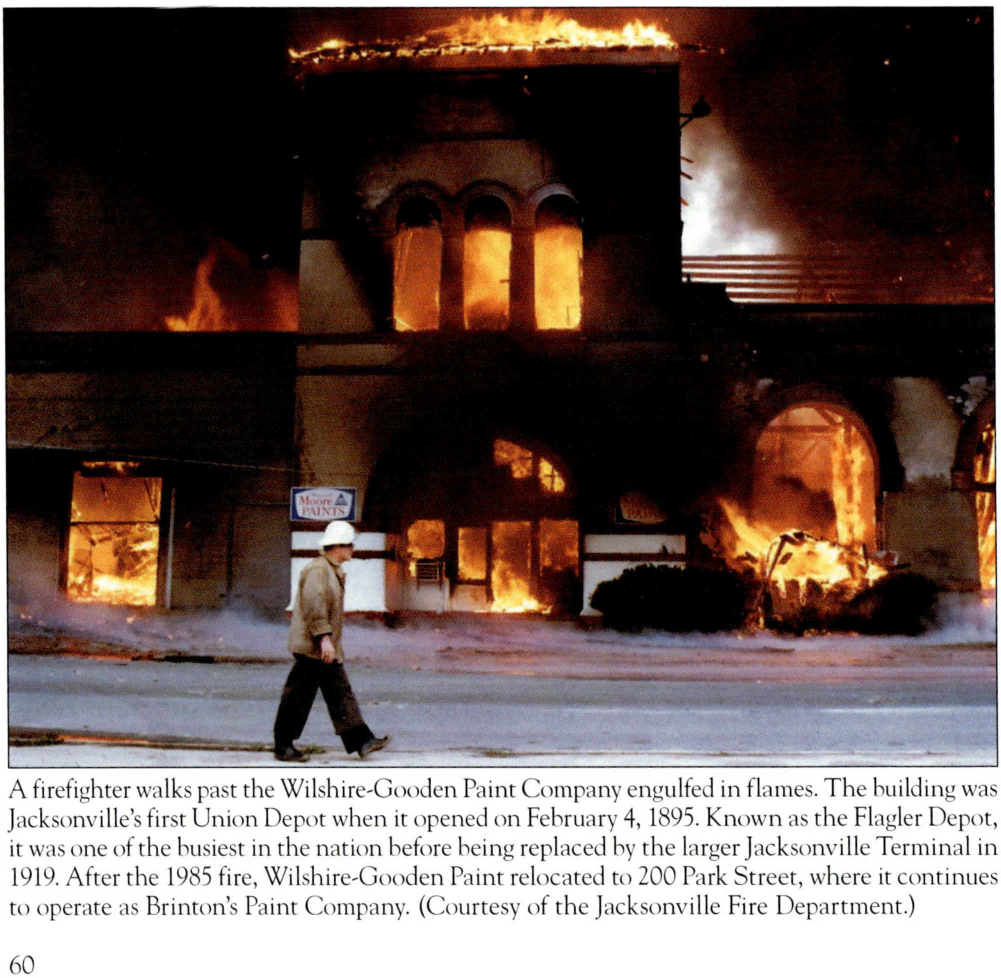

A firefighter walks past the Wilshire-Gooden Paint Company engulfed in flames. The building was Jacksonville's first Union Depot when it opened on February 4, 1895. Known as the Flagler Depot, it was one of the busiest in the nation before being replaced by the larger Jacksonville Terminal in 1919. After the 1985 fire, Wilshire-Gooden Paint relocated to 200 Park Street, where it continues to operate as Brinton's Paint Company. (Courtesy of the Jacksonville Fire Department.)

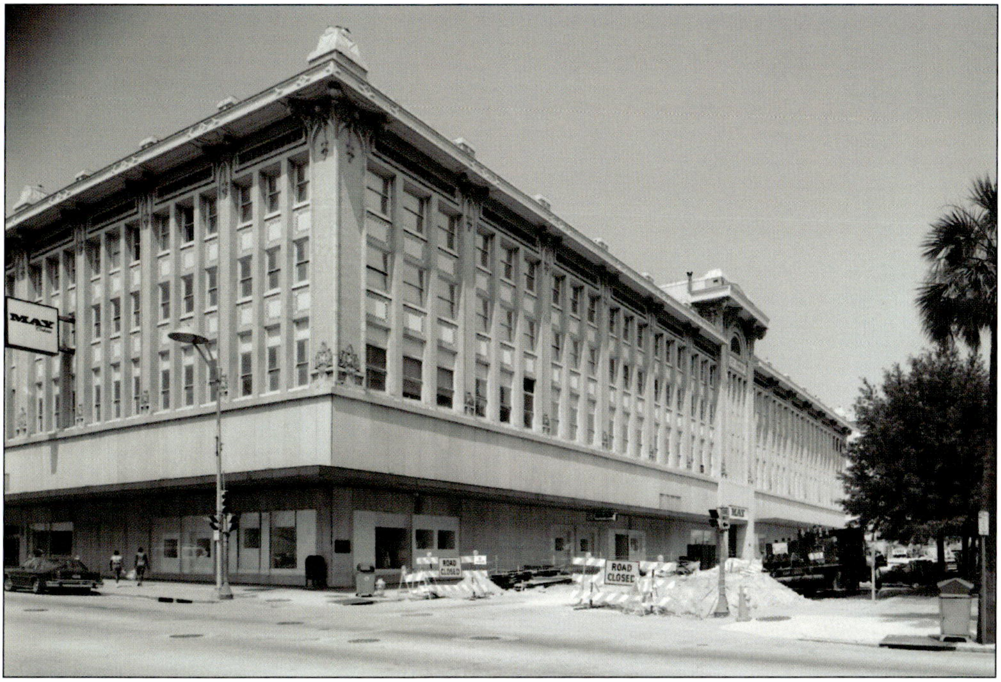

This is a view of the May-Cohens flagship department store during the construction of Hemming Plaza in 1984. Once known as the "Wanamaker of the South," Cohen Brothers department store captured the hearts of thousands of Jacksonville residents since its founding in 1867. When their Hemming Park store was completed in 1912, it was the ninth-largest department store in the United States. Between 1927 and 1960, the store was joined by Levy's, Rosenblum's, Furchgott's of Florida, J.C. Penney, Sears Roebuck and Company, and J.B. Ivey's, transforming downtown into a bona-fide urban retail district. (Courtesy of the Library of Congress.)

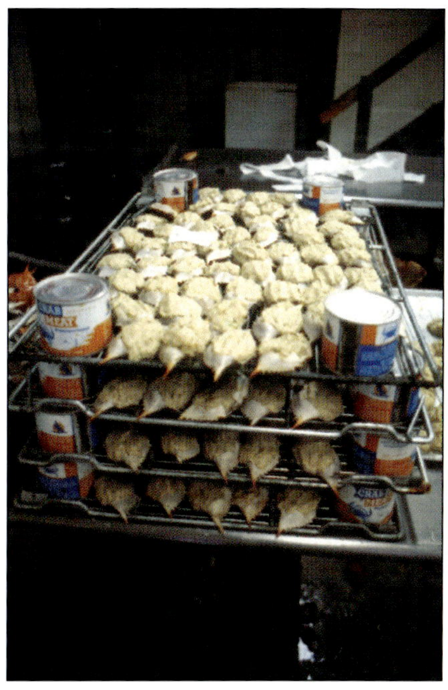

Trays of deviled crab at the Northeast Florida Crab Company are being prepared on August 9, 1985. Blue crab supports one of the largest commercial and recreational fisheries in Florida. Crabmeat processing has been a part of Jacksonville's economy since the establishment of Shaw's Southern Belle Frozen Foods, Inc. along the banks of the Trout River in Panama Park. Founded by Capt. H.W. Shaw and Flossie Russell Shaw in 1934, the company is one of the state's oldest crabmeat-processing businesses and largest specialty seafood packers in the country. Shaws produces deviled crab and crab cakes for clients such as Red Lobster, Shoney's, Captain D's Seafood, Golden Corral Buffet & Grill, Long John Silver's, and Cracker Barrel Old Country Store. Shaw's Southern Belle Frozen Foods employs about 120 people. (Courtesy of the State Archives of Florida and David Alan Taylor.)

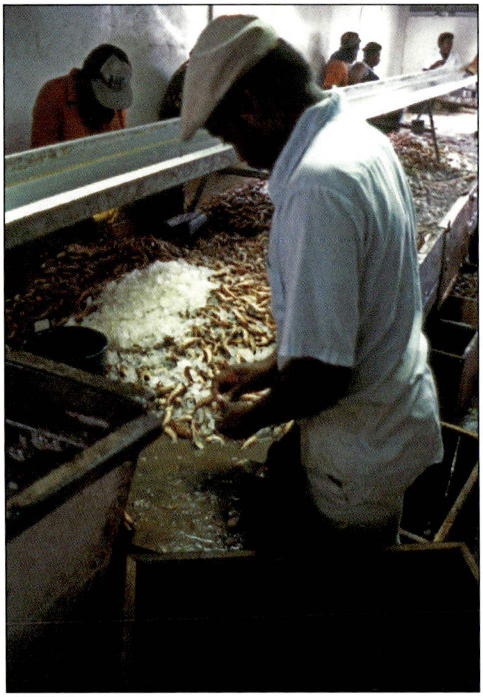

Roland Seafood worker Arthur Mattox is pictured here removing shrimp heads on August 5, 1986. The company was founded by Mat Roland. Roland was born in Portugal but immigrated to Florida with his family in 1937 so that his father, Matias, could fish for bluefish. For years, Roland processed seafood in a metal-covered building located on a timber-decked offshore wharf adjacent to the Atlantic Seafood Company at 4510 Ocean Street in Mayport. Over time, the seafood company expanded with operations in Cape Canaveral, Fernandina Beach, and Fort Myers Beach. Roland also owned many shrimp boats. In 2008, Roland Seafood relocated to 1790 Mayport Road in Atlantic Beach after its waterfront parcel was acquired and demolished by JAXPORT in order to develop a cruise terminal in the heart of the historic fishing village. (Courtesy of the State Archives of Florida.)

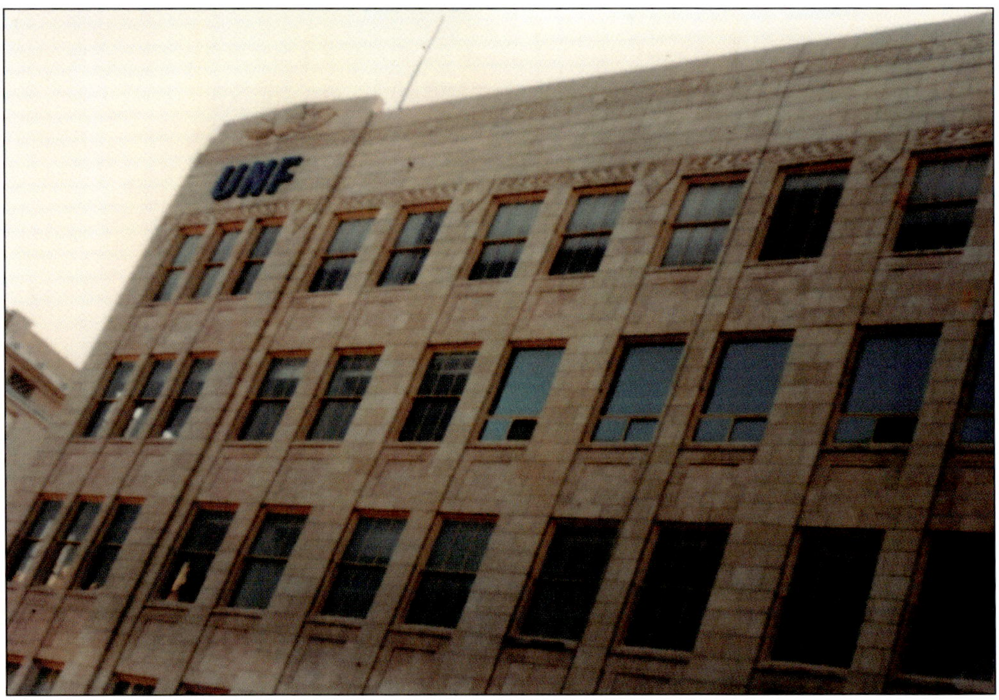

From 1978 to 1987, the University of North Florida (UNF) operated a downtown campus to make courses more accessible to inner-city residents. Enrollment peaked in 1981 with 2,247 students. Enrollment declined to a low of 428 students by 1987, due to a sluggish economy, a reduction in courses offered, and new bus routes to the main Southside campus. UNF closed its downtown center in August 1987. (Courtesy of the City of Jacksonville.)

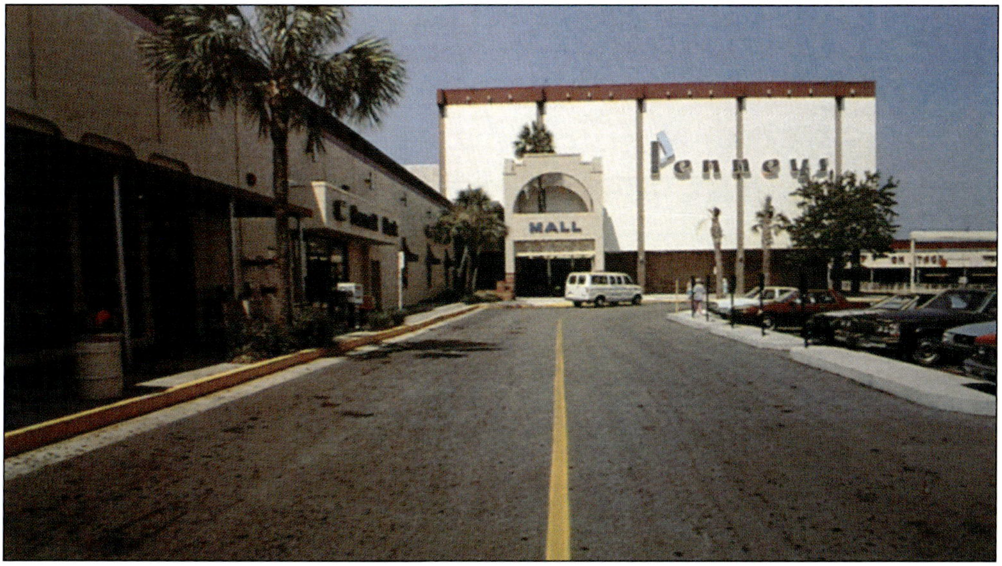

Fresh off the completion of a $2-million face-lift by Toronto-based Bramalea Limited, Gateway Center was northeast Florida's third-largest mall behind Regency Square Mall and Orange Park Mall. Anchored by J.C. Penney, Zarye, May-Cohens, Service Merchandise, and G.C. Murphy, the mall featured as many as 100 specialty shops in 1986. Gateway's face-lift was concentrated on redesigned storefronts and brighter parking lots to deter crime. (Courtesy of the Jacksonville Public Library's Special Collections Department.)

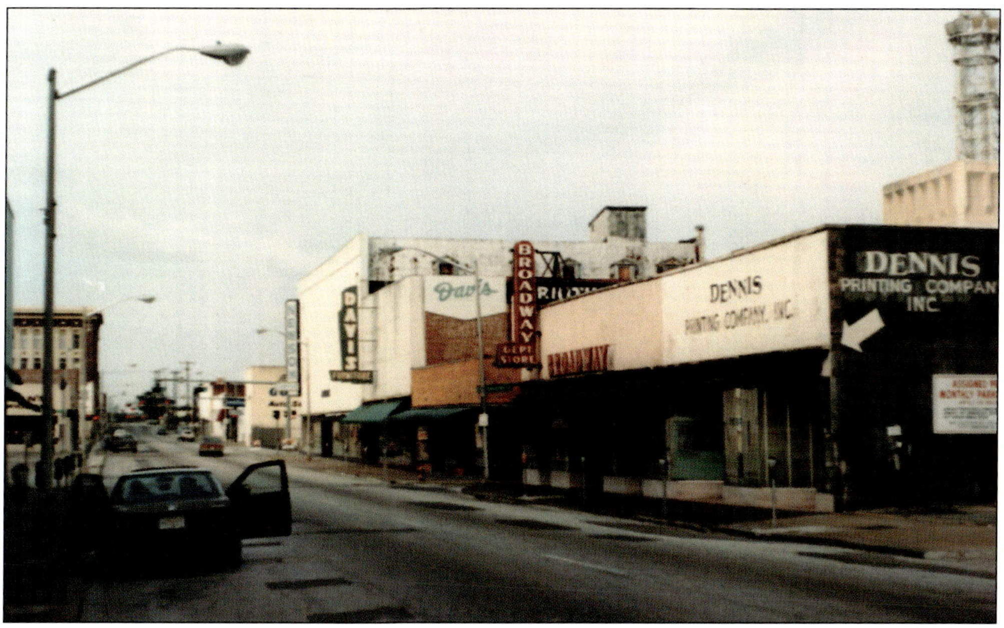

This view is looking north along Broad Street, from Forsyth Street, prior to the 1987 passage of the city's sign ordinance. At one time, signs displayed by E.C. Newsome Furniture, Davis Furniture, and Broadway Department Store were commonplace on the streets of downtown. Intended to improve the aesthetic appearance of the community, primarily for Jacksonville's suburban areas, it can be argued that a piece of what made downtown Jacksonville unique was forever lost in the process. (Courtesy of the City of Jacksonville.)

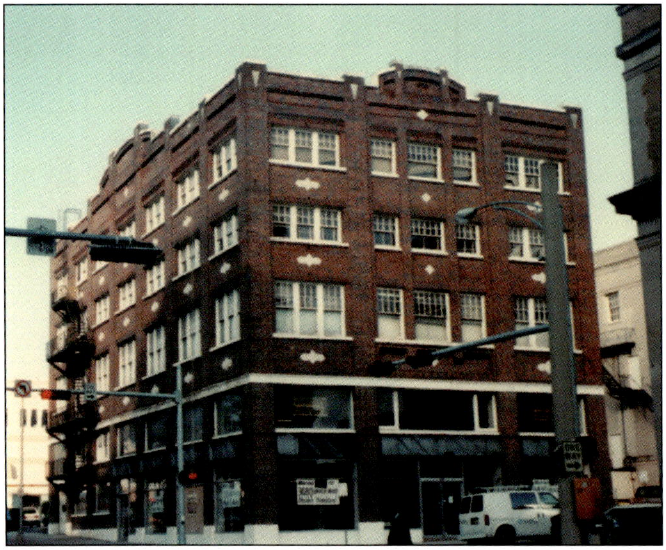

Pictured here is the Mather Furniture Company's downtown location in 1987. The Prairie School structure was originally built in 1927 to house the American Furniture & Carpet Company. In 1987, it was demolished and replaced by a City of Jacksonville parking structure at the intersection East Forsyth and Newnan Streets. Standing in the way of progress, the Mather Furniture Company relocated to 3674 Beach Boulevard. (Courtesy of the City of Jacksonville.)

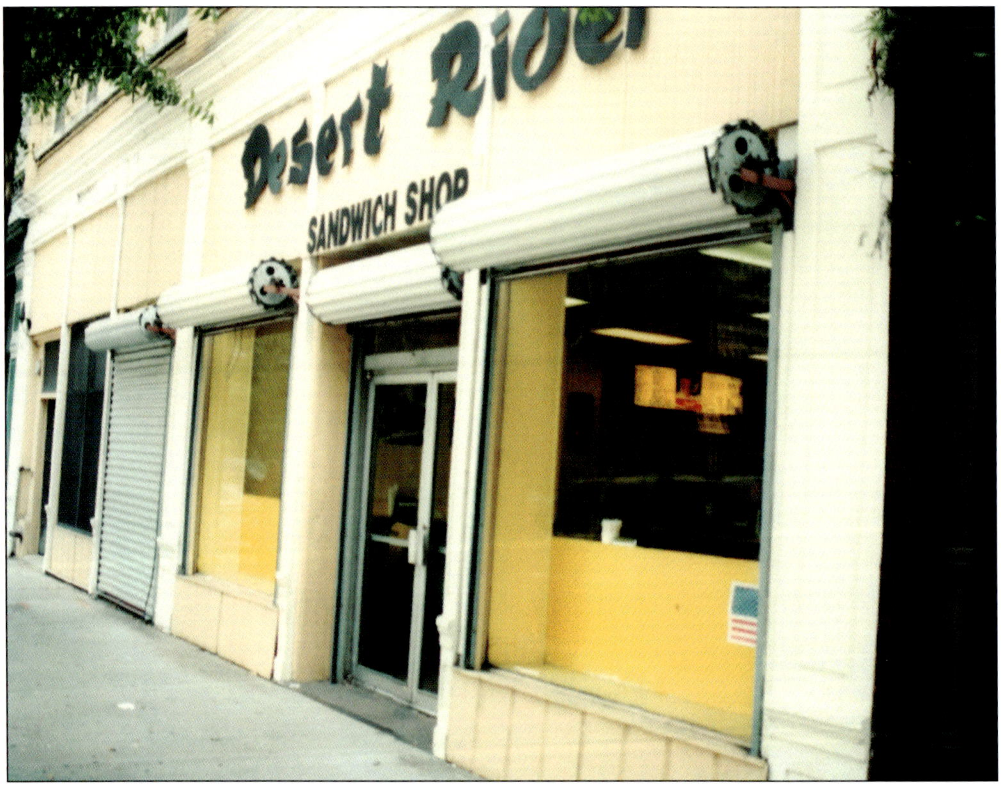

This is the Desert Rider Sandwich Shop, which was located at 319 East Bay Street during the late 1980s. With one of the largest Middle Eastern populations in the United States, Jacksonville has tribes of sandwich shops featuring riders, also known as camel or desert riders. The original rider is a pita pocket stuffed with ham, salami, bologna, cheese, lettuce, tomato, mayonnaise, onions, and dressing. Today, riders denote any sandwich made using a pita pocket. Accompanied by a cherry limeade, this signature sandwich is a staple of Jacksonville's multifaceted food culture. (Courtesy of the City of Jacksonville.)

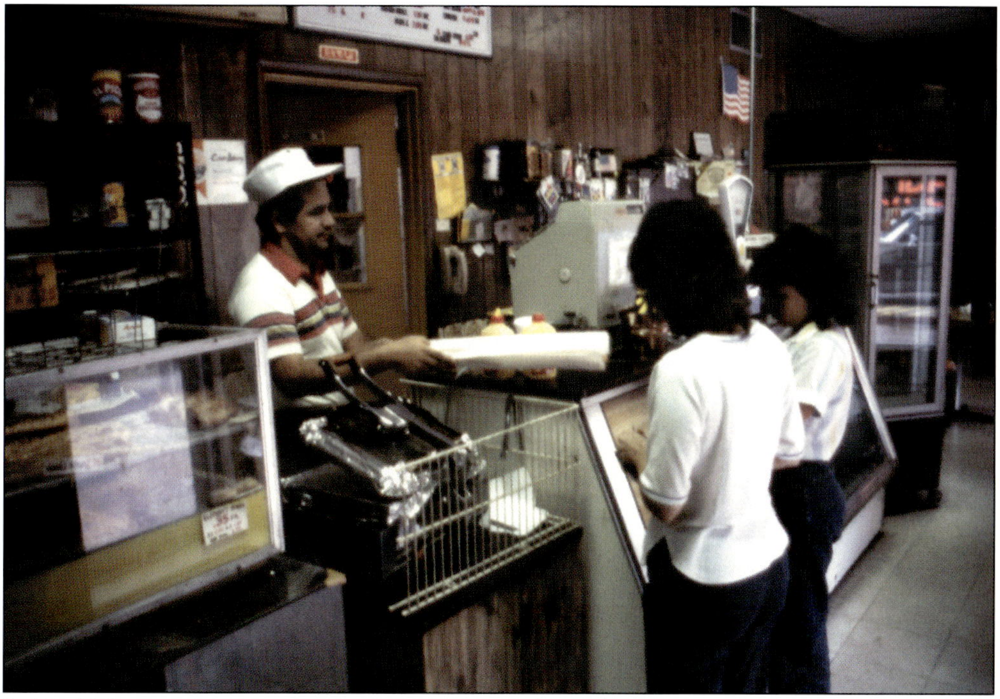

Bobby Ulloa serves two customers at Spring Park's Cuban Bakery of Jacksonville in 1984. Jacksonville's ties to Cuba date back to the 19th century. Prior to the embargo, Jacksonville was the hub for trade with Cuba in Florida. Ulloa's bakery was located at 3715 Emerson Street, near Spring Park Road. (Courtesy of the State Archives of Florida.)

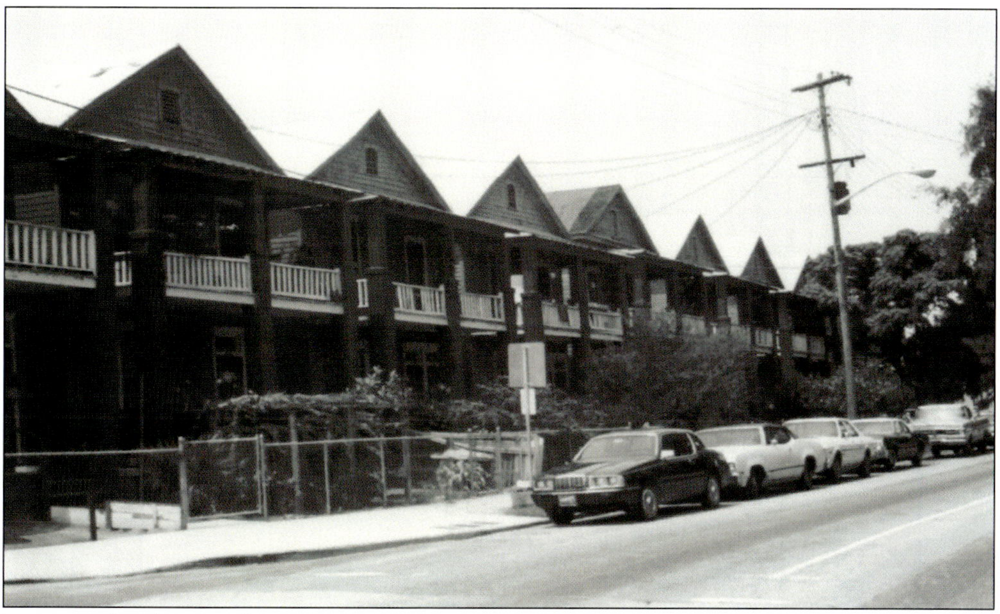

During its heyday, LaVilla was one of South's most dense, colorful, and diverse mixed-use walkable neighborhoods. Intended to revitalize the 1980s crack epidemic–stricken section of downtown, the 1994 River City Renaissance urban-renewal project ultimately transformed the storied district into a wasteland of vacant parcels and surface parking lots. (Courtesy of the City of Jacksonville.)

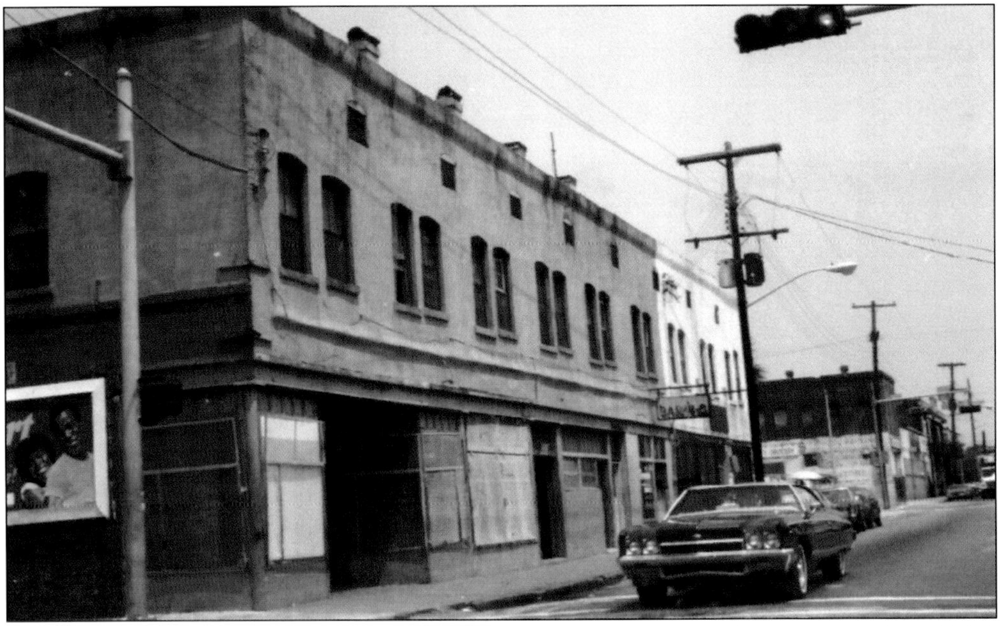

Looking north along Davis Street from West Beaver Street, 86 years earlier the Great Fire of 1901 originated from this site. Prior to desegregation, North Davis Street was a major thoroughfare through the city's African American community. By 1987, the Longshoreman's Recreation Center, Southern Barbeque Restaurant, and Bosie's Place Restaurant & Lounge were the only businesses occupying the 700 block of North Davis Street. (Courtesy of the City of Jacksonville.)

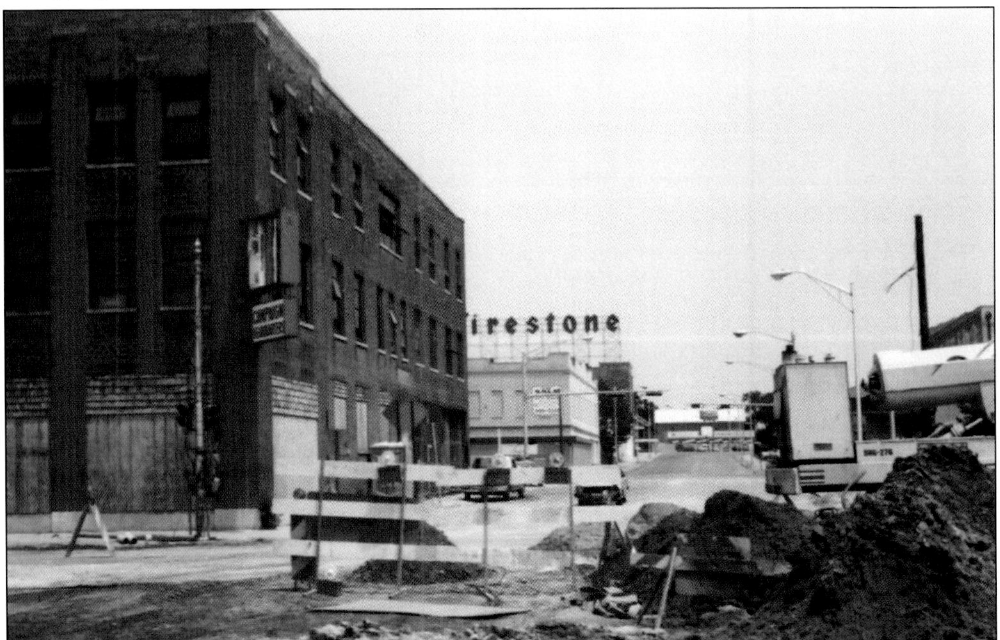

Construction of the Skyway Express along West Bay Street at Lee Street is seen here in 1987. The automated people mover was first proposed in the early 1970s as a solution to the urban core's traffic and parking issues. The first phase between downtown and the convention center was completed in May 1989. (Courtesy of City of Jacksonville Historic Preservation Office.)

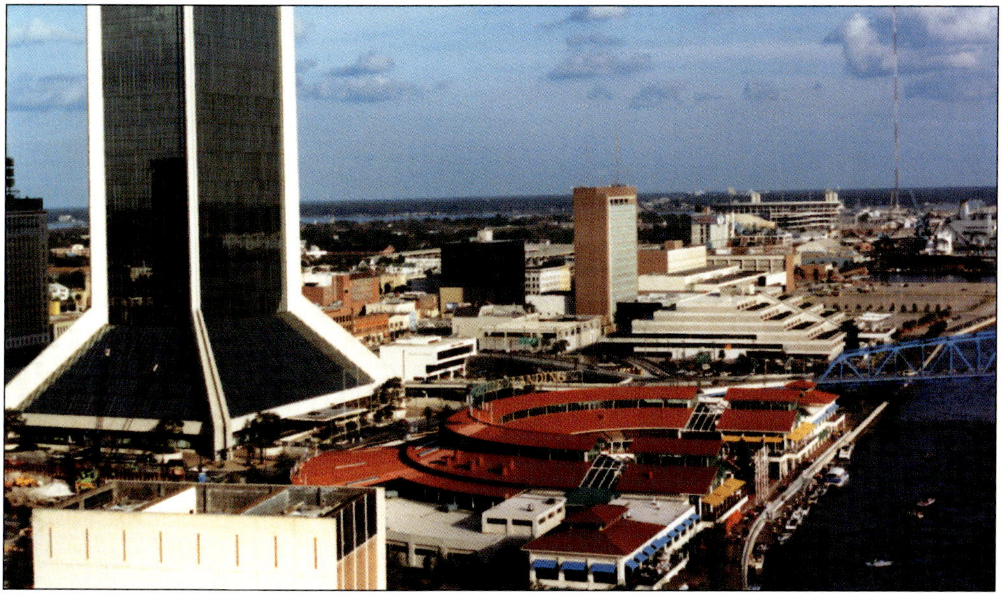

Nestled along the St. Johns River in downtown, the 126,000-square-foot Jacksonville Landing is a festival marketplace that was built by the Rouse Company and opened on June 25, 1987. The Jacksonville Landing hosts more than 350 events each year, including Florida/Georgia Weekend celebrations, the annual Christmas-tree lighting, New Year's Eve, TaxSlayer Bowl celebrations, St. Patrick's Day, and the Fourth of July, as well as live weekend entertainment. (Courtesy of Visit Jacksonville.)

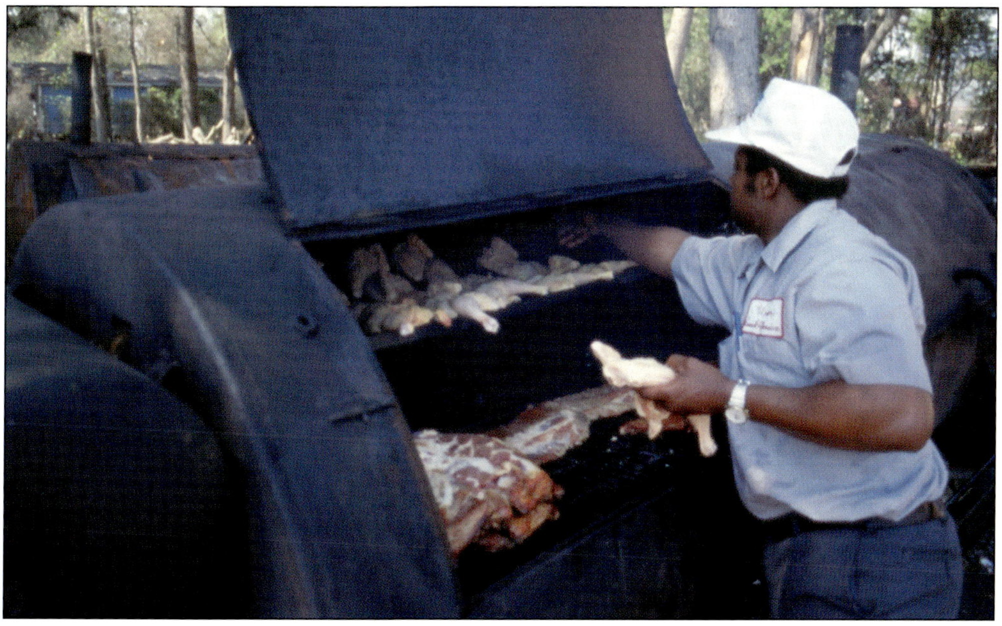

Barbeque has been a fixture in Jacksonville's cuisine scene for centuries. Etymologists believe that barbecue derives from the word *barabicu*, found in the language of the extinct Timucua Indian tribe, which lived in northeast Florida. Pictured here in March 1988 is Hiram Jenkins barbecuing chicken and ribs at his restaurant at 2323 Orange Pickers Road in Mandarin. (Courtesy of Gregory Hansen and the State Archives of Florida.)

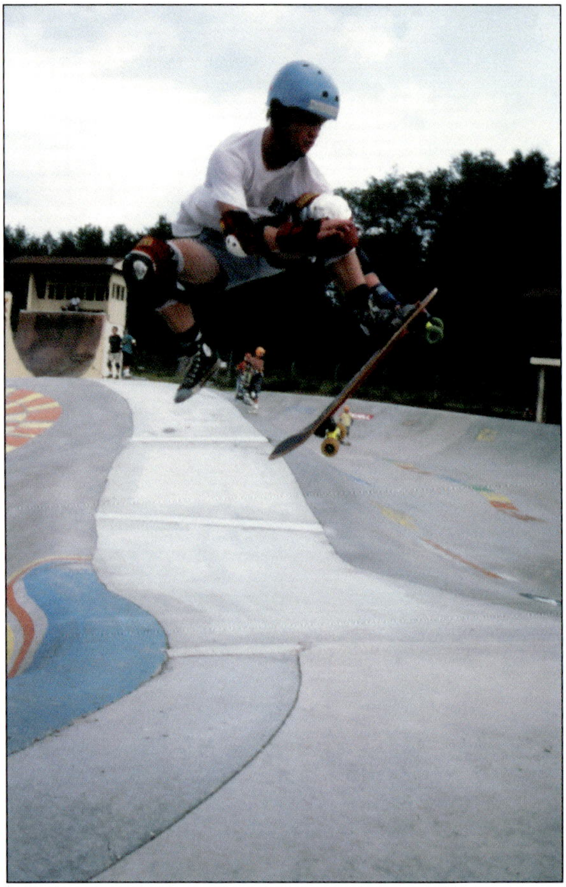

Ben French performs an aerial move with his skateboard at Kona Skatepark in June 1988. Established in 1977, Kona is the longest-surviving private skate park in the world. In 2013, it was named the 16th-best skate park in the country. (Courtesy of Gregory Hansen and the and the State Archives of Florida.)

Officially the Napoleon Bonaparte Broward Bridge, the Dames Point Bridge opened on March 10, 1989. Construction on the 10,646-foot-long, cable-stayed bridge began in 1985. Crossing the St. Johns River with a clearance of 175 feet, it is one of the largest cable-stayed bridges in the country, with 21 miles of cable. (Courtesy of the Leware Construction Company.)

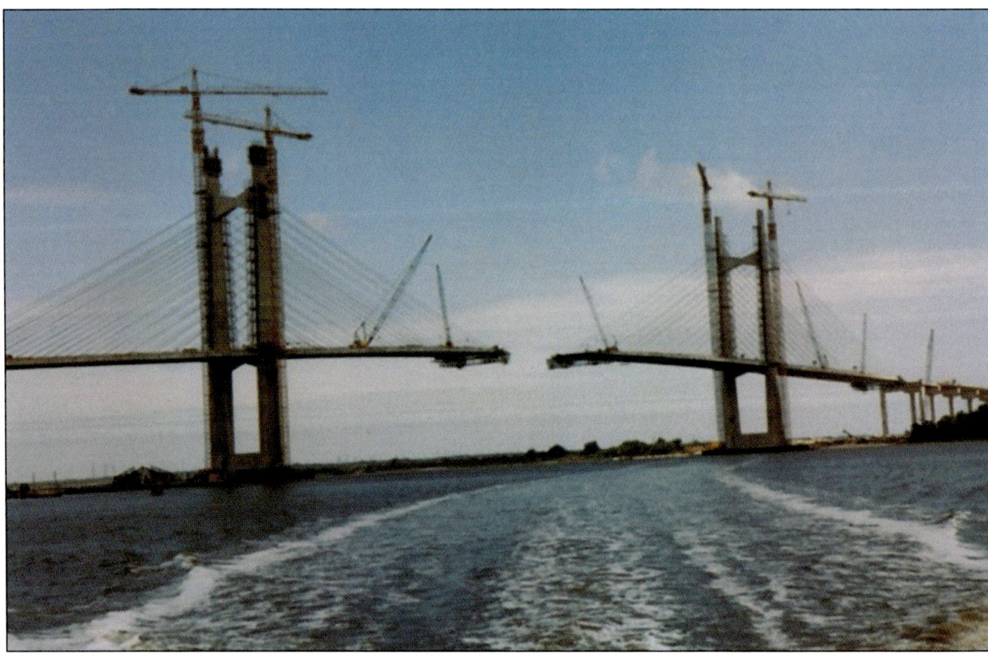

Five

1990s

River City Renaissance

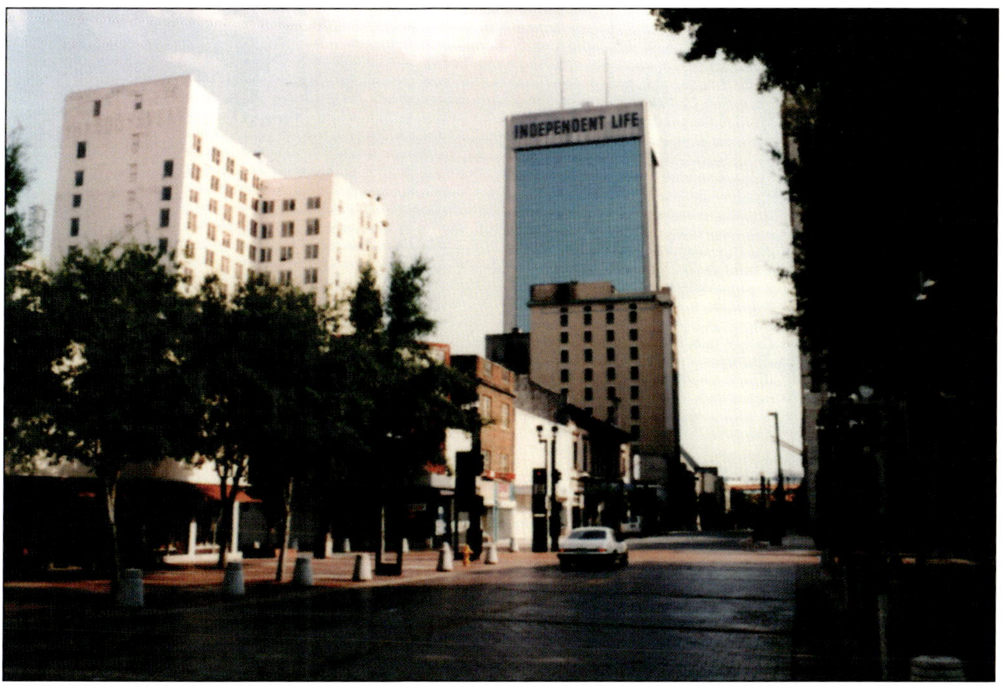

This photograph was taken looking south down Laura Street from Hemming Plaza during the early 1990s. Construction began on the Hemming Plaza streetscape in September 1984. By the time a crowd of 400 welcomed the plaza's reopening on July 26, 1986, downtown's J.C. Penney and Ivey's department stores had closed. On July 27, 1987, May-Cohens announced the closure of its historic 300,000-square-foot flagship store facing Hemming Plaza. (Courtesy of the City of Jacksonville Planning and Development Department.)

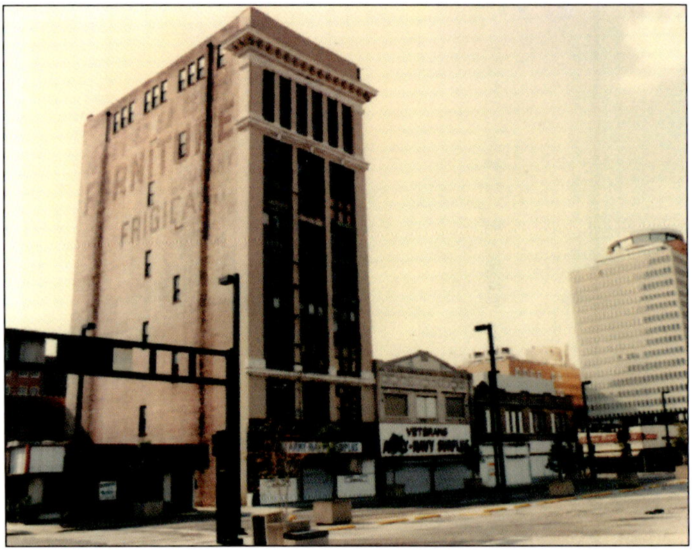

Completed in 1914, the Rhodes-Futch-Collins Building was the last tall structure constructed in the city's post–Great Fire of 1901 building surge. Developed by Amos G. Rhodes, an Atlanta-based furniture magnate, the 11-story tower was the home of Rhodes Furniture for most of the 20th century. On August 17, 2002, it was imploded to make room for a new public library. (Courtesy of the City of Jacksonville.)

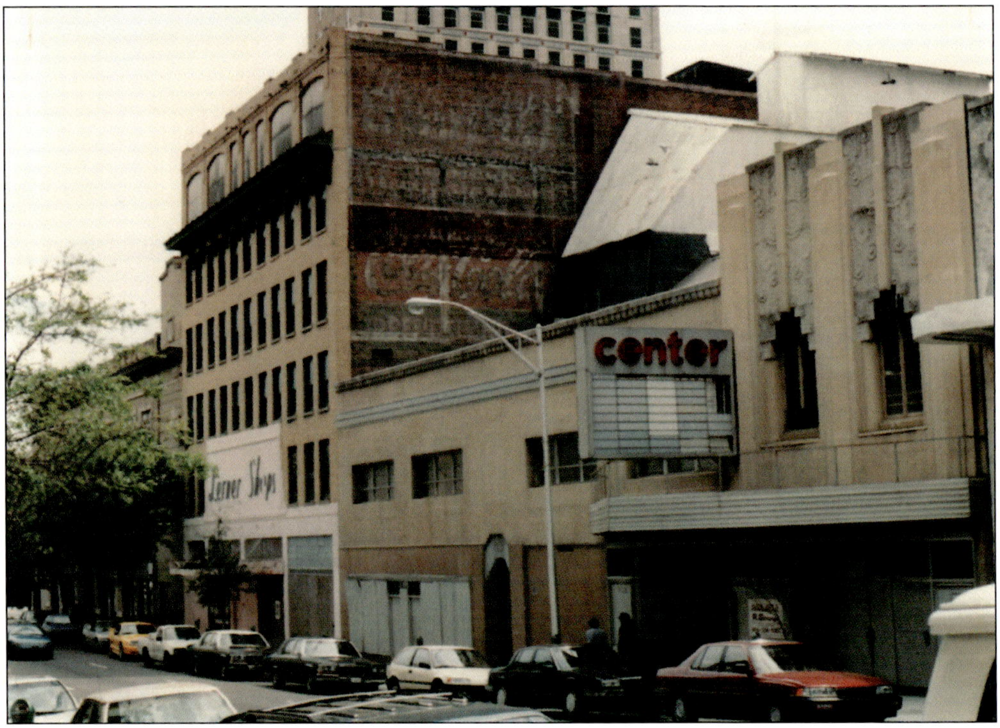

Center Theatre had become a quiet site by the 1990s. Originally constructed as a vaudeville house in 1912, the building was converted into the Arcade Theatre in 1915. It was called the Arcade because the box office was inside of an arcade full of shops that connected Adams and Forsyth Streets through the first level of the adjacent Bisbee Building. In 1960, the theatre was renovated and rebranded as the Center Theatre. Its first film was *Ben Hur.* At its height, the single-screen theatre could seat as many as 1,580 viewers at each showing. By the 1970s, the struggling theater showed kung fu movies. The Center Theatre closed for good on January 2, 1983. On September 5, 2002, the building collapsed, leaving the Florida Theatre as the only remaining movie house from early Jacksonville's theatre district. (Courtesy of the City of Jacksonville.)

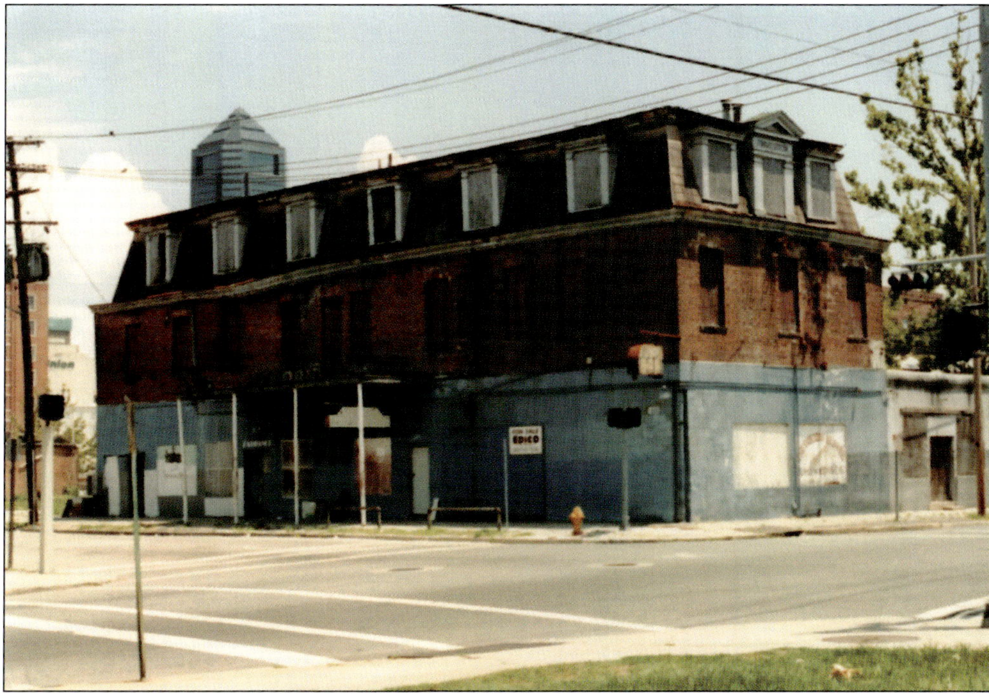

Built in 1895, Genovar's Hall became one of Jacksonville's most culturally significant early-20th century sites. During the 1920s, it was where musicians such as Louis Armstrong lodged while performing in town. The first floor's Lenape Bar is where local waiters and musicians would wait for a chance at stardom. One of those musicians was Ray Charles Robinson, who briefly lived at 633 Church Street. (Courtesy of the City of Jacksonville.)

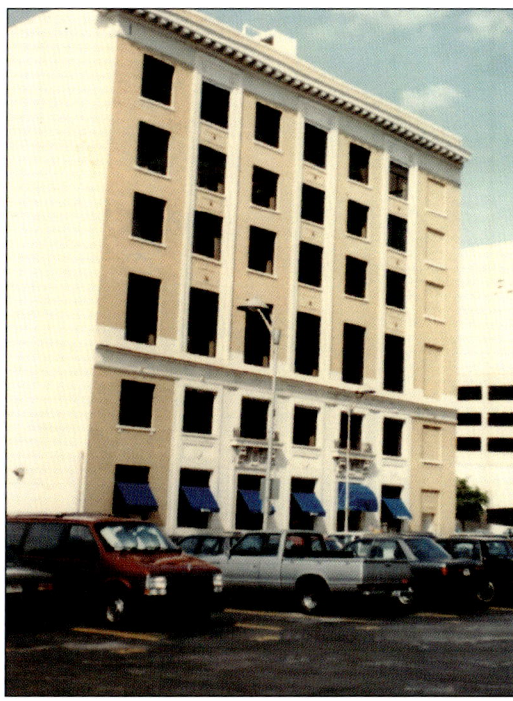

The Southern Bell Telephone and Telegraph Company was one of several buildings that formed a skyscraper canyon along West Adams Street. Completed in 1913 at the cost of $150,000, the main exchange had over 750 operators working inside of it at its peak in the 1960s. Located near Pearl Street, the building was demolished in 2000 to clear space for a new county courthouse. (Courtesy of the City of Jacksonville.)

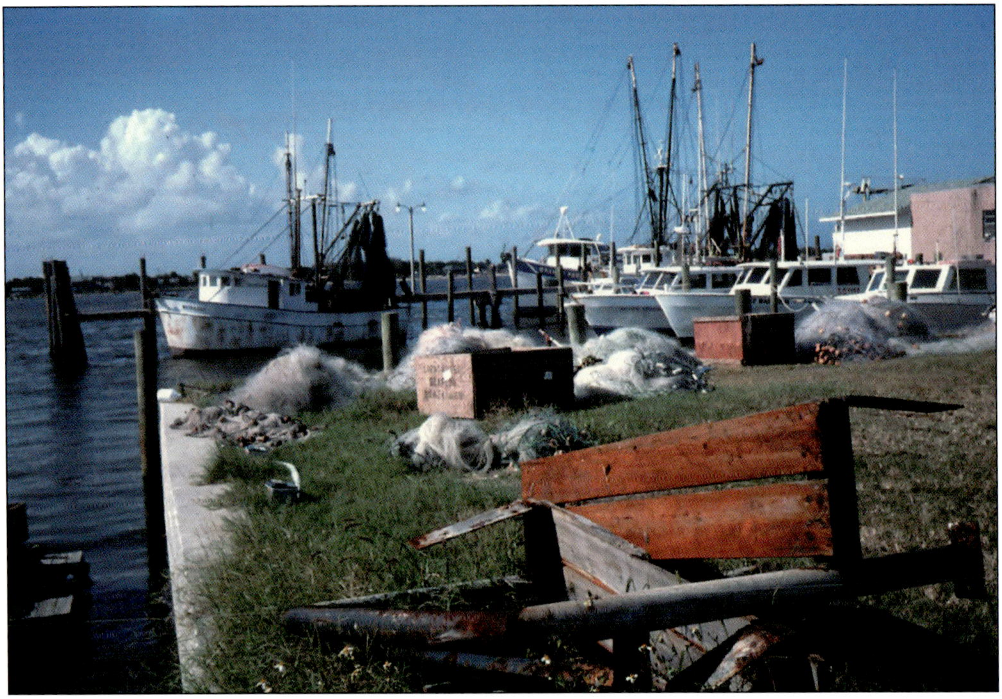

The Mayport shrimp docks are pictured here in 1991. There are two species that make up the majority of the local catch. White shrimp (late August through early February and late April through early June) makes up 80 to 90 percent of the haul, and brown shrimp (June through late August) makes up most of the remaining 20 percent. While white shrimp are mild and tender, brown shrimp are more flavorful and firmer in texture. Pink shrimp make up a negligible portion of the local catch but constitute the majority of landings in the southern part of the state. According to the Shrimp Producers Association based in Fernandina Beach, 10.1 million pounds of shrimp were landed on Florida's East Coast alone in 2011. Mayport's Safe Harbor Seafood is a popular destination for those wanting to taste the local catch. Safe Harbor Seafood Market and Restaurant catches and prepares fresh local seafood daily, while its market features freshly caught lobster, shrimp, mussels, clams, scallops, tuna, and more. (Courtesy of State Archives of Florida.)

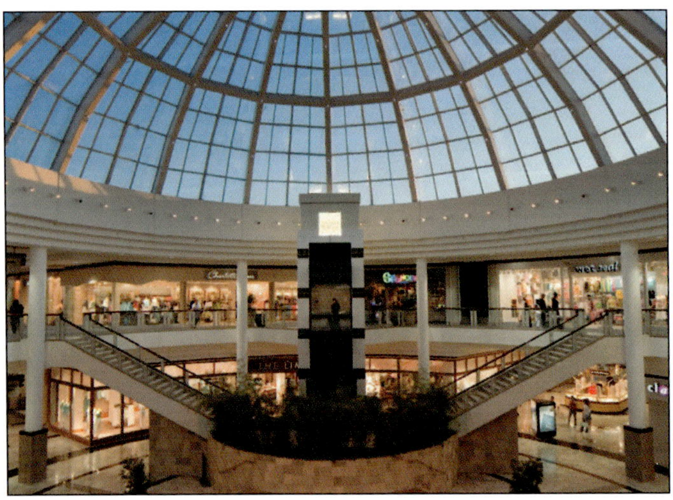

The Avenues, Jacksonville's most dominant enclosed shopping destination, opened its doors in 1990 at the intersection of Philips Highway and Southside Boulevard near Interstate 95. The 1.12-million-square-foot, 150-store mall's original anchors were Maison Blanche, Dillard's, J.C. Penney, and Sears. A fifth anchor, a Parisian department store, was added in 1994. (Courtesy of Simon Property Group, Inc.)

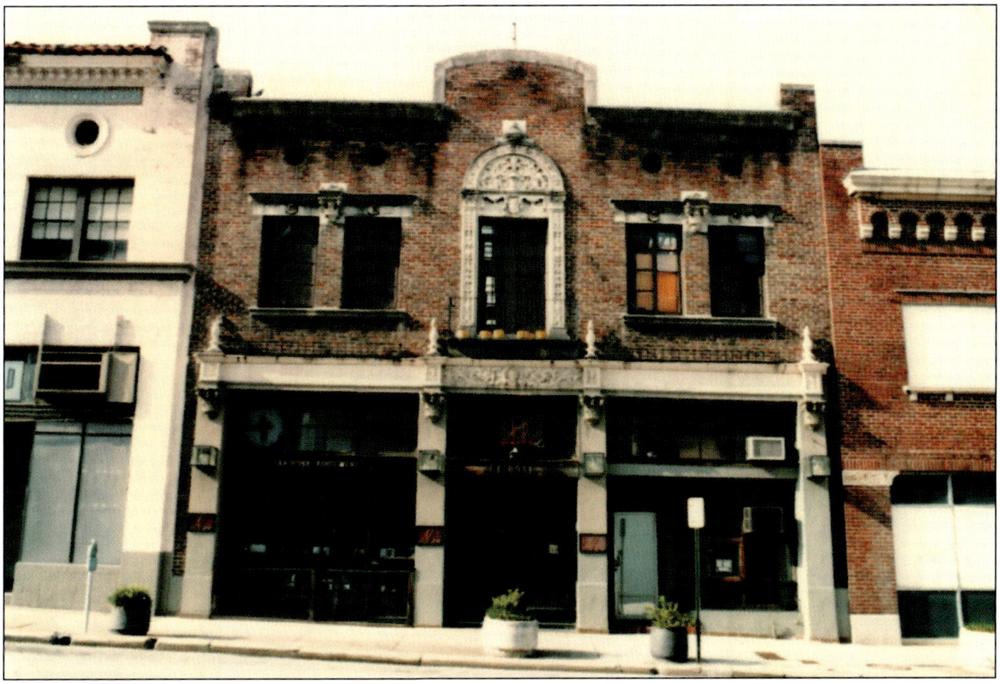

Joseph LaRose's shoe store was located at 33 West Monroe Street. Established in 1949, LaRose's customers included Jackie Kennedy, Abigail Van Buren (of *Dear Abby* fame), and Jayne Mansfield. When LaRose passed in 1999, he left a warehouse with 200,000 pairs of shoes. Acquired and relocated to New York, the LaRose Shoe Collection is showcased at Cherry, a vintage store in the West Village. (Courtesy of the City of Jacksonville.)

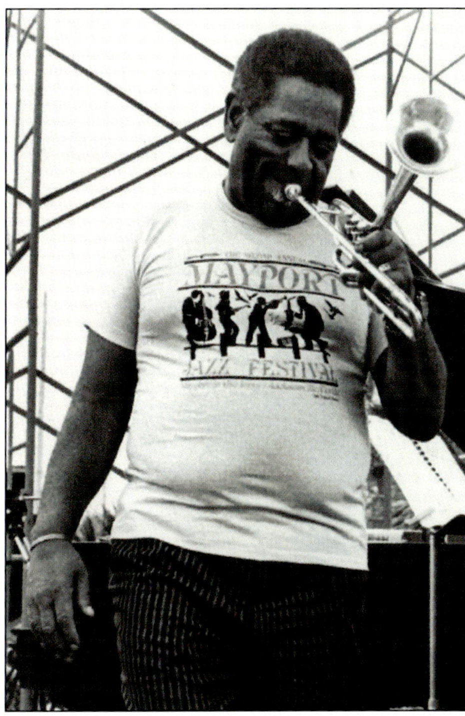

Dizzy Gillespie entertains Jaxsons at the Jacksonville Jazz Festival in Mayport in 1981. Coinciding with Memorial Day weekend, the event has been dubbed by experts as one of the 20 best jazz festivals in the nation. It was founded in 1980 by Mayor Jake Godbold and aide Mike Tolbert as an event to help the struggling village of Mayport. Expecting a few hundred to show up, a crowd of 25,000 turned out for the inaugural event. With crowds increasing in the following years, Mayport was unable to handle the festival, and the event was relocated to downtown Jacksonville in 1982. By the late 1980s, over 100,000 people were attending the annual event. During Mayor John Peyton's administration, the festival underwent a resurgence when it was relocated from Metropolitan Park to the heart of downtown. (Courtesy of Robert M. Overton and the State Archives of Florida.)

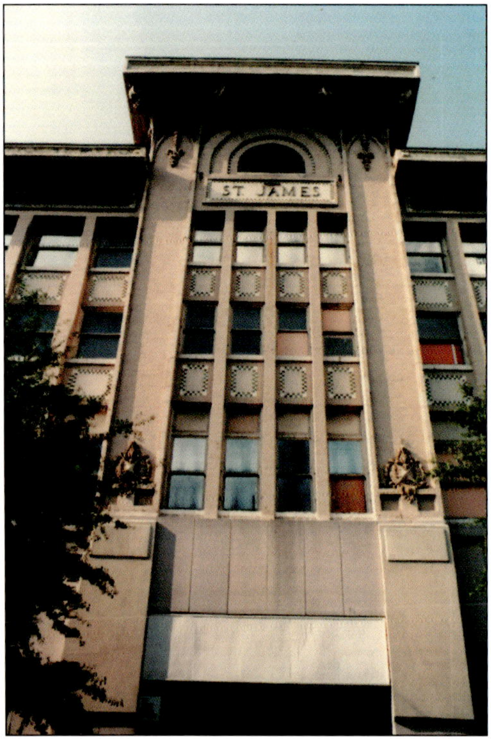

The weathered main entrance of the May-Cohens flagship downtown department store is pictured here after its 1987 closure. In September 1987, Councilwomen Ginny Myrick and Sandra Darling proposed moving city hall into the massive building. In December 1992, Mayor Ed Austin announced his intention to turn downtown's former Cohen Brothers flagship department store into the new city hall. In September 1993, the city council gave official approval of Austin's River City Renaissance plan, which included $20 million for the St. James Building's renovation. Designs for the facility called for the restoration of architect H.J. Klutho's long-lost atrium and octagonal skylight in the center of the building. After 19 months of renovation, 620 city employees began moving into the restored building on December 1, 1997. An official grand opening was held on December 12, 1997. (Courtesy of the City of Jacksonville Historic Preservation Office.)

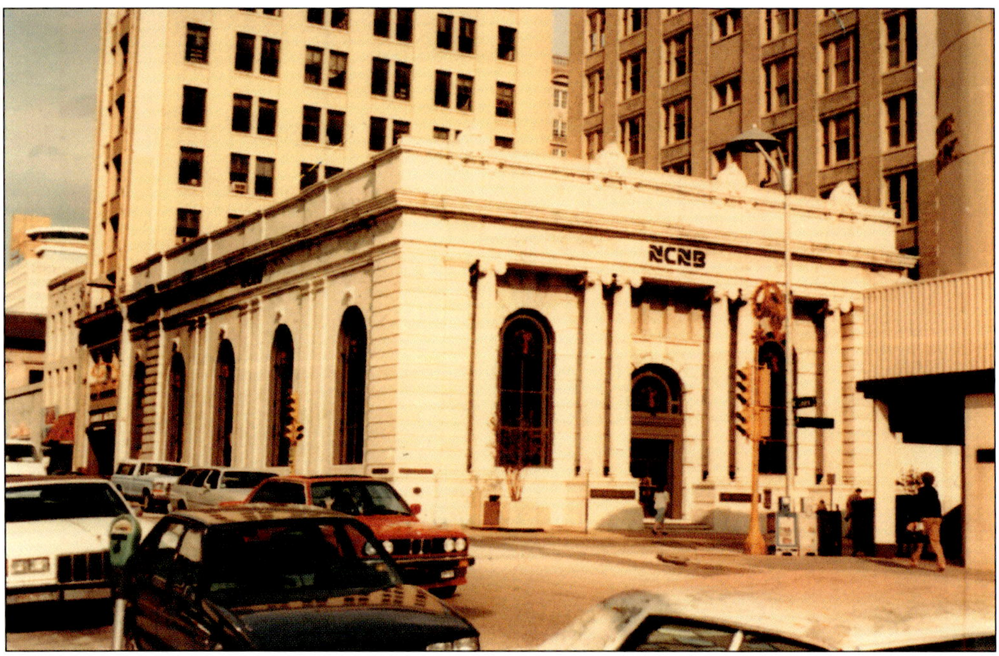

North Carolina–based NCNB National Bank occupied the Marble Bank, Bisbee, and Florida Life Buildings, also known as the "Laura Trio," between 1984 and 1992. In 1992, NCNB merged with the C&S/Sovran Corporation to form NationsBank, abandoning the Laura Trio as a result. Prior to the 1961 construction of the Ed Ball Building, the Laura Trio was the longtime headquarters of Jacksonville-based Florida National Bank. (Courtesy of the City of Jacksonville.)

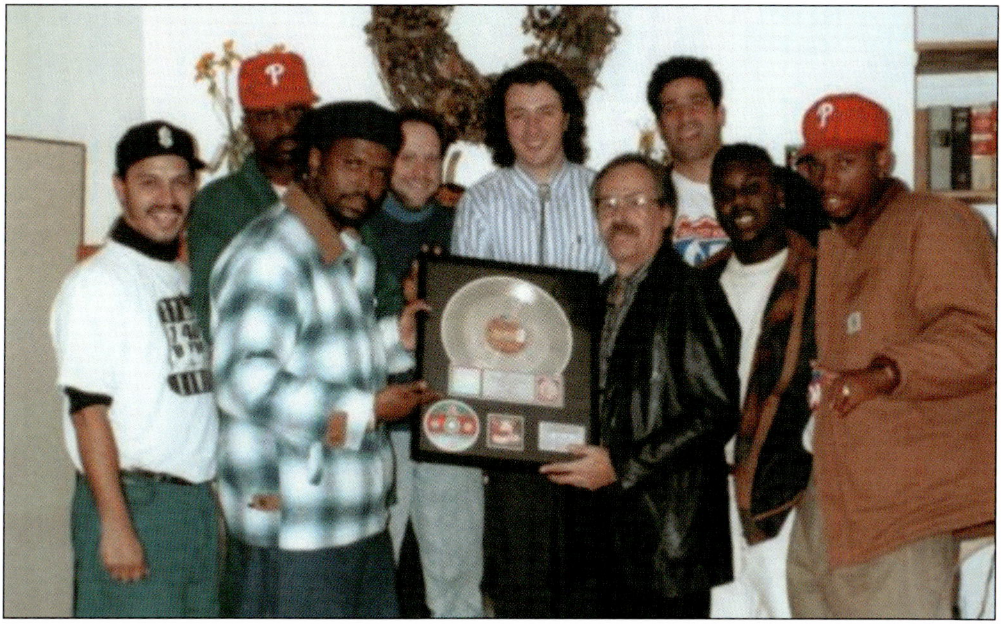

Miami bass is a subgenre of hip-hop music. During the 1990s, the nation's sights were on Jacksonville's C.C. Lemonhead and Jayski McGowan. Their first major hit with 95 South, "Whoot, There It Is," sold over four million copies. More success came in the form of 1994's "Tootsie Roll" with the 69 Boyz and Quad City DJ's "C'mon 'N Ride It (The Train)" in 1996. (Courtesy of www.cozycornerradio.com.)

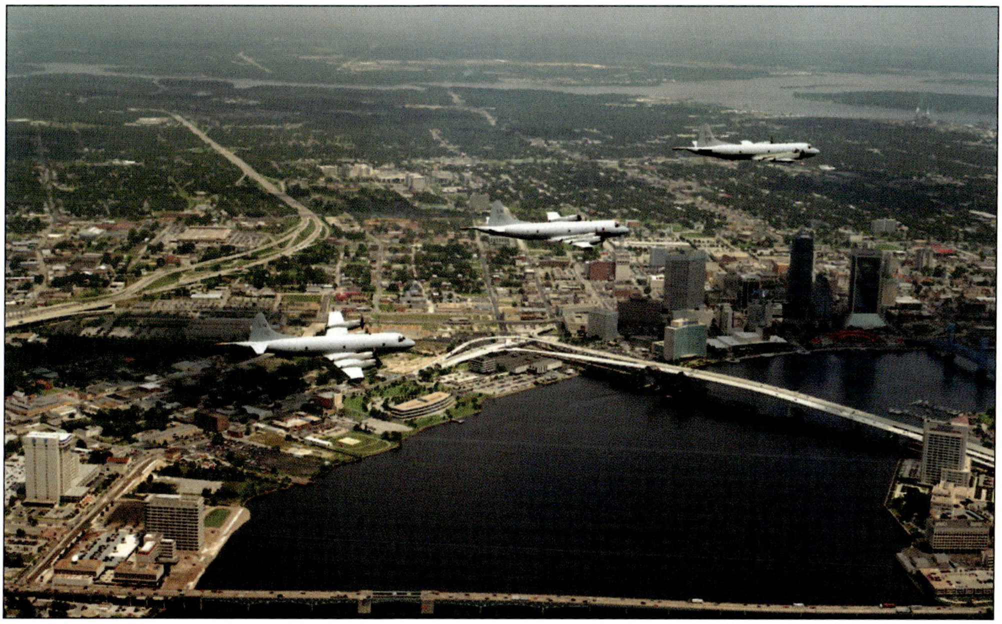

P-3 Orion aircraft overfly downtown in 1994. Developed during the Cold War, the P-3's primary mission was to track Soviet navy ballistic missiles and fast-attack submarines and eliminate them in the event of full-scale war. The last East Coast squadron to deploy the P-3 Orion took off from NAS Jacksonville on January 22, 2015. (Courtesy of Navy Camera Operator: PH1 J.F. Slaughenhaupt and the US Government.)

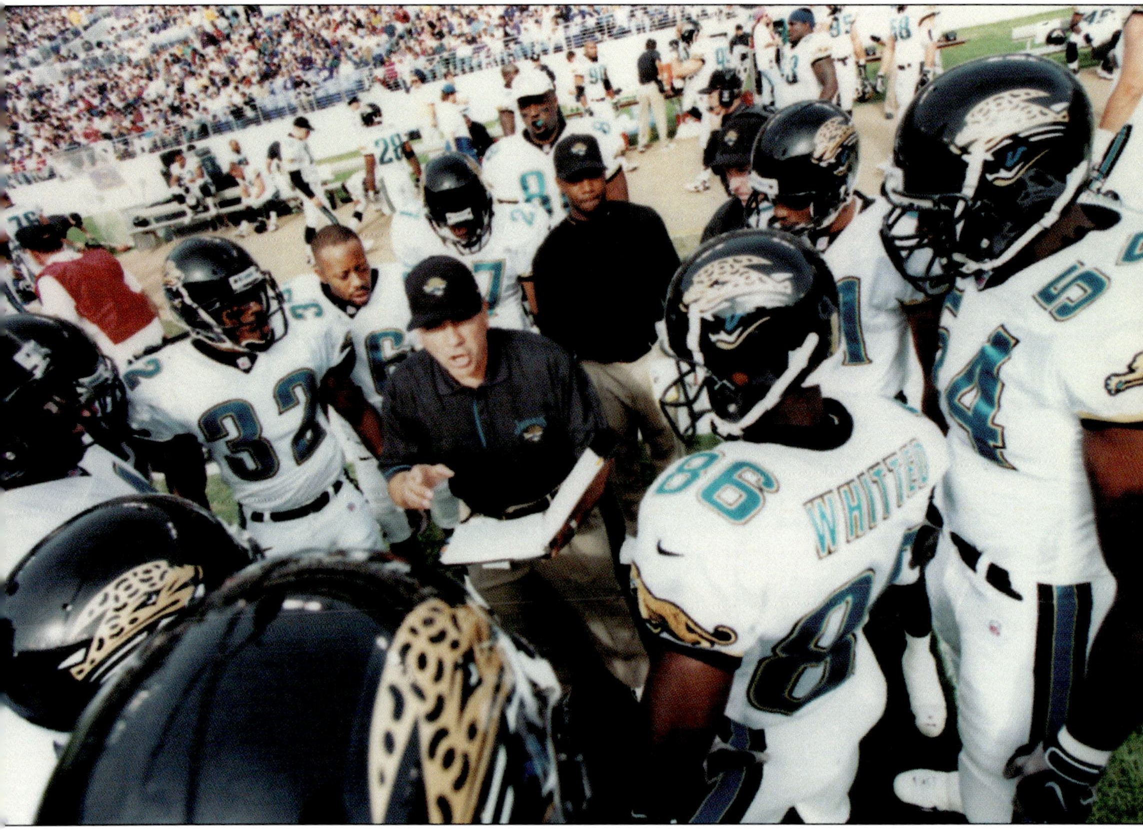

Pictured here is the Jacksonville Jaguars' special teams unit at Alltel Stadium in 1997. In 1993, Jacksonville shocked the nation when NFL owners voted 26-2 in favor of awarding the league's 30th franchise to the city. Because the city's metropolitan area and television market were smaller than most teams in the league, Jacksonville was considered one of the least likely expansion candidates. Along with Charlotte, Jacksonville overcame bids from St. Louis, Missouri; Baltimore, Maryland; and Memphis, Tennessee. The first home Jaguars game occurred on August 18, 1995, with a preseason game against the St. Louis Rams. The Jaguars would quickly rise from an expansion team to one of the top teams in the league by making the playoffs four out of their first five years under head coach Tom Coughlin. In 2012, the franchise was sold to Illinois automobile parts manufacturer and Fulham F.C. (English Football League Championship) owner Shahid Khan.

Six

2000s
The Better Jacksonville Plan

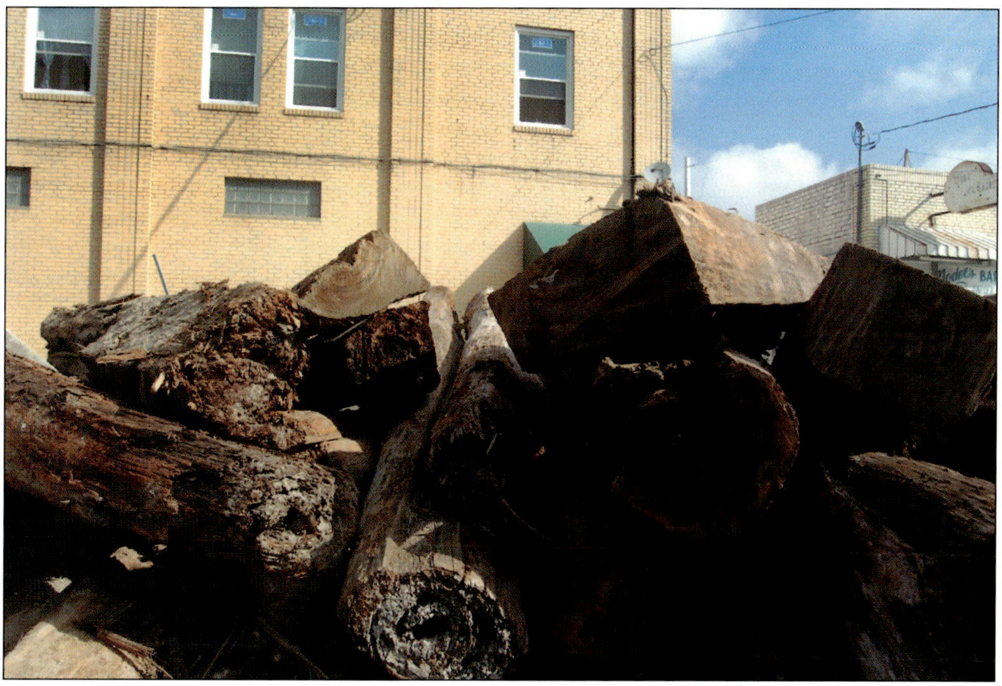

The remains of the Jacksonville Traction Company's Main Street streetcar line were unearthed during the 2009 reconstruction of the highway in the heart of the Springfield Historic District. Prior to World War II, with 61 miles of streetcar lines connecting downtown with its suburbs, Jacksonville's streetcar system was the largest in Florida and one of the largest in the South. In fact, in 1912, there were 13,828,904 passengers who rode the system. (Courtesy of Daniel Herbin and MetroJacksonville.com.)

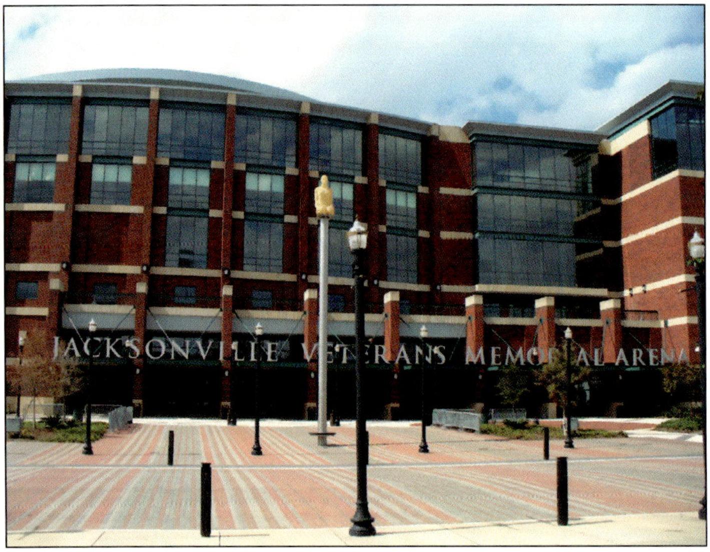

The $130-million Veterans Memorial Arena is a 15,000-seat venue that opened on November 28, 2003, as a part of Mayor John Delaney's Better Jacksonville Plan. Elton John was the first artist to hold a concert in the arena, which was designed with the acoustical characteristics necessary for concerts.

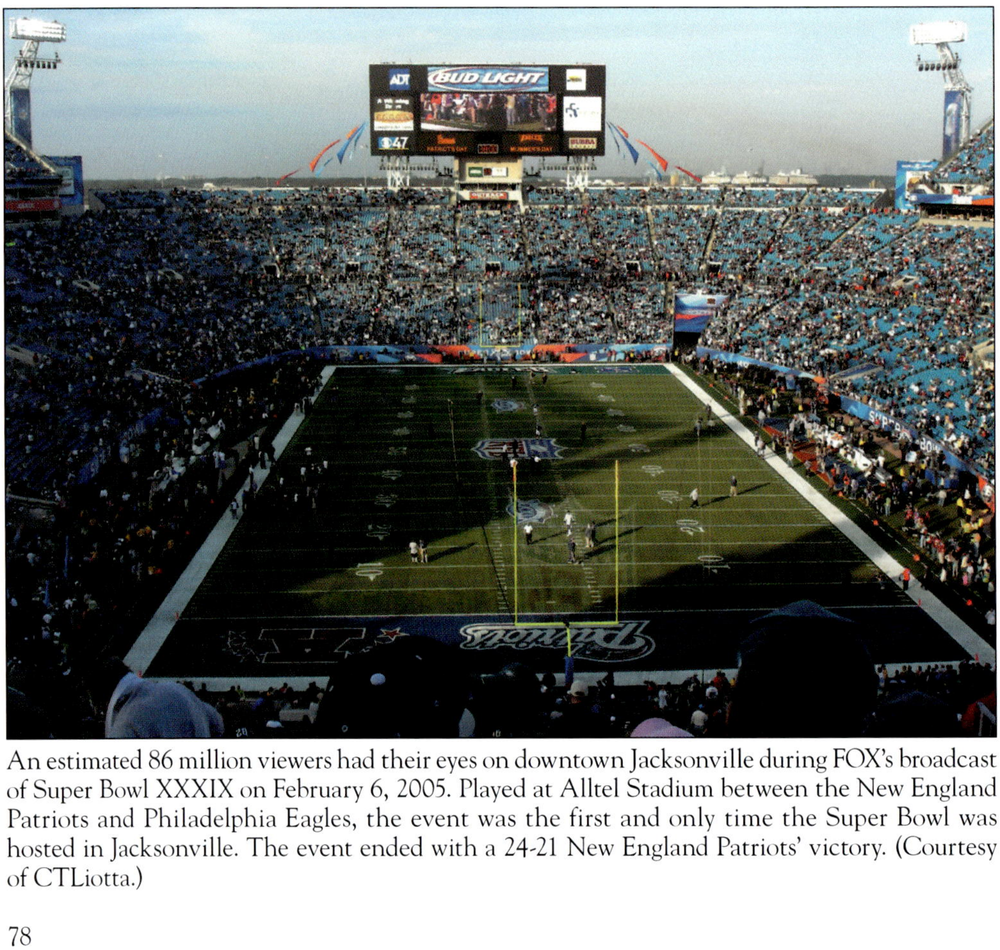

An estimated 86 million viewers had their eyes on downtown Jacksonville during FOX's broadcast of Super Bowl XXXIX on February 6, 2005. Played at Alltel Stadium between the New England Patriots and Philadelphia Eagles, the event was the first and only time the Super Bowl was hosted in Jacksonville. The event ended with a 24-21 New England Patriots' victory. (Courtesy of CTLiotta.)

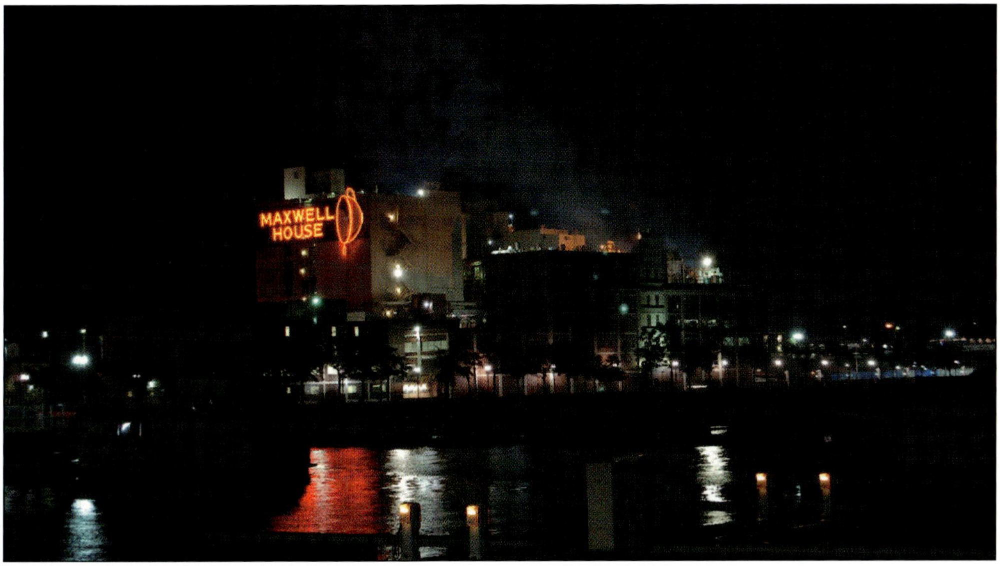

Producing up to one million pounds of coffee a day, East Bay Street's Maxwell House Coffee is the last remaining large industrial facility in downtown, west of Hogans Creek. After a century of continuous operation, the 400,000-square-foot plant, with its iconic coffee cup sign, is one of the world's largest coffee plants and one of the city's oldest manufacturers. Maxwell House opened in Jacksonville in 1910 under a different name, Cheek-Neal Coffee Co. West Bay Street was selected for the plant site because of its ability to receive coffee beans by barge. While the company itself has had notable success, it was not always easy for the Jacksonville plant. In 1990, it was almost shut down. The company was faced with the decision to close one of its major plants. A city-wide protest in Jacksonville, "Keep Max in Jax," helped the plant in Jacksonville win. It operates around the clock, employs over 200 workers, and is said to have a $600-million impact annually. (Courtesy of Daniel Herbin and MetroJacksonville.com.)

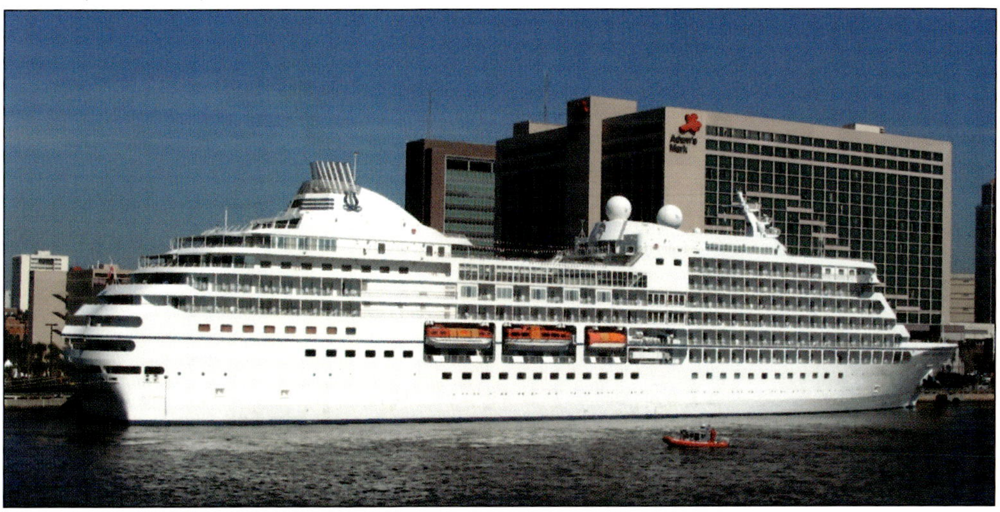

The 490-passenger Radisson *Seven Seas Navigator*, parked in front of the Adam's Mark hotel downtown, was the most luxurious of the five cruise ships brought to town for Super Bowl XXXIX. Along with the Carnival *Miracle*, and Holland America Line's *Volendam*, *Zaandam*, and *Zuiderdam*, the vessels alleviated a critical shortage of high-end hotel rooms that would have prevented Jacksonville from bidding for the Super Bowl. (Courtesy of Edward Graham.)

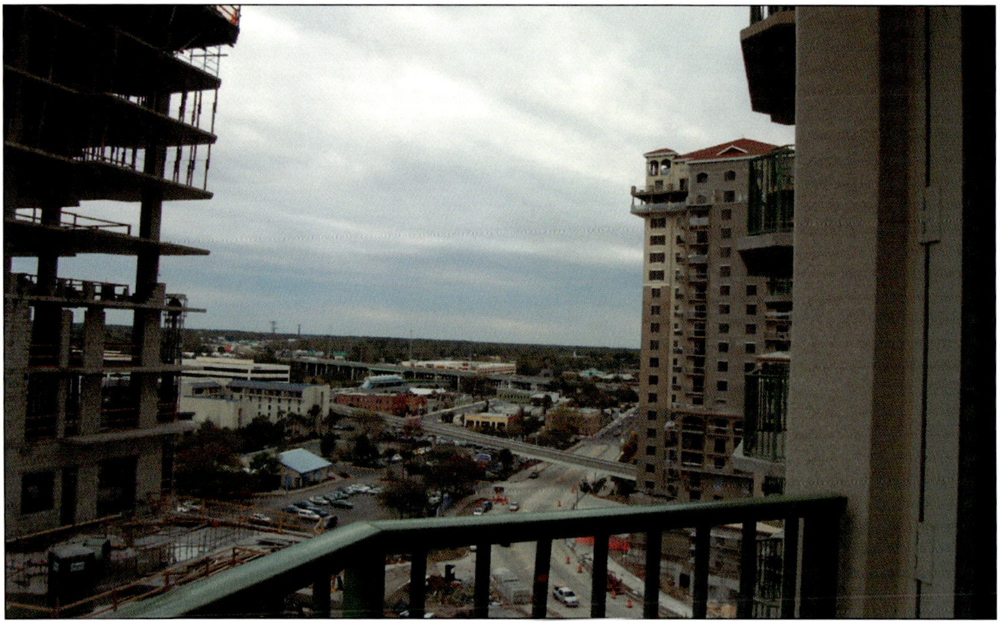

This is a 2007 construction view of the Peninsula (left) and San Marco Place (right) condominium towers from a balcony of the recently completed Strand. The 28-story Strand is Jacksonville's tallest apartment tower, offering spectacular views of the city's skyline. Together, these three Southbank towers are representative of Florida's real estate building boom during the first decade of the 21st century. (Courtesy of Daniel Herbin and MetroJacksonville.com.)

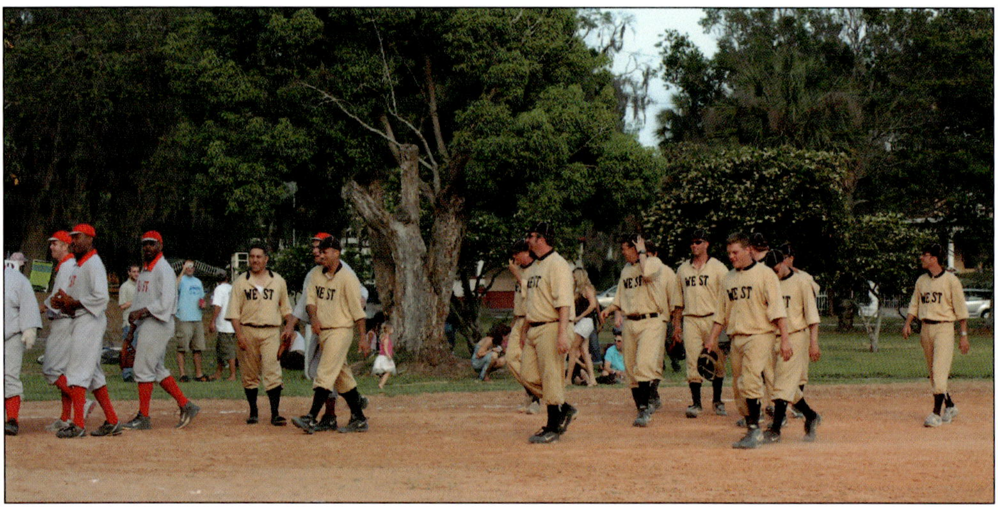

Springfield residents compete in a neighborhood-heritage throwback baseball game at Klutho Park in 2007. Every year, hundreds of fans turn back the clock as Springfield residents are split into East and West teams playing with bats, balls, gloves, and uniforms made to 1910-era specifications. Prior to being renamed in honor of H.J. Klutho in 1984, Klutho Park was a small section of Springfield Park. Most of the park was created between 1899 and 1901 on land donated by the Springfield Company. The park was the site of Jacksonville's first zoo. With no admittance fee, the zoo instantly became a popular destination; however, by 1924, nearby Springfield residents began to protest against foul odors coming from the zoo. This set the stage for the zoo's ultimate relocation to the Trout River site in 1925. (Courtesy of Daniel Herbin and MetroJacksonville.com.)

Jacksonville is a city known for its fireworks displays. Celebrating Independence Day 2007, residents stand in awe of a spectacular fireworks display over the St. Johns River. Viewed from the Northbank and Southbank of the river, fireworks were launched from barges, the roofs of skyscrapers, and bridges. (Courtesy of Daniel Herbin and MetroJacksonville.com.)

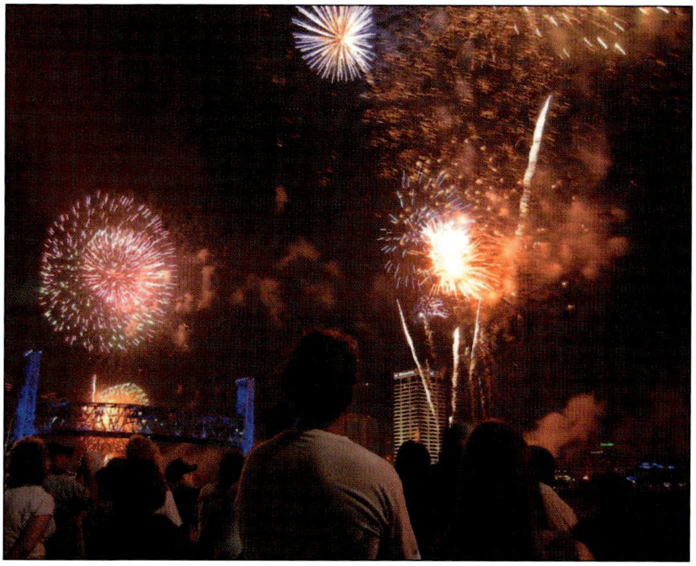

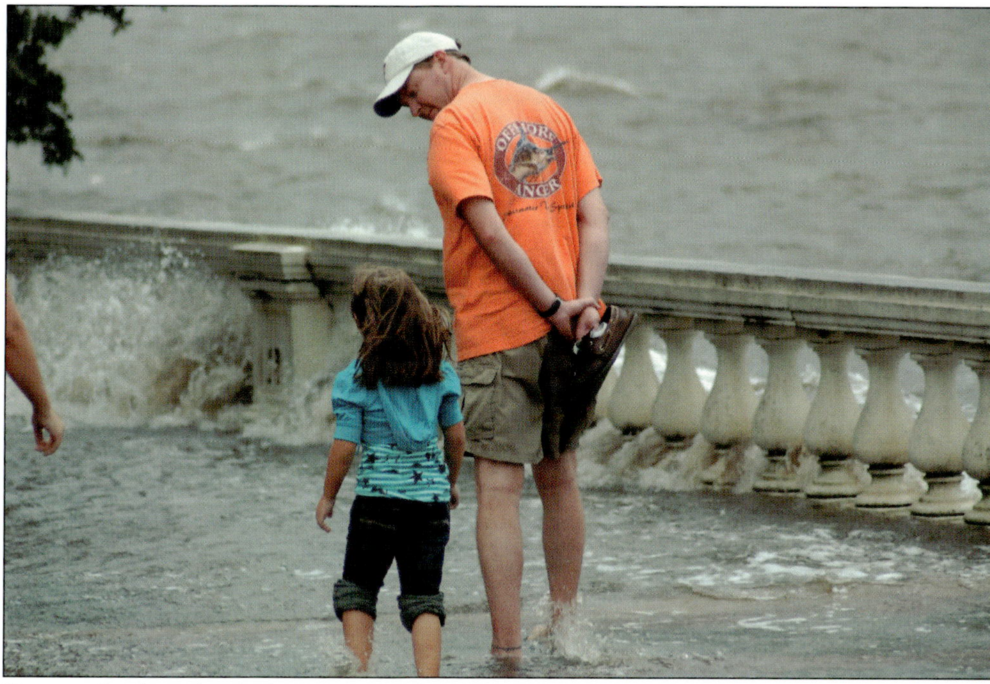

Historically, direct hits by hurricanes and tropical storms are a rare occurrence in Jacksonville, but that did not stop Tropical Storm Fay from leaving its mark on Jacksonville in August 2008. It was a strong and unusual tropical storm in that it moved erratically across the state of Florida over a seven-day period. With its highest winds at 79 miles per hour, the storm caused 13 direct fatalities, 23 indirect fatalities, and $560 million in damage. A total of 81 tornadoes touched down across five states as a result. Already prone to flooding, Jacksonville was no match for Tropical Storm Fay's fury. Low-lying areas around downtown, such as Springfield, San Marco, and Riverside, soon found significant areas of their districts under water. Significant parts of the city were also left without power for days—however, it did not keep curious residents inside. (Courtesy of Daniel Herbin and MetroJacksonville.com.)

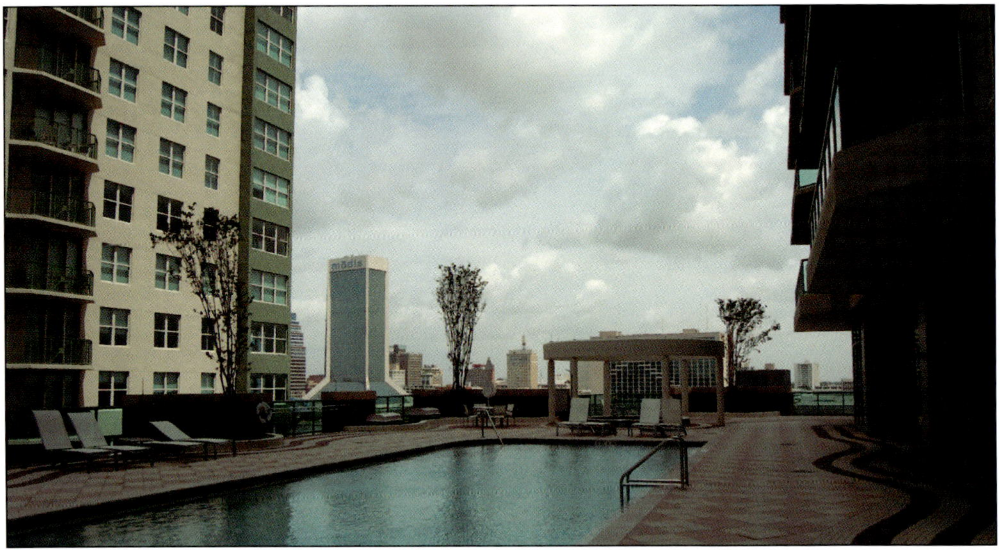

This is a view of downtown Jacksonville from the Peninsula's pool deck and lounge. When completed in 2008, the Peninsula at St. Johns Center became the Southbank's tallest building. Stretching 437 feet into the sky, the 36-story condominium tower is the tallest building constructed in Jacksonville since the completion of the 617-foot-high Bank of America Tower in 1990. (Courtesy of Daniel Herbin and MetroJacksonville.com.)

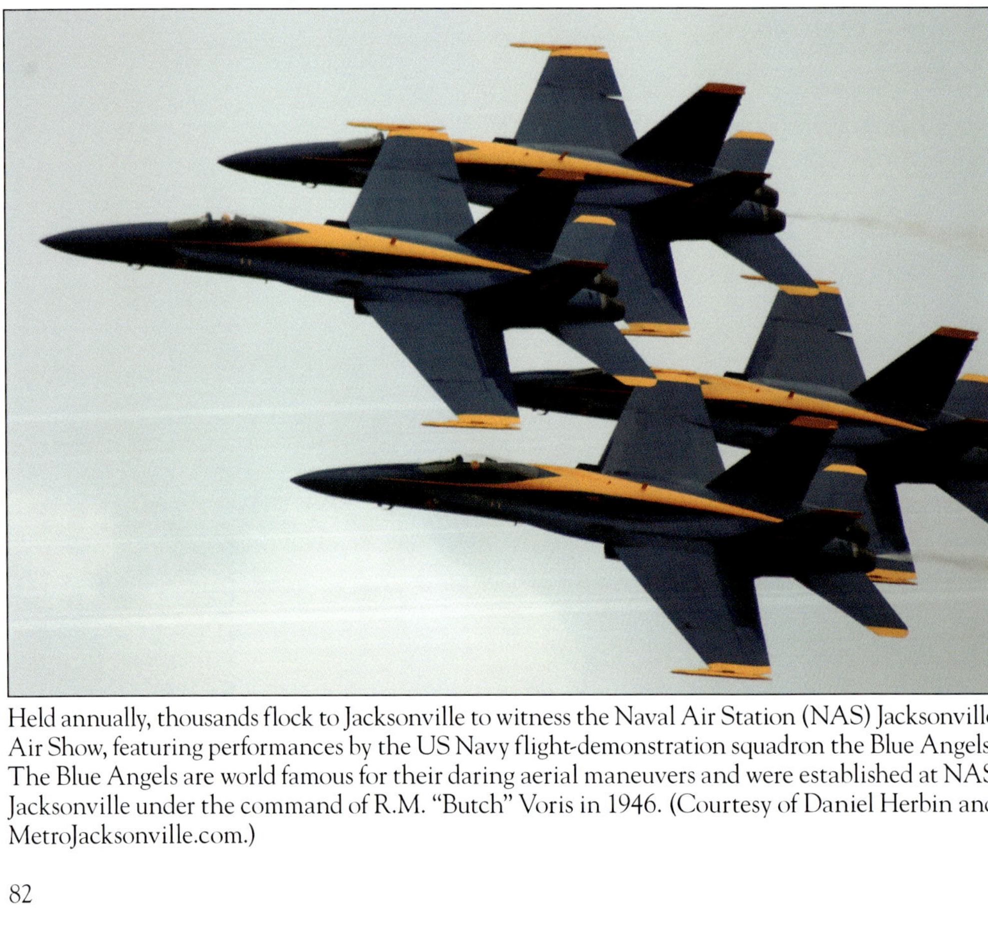

Held annually, thousands flock to Jacksonville to witness the Naval Air Station (NAS) Jacksonville Air Show, featuring performances by the US Navy flight-demonstration squadron the Blue Angels. The Blue Angels are world famous for their daring aerial maneuvers and were established at NAS Jacksonville under the command of R.M. "Butch" Voris in 1946. (Courtesy of Daniel Herbin and MetroJacksonville.com.)

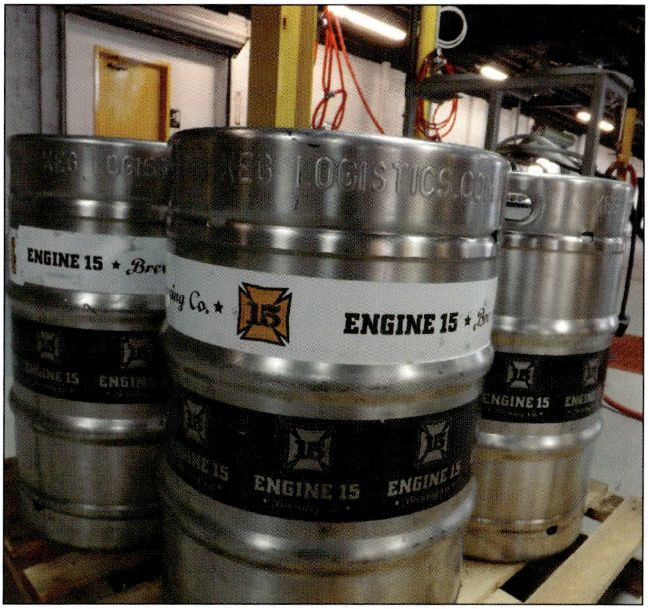

Many say that to see how a small business can reinvigorate a neighborhood, just follow the barrels. Across America, craft breweries are breathing fresh air into aging urban districts. This trend has found its way to Jacksonville, where several local craft breweries, such as Bold City Brewery, Intuition Ale Works, Aardwolf Brewing Company, Green Room Brewing Company, Pinglehead Brewing Company, Veterans United Craft Brewery, and Engine 15 Brewery, have established their roots since 2008. (Courtesy of the author and MetroJacksonville.com.)

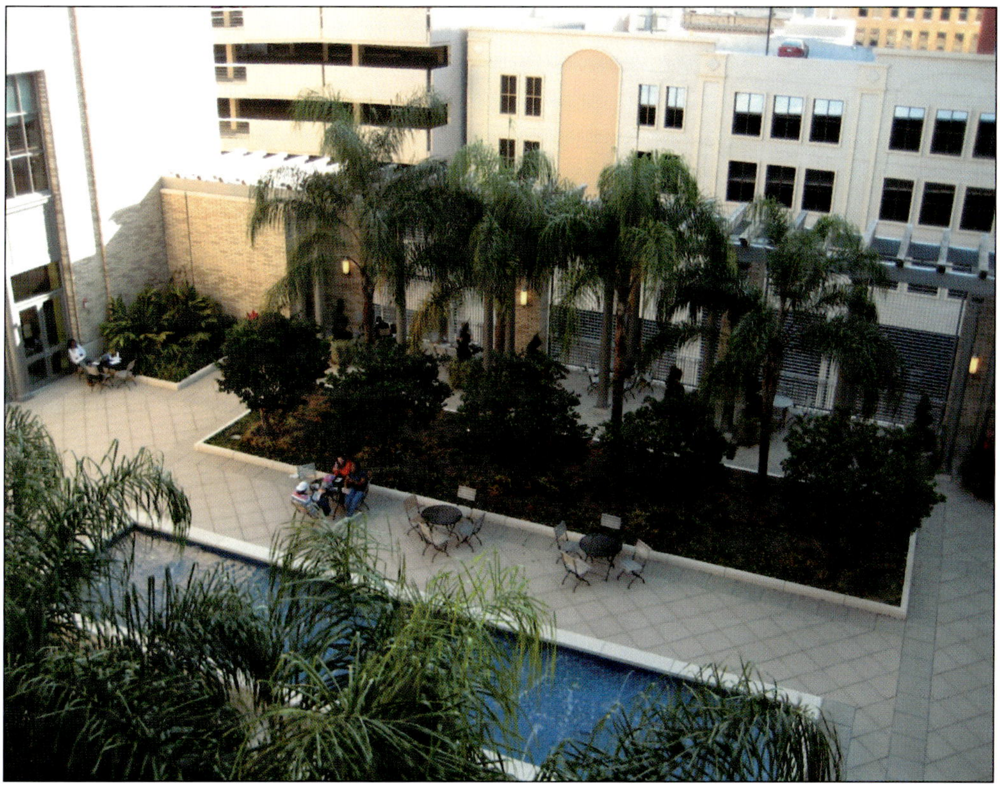

The Betsy Lovett Courtyard is one of Jacksonville's best hidden gems. Located on the library's second floor, it is a quiet urban oasis framed by surrounding downtown buildings and anchored with palm trees and reflecting pools with fountains. Completed on November 12, 2005, as the final library project in the Better Jacksonville Plan, the main library is the largest public library in the state of Florida. (Courtesy of the author and MetroJacksonville.com.)

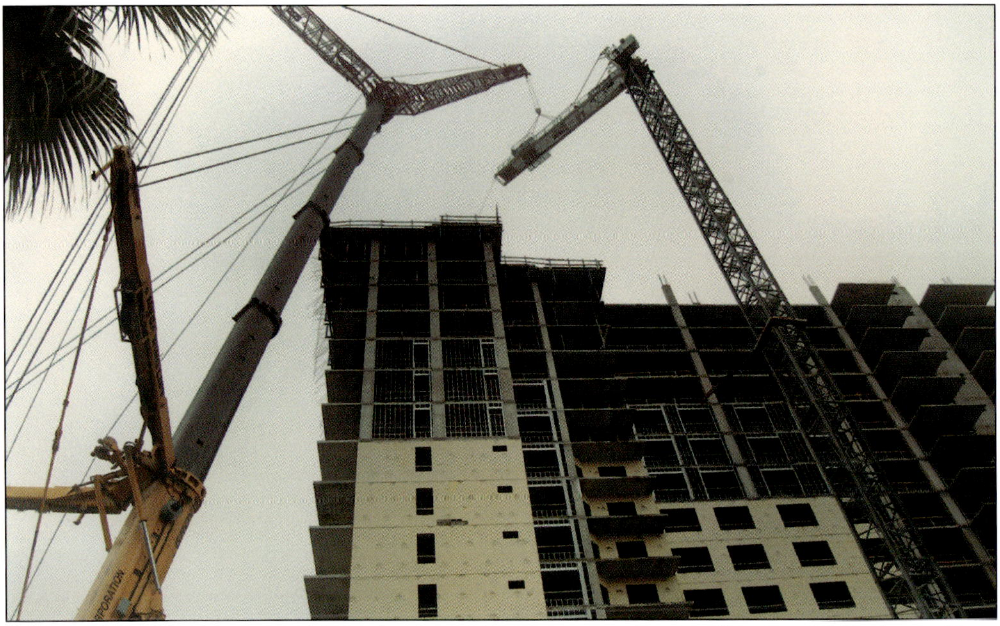

A giant mobile crane is utilized to take down the large tower crane affixed to the Berkman Plaza II construction site on August 17, 2009. The incomplete ruins of Berkman Plaza II stand as a local reminder of the economic pain felt by the 2008 financial crisis. When construction began in early 2006, Berkman Plaza II was envisioned as being a 23-story, 223-unit condominium tower. (Courtesy of Daniel Herbin and MetroJacksonville.com.)

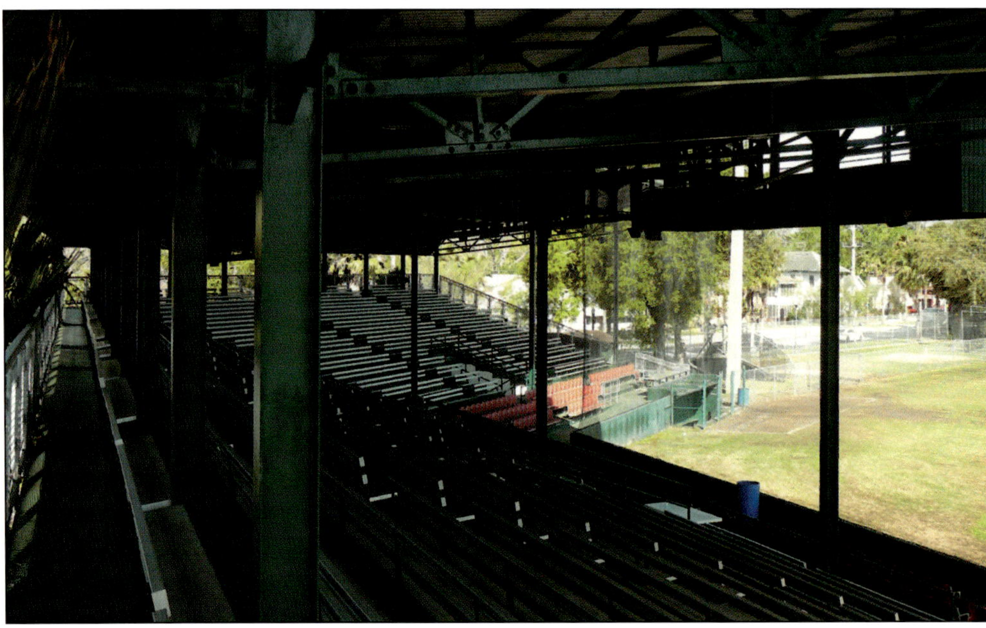

The brick-and-steel grandstand of Durkeeville's J.P. Small Field was completed in 1935 after the original facility was destroyed by fire. Originally known as Durkee Field, it was the home to the Negro League's Jacksonville Red Caps. Players such as Henry Aaron, Leroy "Satchel" Paige, and Roy Campanella passed through on their way to baseball's Hall of Fame. (Courtesy of the author and MetroJacksonville.com.)

Seven

2010s

Taking Jacksonville to the Next Level

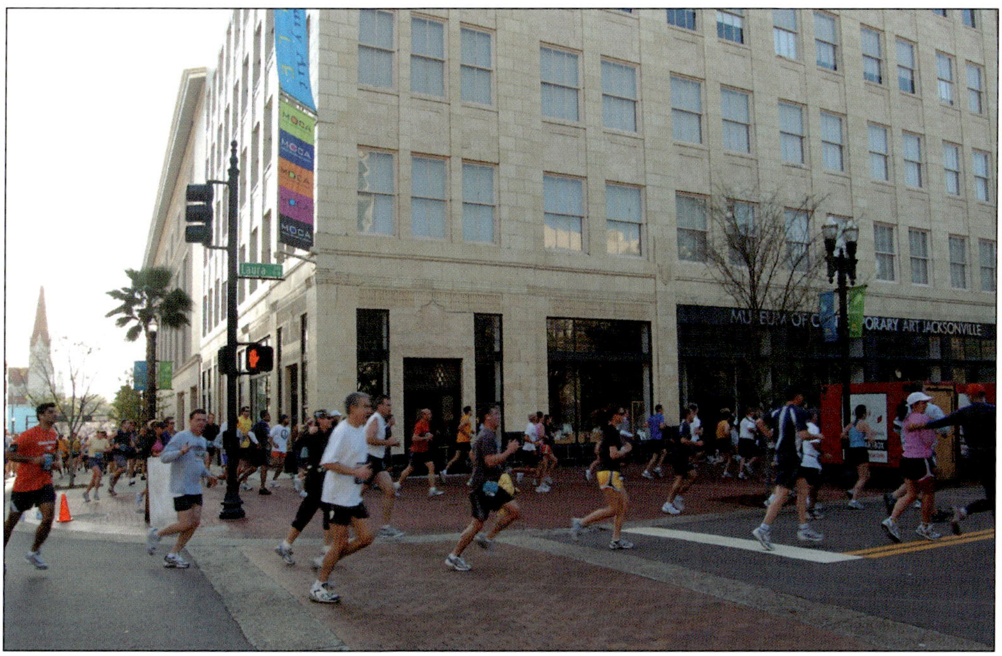

Attracting both competitive and recreational runners, the Gate River Run is the largest 15-kilometer race in the country. Described by local news media as "one of Jacksonville's premiere annual events," the race has been voted as one of the top US road races for the last two decades by *Runner's World* magazine. The course crosses two bridges spanning the St. Johns River, giving the race its name. (Courtesy of Daniel Herbin and MetroJacksonville.com.)

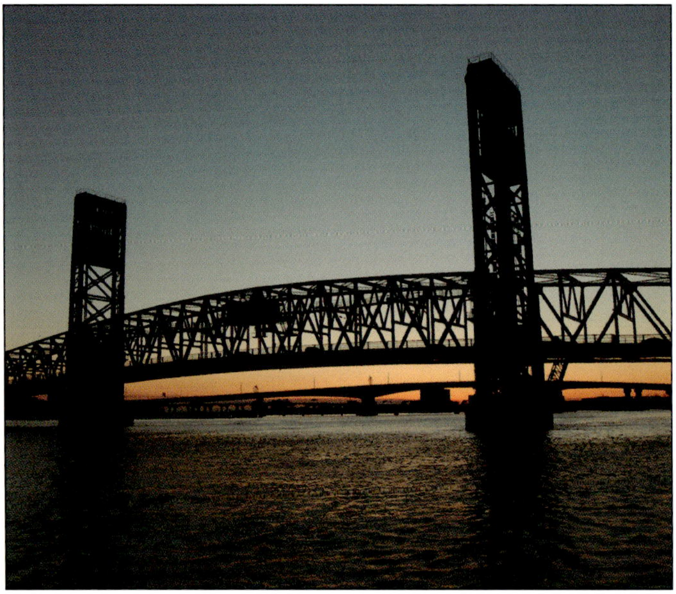

Jacksonville's unique assortment of bridges spanning the St. Johns River provide the city with a distinct identity amongst its regional peers. Eight bridges tie the city together; six of those are iconic fixtures in the heart of downtown. The oldest is the FEC Strauss Trunnion Bascule Bridge. This double-track railroad bridge dates back to January 5, 1890. It is largely responsible for the development of south Florida. (Courtesy of Daniel Herbin and MetroJacksonville.com.)

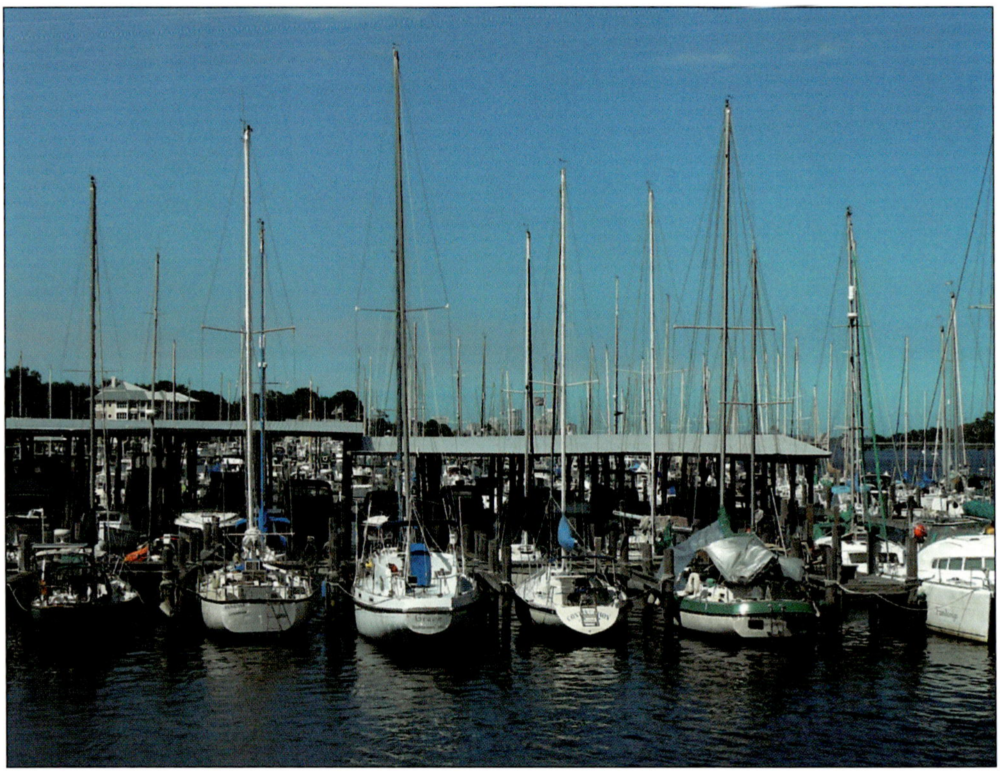

The Ortega River is the recreational-boating center of northeast Florida. Situated along Lake Shore Boulevard and Lakeside Drive, "Marina Mile" features several marinas, boat-repair shops, yacht sales, and similar marine-oriented businesses. Due to pleasure boats from more than a dozen marinas passing underneath it to reach the St. Johns River, Marina Mile's Ortega River Bridge is the most frequently opened drawbridge in Florida, with 15,000 lifts annually. (Courtesy of the author and MetroJacksonville.com.)

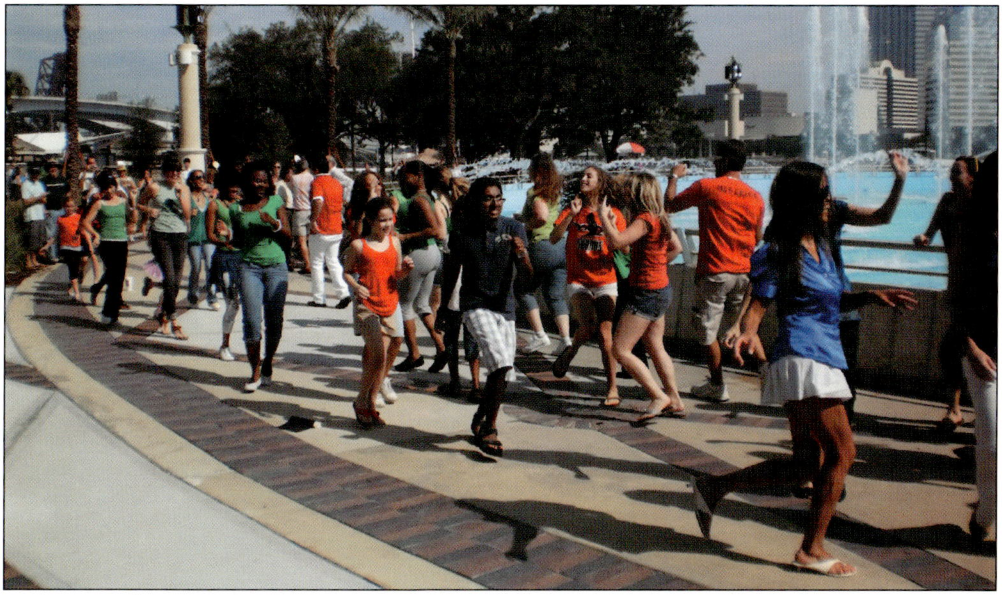

Following a $3.1-million, nine-month restoration, Friendship Fountain reopened Saturday, June 18, 2011, on Jacksonville's Southbank. Among the dignitaries present for the reopening ceremony were Mayor John Peyton and Taylor Hardwick, the architect who designed the original Friendship Fountain Park. The 200-foot-diameter fountain projects a curved radiating walkway to the river, accentuated by 22 Medjool date palms that are 25 feet high, 135 color-changing LEDs, and synchronized music. (Courtesy of the author and MetroJacksonville.com.)

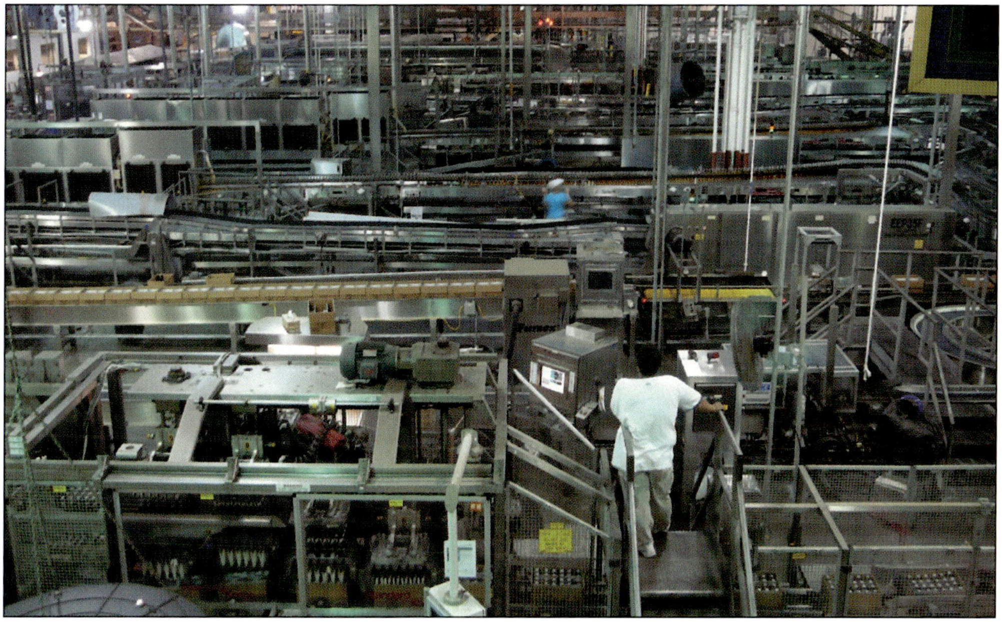

Anheuser-Busch's Jacksonville brewery produces more than 125 million cases of beer each year, serving Florida, southern Georgia, and southern Alabama markets. Completed in 1969, the Jacksonville brewery operates 24 hours a day, filling up to 8.5 million cans of beer daily, and offers free tours for a behind-the-scenes look at the brewing and packaging process. (Courtesy of the author and MetroJacksonville.com.)

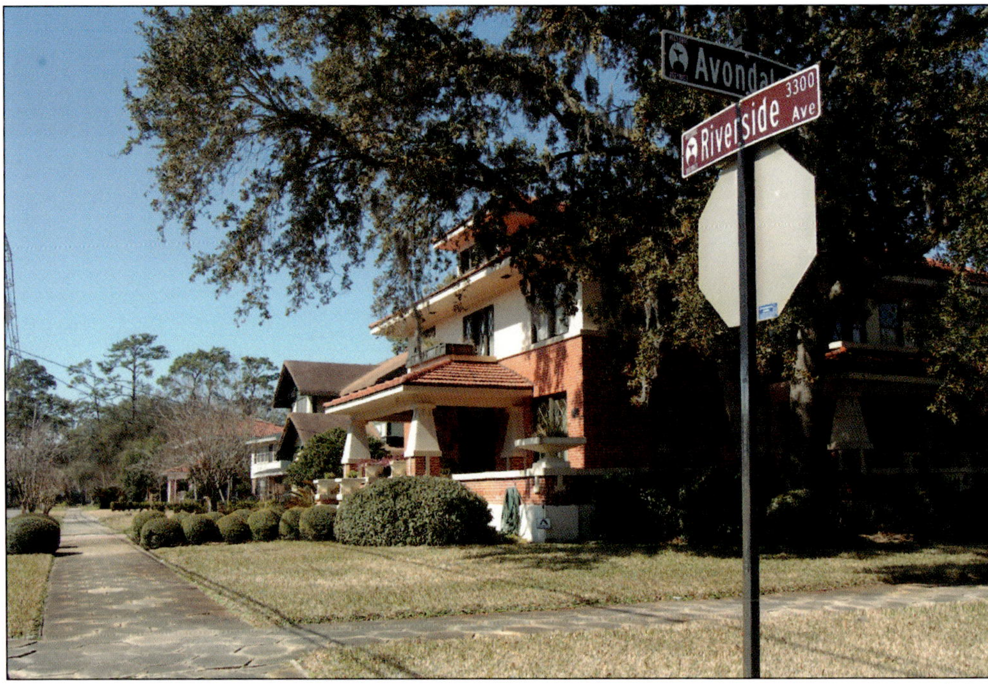

Over time, many cities have left their mark on the country's architectural landscape. New York has its brownstones, Charleston its single house, and Chicago has the Chicago School of Architecture. Believe it or not, Jacksonville has more examples of the Prairie School style than any city outside of the Midwest. Many great residential examples of this architecture style can be found in the Riverside/Avondale Historic District. Located southwest of downtown, the Riverside/Avondale Historic District became the city's first to be added to the National Register of Historic Places, in 1985. Although sections of the district date back to 1868, its greatest period of growth occurred between the Great Fire of 1901 and the Great Depression. Primarily residential, the neighborhood contains several pedestrian-friendly, mixed-use districts and has rapidly grown in popularity with millennials. (Courtesy of Daniel Herbin and MetroJacksonville.com.)

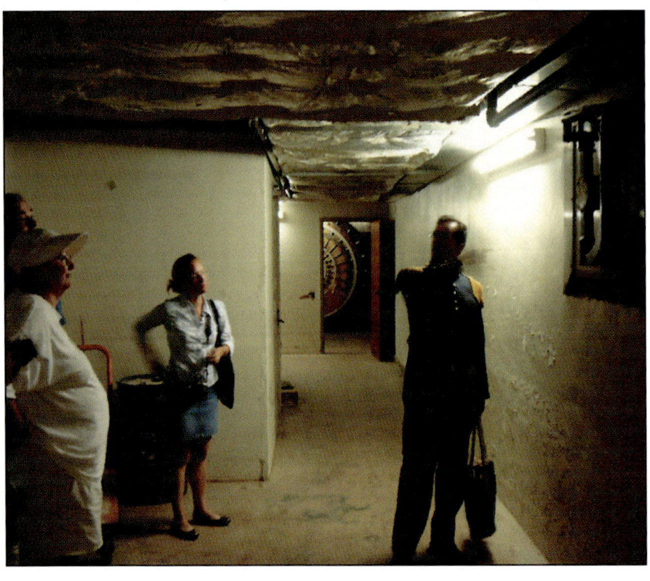

A 2011 Top to Bottom Walking Tour of downtown by AdLib Luxury Tours reveals a piece of underground Jacksonville. Home to the headquarters of Atlantic National Bank, Barnett Bank, and Florida National Bank, the city was considered the banking and financial hub of Florida during the early 1900s. Before the days of automated deposits, bank employees used this tunnel system to safely transport money from one building to another. (Courtesy of the author and MetroJacksonville.com.)

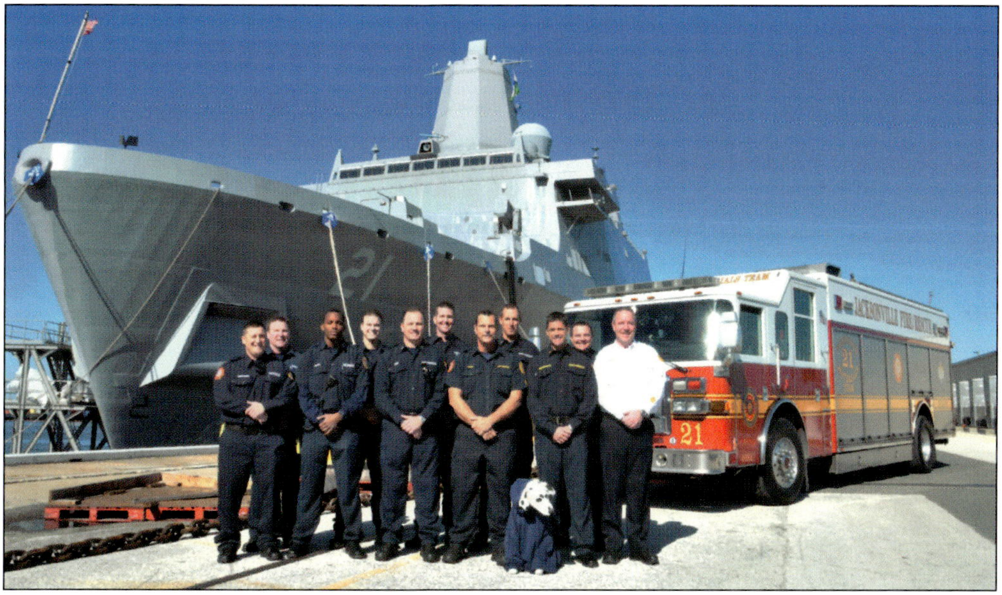

Mayport Naval Station's USS *New York* (LPD-21), the fifth San Antonio–class amphibious-transport dock, has a crew of 360 and can carry up to 700 Marines. It is notable for using a symbolic amount of steel salvaged from the World Trade Center after it was destroyed in the 9/11 attacks. Christened on March 1, 2008, the *New York* shifted homeport from Norfolk, Virginia, to Naval Station Mayport in 2013. (Courtesy of the US Navy.)

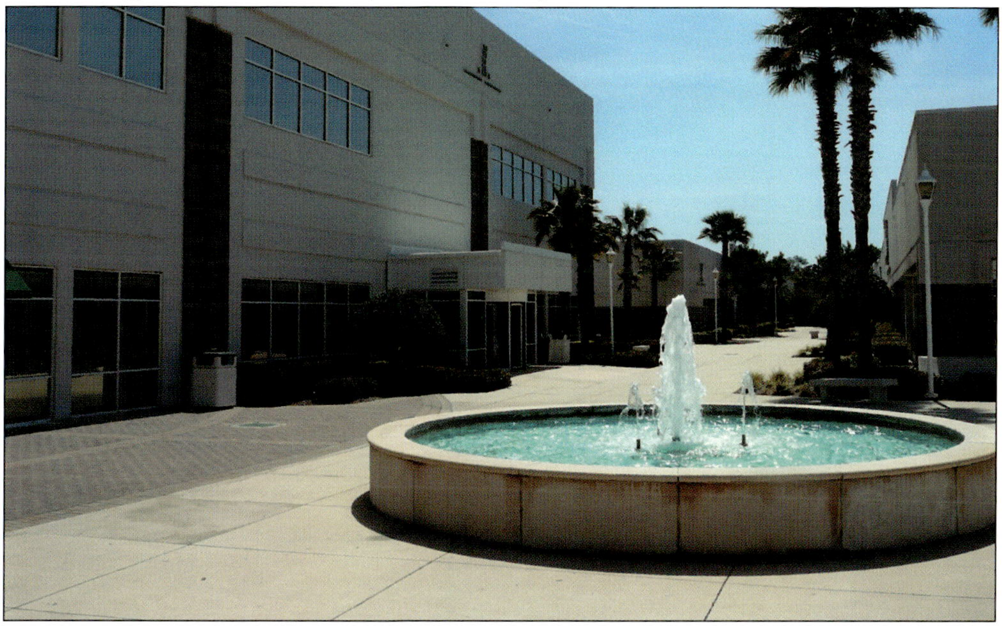

Pictured here is the former Montgomery Ward store at Metro Square Office Park in 2013. Philips Highway Plaza was the Southeast's largest shopping center and city's first mall when it opened in November 1960. By the 1990s, the mall had fallen into despair and decline. In 1996, developers Charles Price, Craig Meek, and ING Realty Partners acquired the property, removed the mall's roof, and successfully converted the shopping center into an office park. (Courtesy of the author and MetroJacksonville.com.)

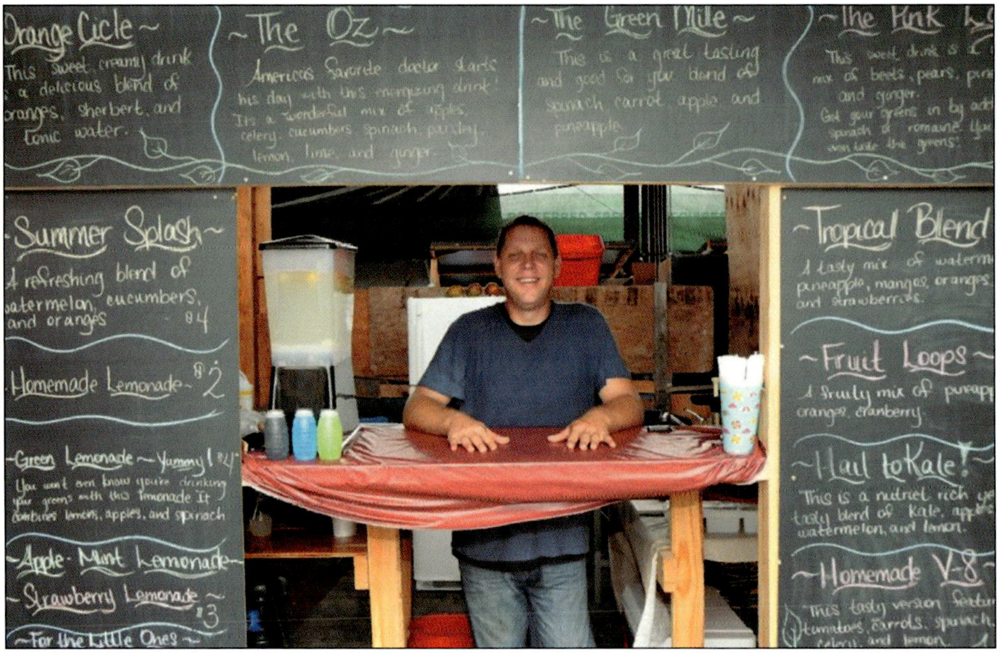

Pictured here is the Fountain of Youth All Natural Juice Bar at the Jacksonville Farmers Market during the market's 75th anniversary. Founded in 1938, the Jacksonville Farmers Market is one of the few working, authentic farmers' markets in the region and the oldest continuously operated public market in Florida. Visited year-round by up to 25,000 people a week, the market is the type of enjoyable travel destination that helps a city create a name for itself. (Courtesy of Jacksonville Farmers Market.)

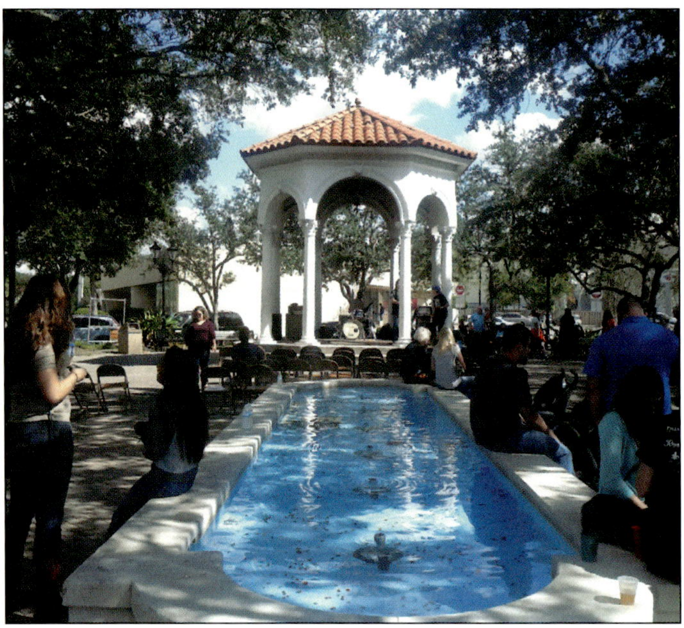

Balis Park is pictured here shortly after its 2013 expansion. Originally a large roadway intersection, a community-driven reclamation project resulted in the modification of the San Marco Boulevard/Atlantic Boulevard intersection into a bona fide centralized public square for the San Marco Square shopping district. As a result, automobile movement has been improved on existing streets, and the community gained a great public amenity. (Courtesy of the author and TransformJax.org.)

A product of the Rails-to-Trails Conservancy's Urban Pathways initiative, the S-Line Urban Greenway is Jacksonville's first dedicated urban multiuse path. The S-Line Urban Greenway is a 4.8-mile rails-to-trails multiuse path that connects New Town and Durkeeville with Springfield and Brentwood. The opportunity to create this multiuse trail came as a result of the City of Jacksonville gaining possession of an abandoned length of CSX railroad right-of-way, appropriately in the shape of an S. (Courtesy of the and MetroJacksonville.com.)

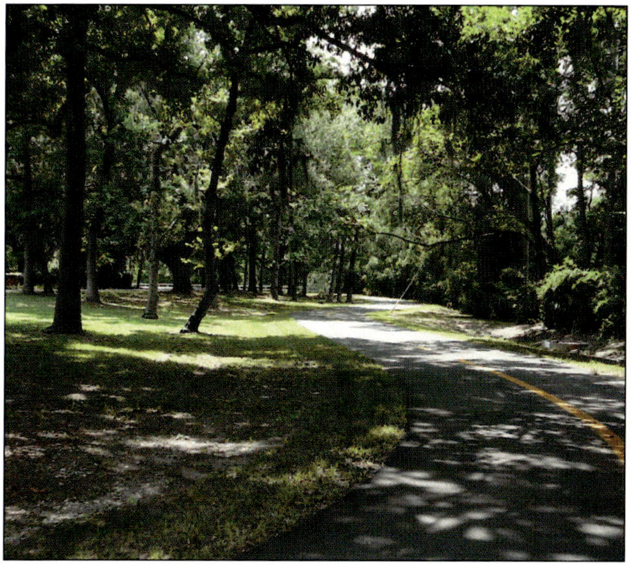

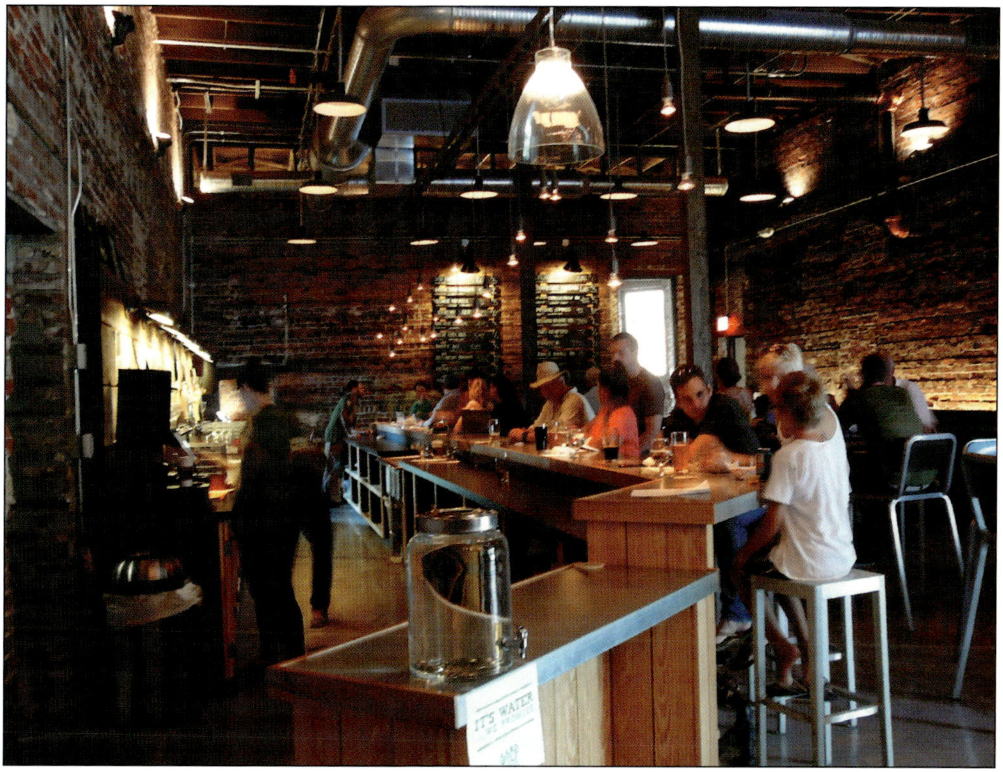

The understanding and importance of Jacksonville becoming a sustainable city is becoming a major desire amongst residents. As a result, the Florida chapter of the US Green Building Association established the Green Lion Festival in summer 2013. Hosted by Aardwolf Brewing, the annual event is designed to introduce people interested in a sustainable city, from building materials and techniques to food sources and energy independence. (Courtesy of the author and MetroJacksonville.com.)

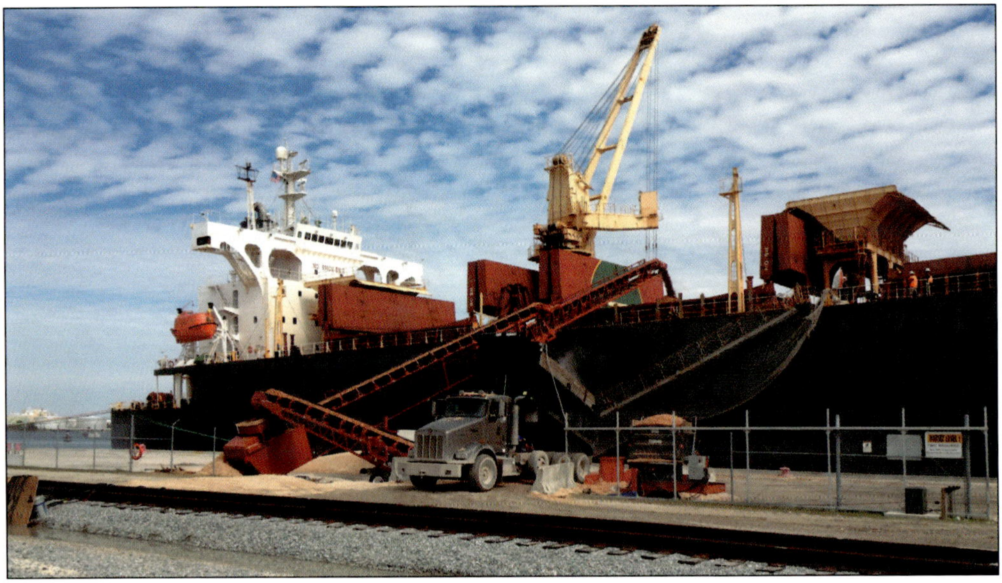

In 2010, Keystone Coal's $20-million,70-acre terminal on the old Jefferson Smurfit paper mill site was constructed. After overcoming Jacksonville Port Authority's attempt to take the land by eminent domain, Keystone's plans involve retrofitting the old mill to process and store lime, petroleum coke, South American coal, and grain, along with the addition of a 1,000-foot berth able to handle break bulk shipments. (Courtesy of Robert Mann and MetroJacksonville.com.)

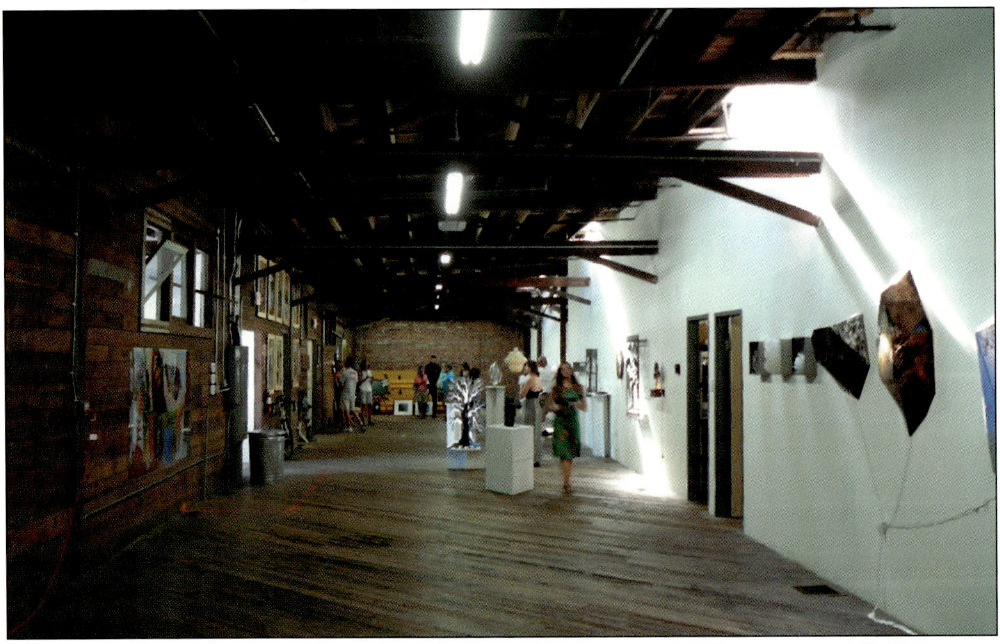

Located at the corner of Rosselle and King Streets, the acronym CoRK represents 100,000 square feet of artist studios, gallery space, and performing-arts space in Riverside's Brewing District. CoRK's network of warehouses dates back to the 1920s, as businesses such as the Atlantic Match Company, Peter Ballantine & Sons, Francis H. Leggett & Company, Schell-Sasse, and Dixon Powdermaker established an industrial presence on the edge of Riverside. (Courtesy of the author and MetroJacksonville.com.)

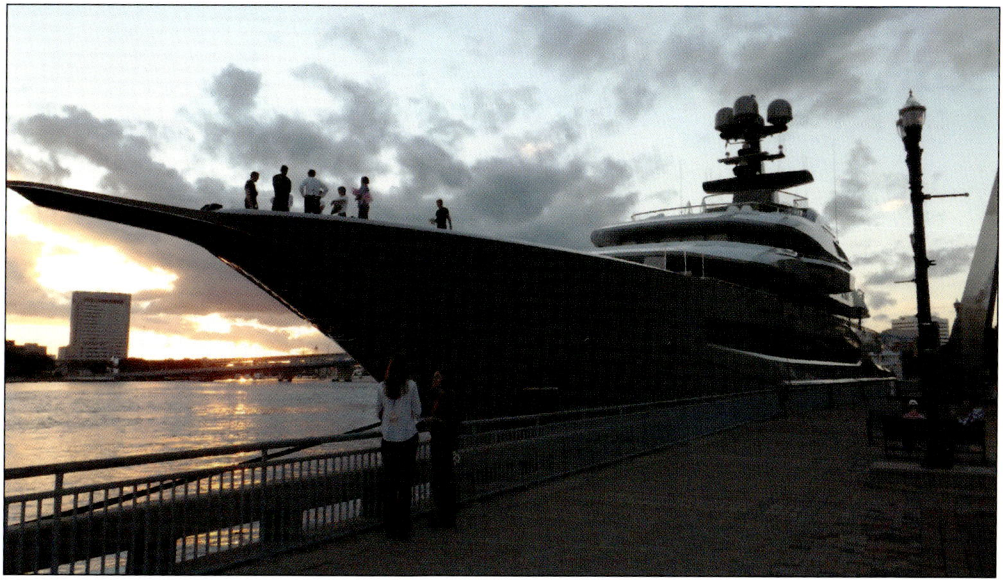

An evening stroll along the Northbank Riverwalk reveals a super-yacht available for charter for $1.47 million a week. Launched in September 2014, the 312-foot-long *Kismet* is the latest toy of Jacksonville Jaguars owner Shahid Khan. The impressive craft boasts eight staterooms, three decks, a helicopter landing pad, and a private sundeck with a pool-Jacuzzi-BBQ area. (Courtesy of the author and MetroJacksonville.com.)

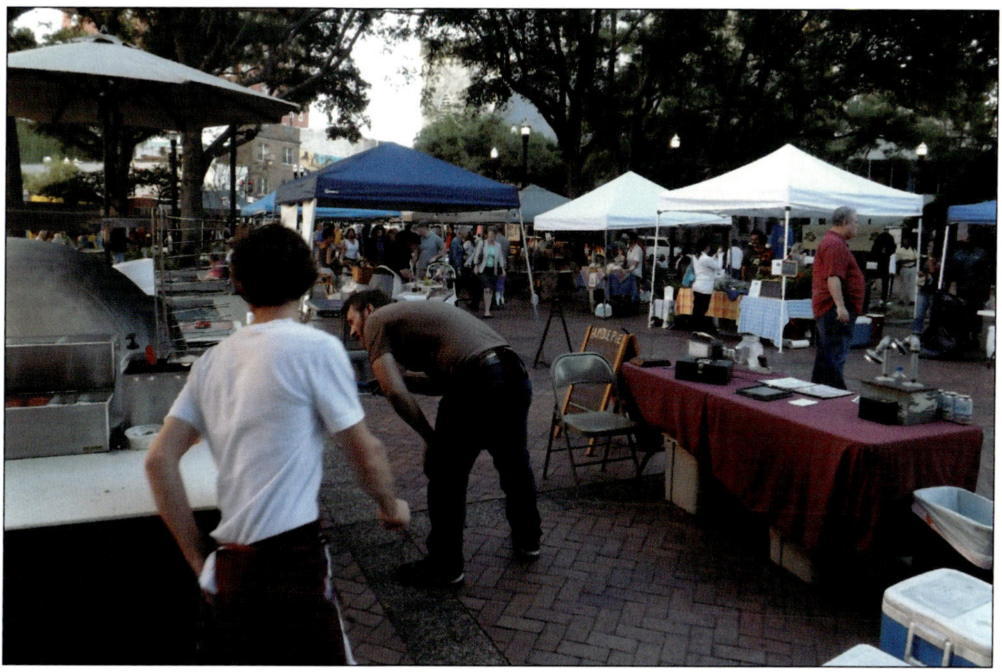

Held from 5:30 p.m. until 9:00 p.m. on the third Thursday of each month, Jaxsons Night Market is an open-air market in the heart of downtown that features local farmers, artisan and craft makers, street-food vendors, fashion retailers, and a craft-beer garden by Intuition Ale Works. For Jaxsons, by Jaxsons, the market celebrates an array of locally owned businesses that help make Jacksonville unique. (Courtesy of the author and MetroJacksonville.com.)

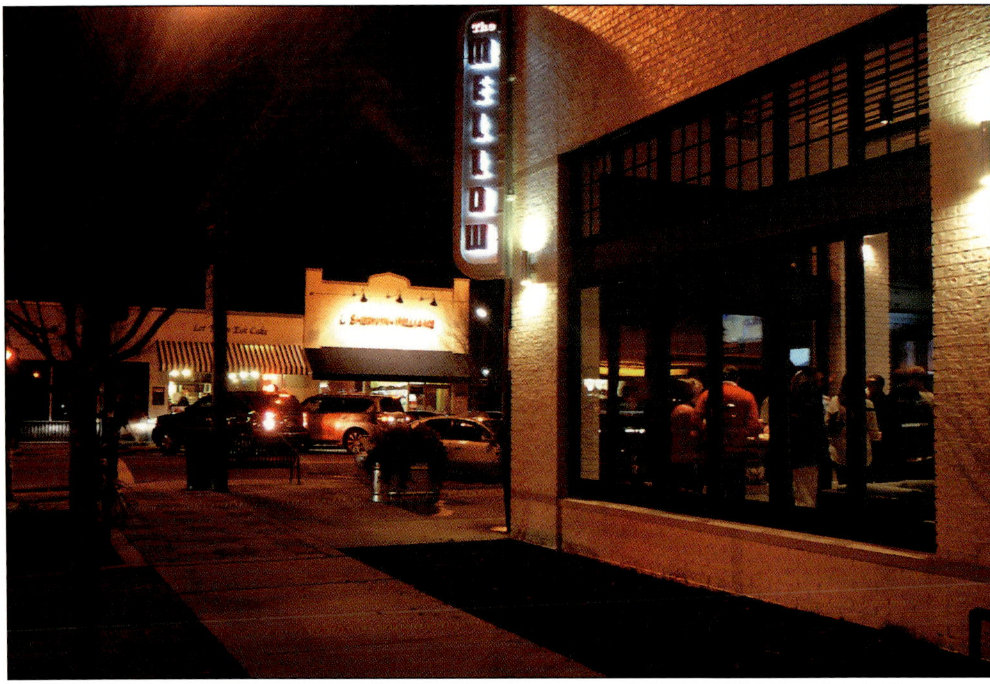

A new Mellow Mushroom Pizza Bakers anchors the center of Riverside/Avondale's Shoppes of Avondale during its 2014 grand opening. For nearly 24 months, the pending opening of the restaurant was one of the most controversial infill-development projects in Jacksonville, symbolizing a cultural and demographic shift impacting revitalizing older neighborhoods nationwide. (Courtesy of the author and MetroJacksonville.com.)

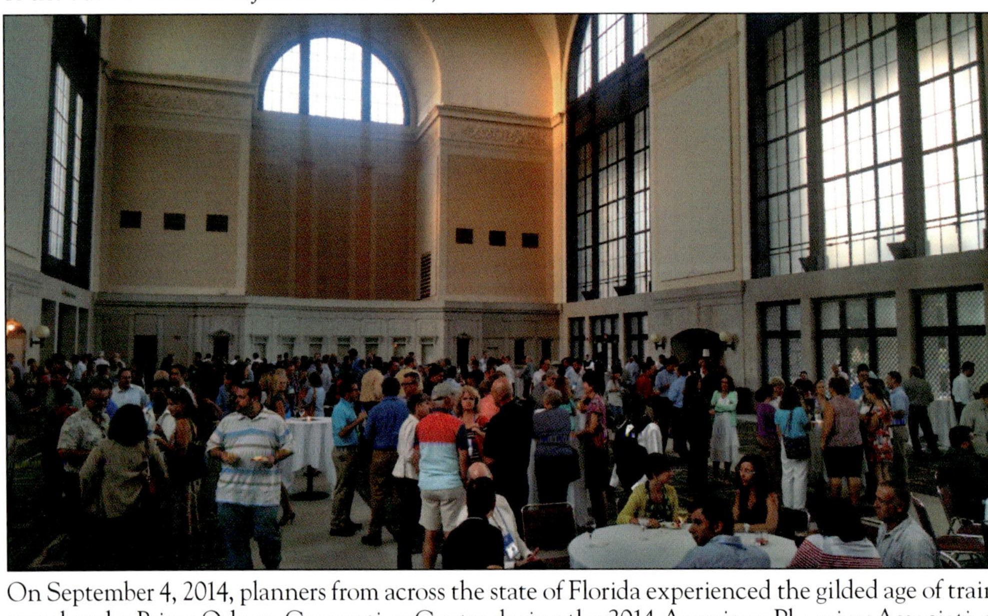

On September 4, 2014, planners from across the state of Florida experienced the gilded age of train travel at the Prime Osborn Convention Center during the 2014 American Planning Association (APA) Florida Conference's All Aboard Reception. From 1919 to 1974, this 75-foot-high vaulted-ceiling space served as the grand lobby of a station that was the gateway to Florida. (Courtesy of the First Coast Section of the Florida chapter of the American Planning Association.)

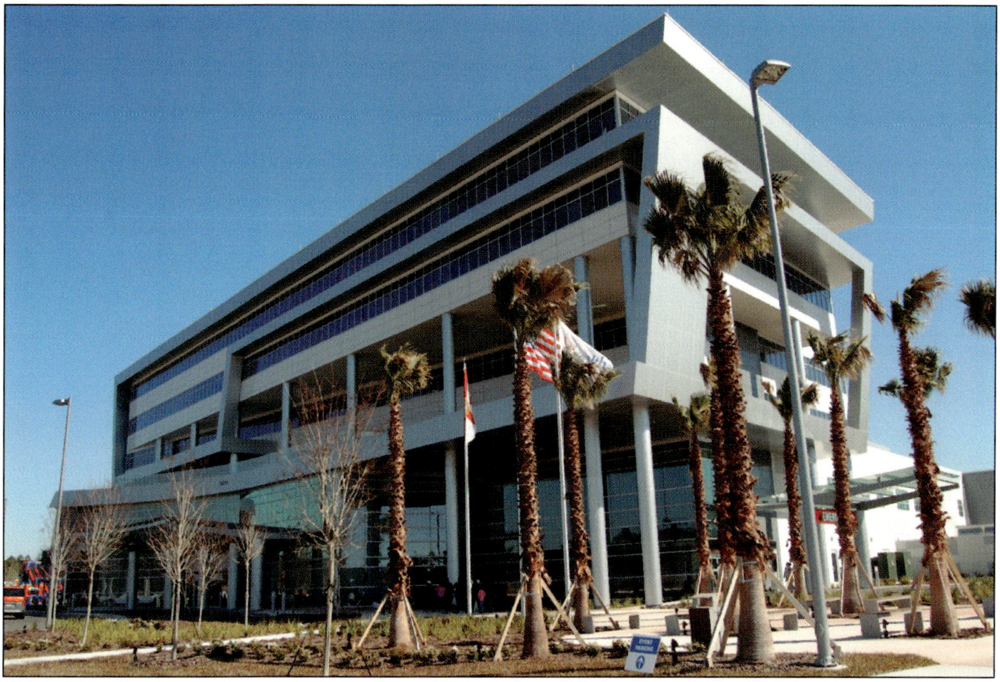

As Jacksonville continues to grow outward, its medical institutions continue to position themselves to meet the needs of the city's expanding population. UF Health North is one of Jacksonville's newest major medical centers. The 210,000-square-foot, state-of-the-art outpatient medical complex is positioned to make access to high-quality medical care more convenient for residents throughout northeast Florida and southeast Georgia. Located on Max Leggett Parkway, the initial phase includes a 28-bed emergency room, five operating rooms, two endoscopy suites, a catheterization laboratory, a natural-birthing center, complete diagnostic imaging, and a full laboratory. Additional plans call for UF Health Jacksonville to add a 92-bed hospital tower on the northern end of the campus by 2017. It is believed that profits from this facility will eventually help subsidize the operation of UF Health's main campus in Springfield. (Courtesy of Daniel Herbin and MetroJacksonville.com.)

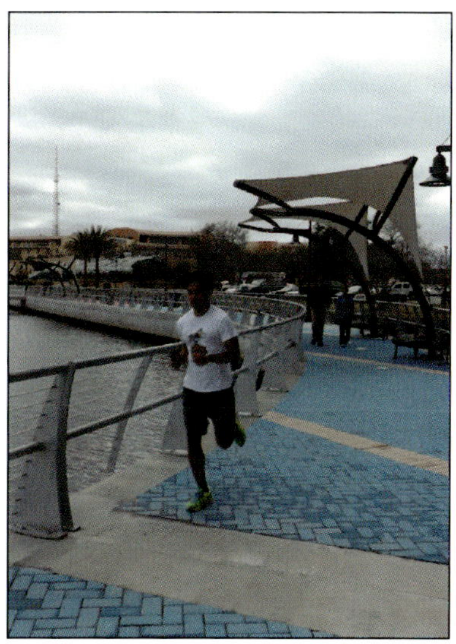

"This newly redesigned Southbank Riverwalk will add even more momentum to our Downtown riverfront and serve as a destination for our residents and visitors. This new 4,000-foot Riverwalk provides a unique experience for the public to enjoy our treasured St. Johns River, and represents a great investment in the quality of life and future of our community," according to Jacksonville mayor Alvin Brown. The original Southbank Riverwalk opened on November 8, 1985. The 1.2-mile walk was envisioned to be a festive waterfront public space linking Friendship Fountain with several hotels, restaurants, and office buildings along the riverfront. Many amenities originally proposed were never built, including a wharf offering an open-air marketplace, aquarium, great lawn, sidewalk café under the Main Street Bridge, and amphitheater. (Courtesy of the author and MetroJacksonville.com.)